ELEMENTS OF REFUSAL

ELEMENTS OF REFUSAL

ESSAYS BY JOHN ZERZAN

LEFT BANK BOOKS

Left Bank Books
Box B, 92 Pike St.
Seattle, Wa. 98101
(206)622-0195

Editorial and Distribution offices:
Left Bank Distribution
5241-University Way NE
Seattle, Wa. 98105
(206)522-8864

Acknowledgments: Typesetting by Jennifer Glod, Sue Letsinger, Brian Kane, Tom O'Keefe, Shawn Crowley and David Brown. Cover design by David Brown.
Many thanks to John Zerzan and Alice Carnes for editorial assistance and—most especially—for their enduring patience.
Thanks also to a number of individuals supporting this and other of our publication efforts with loans and coffee to keep us all dancing far into the wee hours.

ISBN: 0 939306 08 5

Left Bank Books is a collectively owned and operated project, now in its 15th year. We operate with a tiny under-paid staff and the aid of volunteers (and mostly by the seat of our pants).

We have two bookstores. *Left Bank Books* (92-Pike St.) carries new and used books, specializing in anti-authoritarian, independent left-wing and contemporary literature.

a/k/a Books (5241-University Way NE) carries used books, specializing in collectible and out-of-print labor, economic, left-wing politics, and contemporary literature and first editions.

Under the auspices of Left Bank Books we also publish books, pamphlets and other materials. Furthermore, we also operate *Left Bank Distribution*, providing retail mail-order to individuals and wholesale distribution to bookstores and institutions. In addition to our own books, we distribute over 30 other small publishers on an international basis.

Lastly, we sponsor a *Books-to-Prisoners* project (Box A, 92 Pike St.), providing books free to prisoners in North America (we receive over 100 requests a month (!), so donations of books or postage money is always appreciated).

We issue a number of newsletters and catalogs pertinent to these specific activities and interests. Please contact us for copies, to be on our mailing lists, or for further information regarding our projects.

CONTENTS

PREFACE

The modern world offers a severely degraded texture of life without new compensations to make it other than intolerable. A dying capitalism with nothing in its ideological pocket, nothing up its sleeve, seems mainly to want to take us with it into oblivion.

As illusions die, we are reminded that the real moment of triumph will occur as everyone sees through this global and bereft society.

These articles, especially those in the first section, make use of the ability to fathom the beginnings of something from insights apparent in its terminal state. They make a stab at being informed by this species of "hindsight."

The general withdrawal from the hideous joke which is domination requires both disalienating acts and critical thinking. The negative principle that can draw a final curtain on this obscene and debasing organization of life draws its force from the dialectic between the two.

I can only hope that these selections contribute in some way to the further erosion of power's lingering sources.

—John Zerzan

INTRODUCTION

Elements of Refusal is the first comprehensive collection of John Zerzan's writings. Appearing over the past decade in primarily marginal or "underground" publications, this collection is long overdue.

No less than as they appeared, these essays are provocative and important. For me John's writings have always contained that critical spirit which best characterized both the old "Frankfort School" and the Situationists—but are more radical, and without the debilitating despair of the former or the disgusting love affair with technology and "progress" afflicting the latter.

Present-day "reality," as constituted by those with vested interests in maintaining this domination, is touted as the "best", if not the only possible reality. Accordingly, history is shaped like a monstrous land-fill to legitimize this contemporary high-rise shill.

Still, the designated social strait jacket ill-fits and the the social fabric isn't so smooth as appearances dictate. Daily life, as John makes clear, with its increasingly intensifying alienations, schizophrenia and psychopathology becomes more spectacular and bizarre. No, all is not well in Utopia. It is a weird and peculiar world where the growing destruction of the earth is touted as "progress," an advance for humanity. Every technological innovation promising to bring us closer together drives us farther apart; every revolution promises to liberate us from want, but leaves us more in need.

We grow more dependent on glitter and distraction to fill the void where all that is human is gutted. Our noses are shoved to the window of consumption (a display of lies) and are told that here is life. Life is reduced to a game where, for a price, anyone can play; but there is nowhere to play. Indeed, the word "survive" replaces the word "life" more and more in our everyday speech, as if they were equivalent. A kind of social terror permeates everything, becoming a commonplace in our lives. Because, contrary to the glib, superficial aura (desperately and massively touted by mass media), this "work- buy-consume-die" paradise teeters on the brink of collapse and dissolution.

But it is not enough to suspect something awry, to buy bicycles instead of cars, or eat more grain, less meat. It is not enough to affirm the coherency of our feelings or insights through alternative groupings, structures, cultures, and so forth. We must go much further. Failure to press coherently to the sources of our malaise simply leave us carrying this offal about, endlessly failing to understand anything, repeating forever the stupidities trapping us here, reducing everything to a cynical charade. We will be continually victimized, our best insights nothing if we are not become visionaries, insisting more of life than a never ending series of computer gadgets, new "causes," new mysticisms or re-runs of Dr. Strangelove *ad nauseum*.

John's essays make all this abundantly clear. Here it is axiomatic that time, technology, work and other aspects of our social lives—hailed as the liberators of humanity—are, in fact, the co-conspirators of domestication and domination. Today, more than ever—as you will see from this modest collection—they stand exposed. If some think these efforts are simply a theory of spontaneity they will fail to understand anything, much less the end of illusion, how to separate the authentic from the corrupt and recuperable.

If de-mystification is difficult, finding those prepared to listen or to undertake the necessary doings is more so. The blat of everyday survival threatens to drown out some important voices of our time. A few I would point out, for example, are Fredy Perlman, Frederick Turner, Jacque Cammatte, Pierre Clastres, Marshall Sahlins, Richard Drinnon, Stanley Diamond, Howard Zinn and the lively changing groups of people who have been involved in marginal and periodical publications, such as the *Fifth Estate* in Detroit. These people constitute no school or homogenous group. They are diverse individuals whose disagreements, oppositions and arguments are as integral to their activity as the commonality of their projects. At the core we see much of what is vital to any authentic revolution: to have done with the "civilizing" myths destroying us.

Much of their work is necessarily "anthropologically" grounded. The importance of this digging cannot be underestimated. It isn't a rooting about for utopia or silly sociological role-models. We are so locked in mentally and physically to "what is" that we fail to recognize that our kingdom is a prison. The overwhelming power of present-day ruling notions and the requirements of sheer survival leave many of us virtually incapable of recognizing how diverse are the possibilities of *life*.

It is not the power of the State, of capitalism, mass media, nationalism, racism, sexism, work routine, class, language, schooling, or culturalization doing us in, but the total ensemble that must be attacked. John's writings are an important part of this effort—divested of the dross always undermining the best-intentioned movements—to begin anew rather than on or within the ash- heaps of the old society, for we are not rid of a plague while trucking its diseased baggage all about.

Elements of Refusal is the result of one person's pursuits, musings, concerns, discoveries, possibilities, researches and clarifications where so little is understood. The ideological landscape is insidious in its need to prevail. Everywhere this is confirmed. Even the suspicious, the marginalized or the refusers have few places to turn. This small book is not a how-to manual nor a blueprint of an alternative future, but begins where we must all begin: by questioning the whole in each of its parts. And it reflects the attendant problems of rummaging and researching where so little is understood. This is, ultimately, a book of on-going explorations—not equations.

These articles are loosely grouped in three sections: the first encompasses the more fundamental, sweeping, speculative searches for the sources of our contemporary malaise—origins so deep as to require digging into pre-history; the second group is oriented to events and movements over the past 100 years or so, debunking certain mythologies surrounding technology, the origins of WWI, a variety of "breakdowns," and industrialism with its concomitant actors and movements ; and the last section, focused on the 1980s, draws especially upon mass media's own disparate materials, helping us to understand present-day diversions and the radical contexts of its "breakdowns."

Every pocket of refusal gives us hope and every element of refusal keeps this hope burning: in the "past," as we are the legatees of those before us; "presently," amongst each other; to the "future," *absolutely*. Of some primitive past, some so-called "Golden Age," we cannot and do not want re- implement its time or character; but we can, now, recover and cleave to its temper. And here, lastly, if John's tone is often apocalyptic, so be it; indeed, it is in this spirit *Elements of Refusal* is presented—as a series of provocations and challenges.

—*David Brown*
Left Bank Books

BEGINNING OF TIME, END OF TIME

Just as today's most obsessive notion is that of the material reality of time, self-existent time was the first lie of social life. As with nature, time did not exist before the individual became separate from it. Reification of this magnitude — the beginning of time — constitutes the Fall: the initiation of alienation, of history.

Spengler observed that one culture is differentiated from another by the intuitive meanings assigned to time,[1] Canetti that the regulation of time is the primary attribute of all government.[2] But the very movement from community to civilization is also predicated there. It is the fundamental language of technology and the spirit of domination.

Today the feverish acceleration of time, as well as the failure of the "solution" of spatializing it, is exposing it as an artificial, oppressive force along with its corollaries, progress and Becoming. More concretely, technology and work are being revealed by the palpable thrall of time. Either way, the pressure to dissolve history and the rule of time hasn't been so strong since the Middle Ages, before that, since the Neolithic revolution establishing agriculture.

When the humanization of technology and work appear as dubious propositions, the humanization of time itself is also called into question. The questions forming are, how can basic oppressions be effectively controlled or reformed? Why not abolished?

Quoting Hegel approvingly, Debord wrote, "Man, 'the negative be-ing who *is* only to the extent that he suppresses Being,' is identical to time."[3] This equation is being refused, a situation perhaps best illumined by looking at the origins, evolution and present status of time.

If "all reification is a forgetting,"[4] in Horkheimer and Adorno's pregnant phrase, it seems equally true that all "forgetting" — in the sense of loss of contact with our time-less beginnings, of constant "falling into time" — is a reification. All the other reifications, in fact, follow this one.[5]

It may be due to the huge implications involved that no one has satisfactorily defined the objectification called time and its course. From time, into history, through progress, and to the murderous idolatry of the future, which now kills species, languages, cultures, and possibly the entire natural world. This essay should go no further without declaring an intent and strategy: technological society can only be dissolved (and prevented from recycling) by annulling time and history.

"History is eternal becoming and therefore eternal future; Nature is become and therefore eternally past,"[6] as Spengler put it. This movement is also well captured by Marcuse's "History is the negation of Nature,"[7] the increasing speed of which has carried man quite outside of himself. At the heart of the process is the reigning concept of temporality itself, which was unknown to early humans.

Levy-Bruhl provides an introduction: "Our idea of time seems to be a natural attribute of the human mind. But that is a delusion. Such an idea scarcely exists where primitive mentality is concerned. . ."[8] The Frankforts concluded that primeval thought "does not know time as uniform duration or as a succession of qualitatively indifferent moments."[9] Rather, early individuals "lived in a stream of inner and outer experience which brought along a different cluster of coexisting events at every moment, and thus constantly changed, quantitatively and qualitatively."[10]

Meditating on the skull of a plains hunter-gatherer woman, Jacquetta Hawks could imagine the "eternal present in which all days, all the seasons of the plain stand in an enduring unity."[11] In fact, life was lived in a continuous present,[12] underlying the point that historical time is not inherent in reality but an imposition on it. The concept of time itself as an abstract, continuing "thread," unravelling in an endless progression that links all events together while remaining independent of them was completely unknown.

Henri-Charles Puesch's term "articulated atemporality" is a useful one, which reflects the fact that awareness of intervals, for instance, existed with the absence of an explicit sense of time. The relationship of subject to object was radically different, clearly, before temporal distance intruded into the psyche. Perception was not the detached act we know now, involving the distance that allows an externalization and domination of nature.

Of course, we can see the reflections of this original condition in surviving tribal peoples, in varying degrees. Wax said of the nineteenth century Pawnee Indians, "Life had a rhythm but not a progression."[13] The Hopi language employs no references to past, present or future. Further in the direction of history, time is explicit in Tiv thought and speech, but is not a category of it, just as another African group, the Nuer, have no concept of time as a separate idea. The fall into time is a gradual one; just as the early Egyptians kept two clocks, measuring everyday cycles and uniform "objective" time, the Balinese calendar "doesn't tell what time it is, but rather what kind of time it is."[14]

In terms of the original, hunter-gatherer humanity[15] generally referred to above, a few words may be in order, especially inasmuch as there has been a "nearly complete reversal in anthropological orthodoxy"[16] concerning it since the end of the 1960s. Life prior to the earliest agricultural societies of about 10,000 years ago had been seen as nasty, short and brutish, but the research of Marshall Sahlins, Richard Lee and others has changed this view very drastically. Foraging now represents the original affluent society in that it provided life and cultural pleasures with a minimum of effort; work was regarded strictly as a social cost and the spirit of the gift predominated.[17]

This, then, was the basis of no-time, bringing to mind Whitrow's remark that "Primitives live in a now, as we all do when we are having fun,"[18] and Nietzsche's that "All pleasure desires eternity — deep, deep eternity."

The idea of an original state of pleasure and perfection is very old and virtually universal.[19] The memory of a "Lost Paradise" — and often an accompanying eschatology that demands the destruction of subsequent existence — is seen in the Taoist idea of a Golden Age, the Cronia and Saturnalia of Rome, the Greeks' Elysium, and the Christian Garden of Eden and the Fall (probably deriving from the Sumerian laments for lost happiness in lordless society), to name but a few. The loss of a paradisal situation with the dawn of time reveals time as the curse of the Fall, history seen as a consequence of Original Sin. Norman O. Brown felt that 'Separateness, then is the Fall — the fall into division, the original lie,"[20] Walter Benjamin that "the origin of abstraction...is to be sought in the Fall."[21] Conversely, Eliade discerned in the shamanic experience a "nostalgia for paradise," in exploring the belief that "what the shaman can do today *in ecstasy*" could, prior to the hegemony of time, "be done by all human beings *in concreto*."[22] Small wonder that Loren Eisely saw in aboriginal people "remarkably effective efforts to erase or ignore all that is not involved with the transcendant search for timelessness, the happy land of no change,"[23] or that Lévi-Strauss found primitive societies determined to "resist desperately any modification in their structure that would enable history to burst forth into their midst."[24]

If all this seems a bit too heady for such a sober topic as time, a few modern cliches may give pause as to where an absence of wisdom really lies. John G. Gunnell tells us that "Time is a form for ordering experience,"[25] an exact parallel to the equally fallacious assertion of the neutrality of technology. Even more extreme in its fealty to time is Clark and Piggott's bizarre claim that "human societies differ from animal ones, in the final resort, through their consciousness of history."[26] Erich Kahler has it that "Since primitive peoples have scarcely any feeling for individuality, they have not individual property,"[27] a notion as totally wrong as Leslie Paul's "In·stepping out of nature, man makes himself free of the dimension of time."[28] Kahler, it might be added, is on vastly firmer ground in noting that the early individual's "primitive participation with his universe and with his community begins to disintegrate" with the acquiring of time.[29] Seidenberg also detected this loss, in which our ancestor "found himself diverging ever farther from his instinctual harmony along a precarious path of unstable synthesis. And that path is history."[30]

Coming back to the mythic dimension, as in the generalized ancient memory of an original Eden — the reality of which was hunter-gatherer life — we confront the magical practices found in all races and early societies. What is seen here, as opposed to the time-bound mode of technology, is an atemporal intervention aimed at the "reinstatement of the usual uniformities of nature."[31] It is this primary human interest in the regularity, not the supersession, of the processes of nature that bears emphasizing. Related to magic is totemism, in which the kinship of all living things is paramount; with magic and its totemic context, participation with nature underlies all.

"In pure totemism," says Frazer, ". . .the totem [ancestor, patron] is never a god and is never worshipped."[32] The step from participation to religion, from communion with the world to externalized deities for worship, is a part of the alienation process of emerging time. Ratschow held the rise of historical consciousness responsible for the collapse of magic and its replacement by religion,[33] an essential connection. In much the same sense, then, did Durkheim consider time to be a "product of religious thought."[34] Eliade saw this gathering separation and related it to social life: "the more extravagant myths and rituals, Gods and Goddesses of the most various kinds, the Ancestors, masks and secret societies, temples, priesthoods, and so on — all this is found in cultures that have passed beyond the stage of gathering and small-game hunting. . ."[35]

Elman Service found the band societies of the hunter-gatherer stage to have been "surprisingly" egalitarian and marked by the absence not only of authoritarian chiefs, but of specialists, intermediaries of any kind, division of labor, and classes.[36] Civilization, as Freud repeatedly pointed out, with alienation at its core, had to break the early hold of timeless and non-productive gratification.[37]

In that long, original epoch, alienation first began to appear in the shape of time, although many tens of thousands of years' resistance stayed its definitive victory, its conversion into history. Spatialization, which is the motor of technology, can be traced back to the earliest sad experiences of deprivation through time, back to the beginning efforts to offset the passage of time by extension in space. The injunction of Genesis to "Be fruitful and multiply" was seen by Cioran as "criminal."[38] Possibly he could see in it the first spatialization — that of humans themselves — for division of labor and the other ensuing separations may be said to stem from the large growth of human numbers, with the progressive breakdown of hunter-gatherer life. The bourgeois way of stating this is the cliche that domination (rulers, cities, the state, etc.) was the natural outcome of "population pressures."

In the movement from the hunter-gatherer to the nomad we see spatialization in the form, at about 1200 B.C., of the war chariot (and the centaur figure). The intoxication with space and speed, as compensation for controlling time, is obviously with us yet. It is a kind of sublimation; the anxiety energy of the sense of time is converted toward domination spatially, most simply.

With the end of a nomadic existence, the social order is created on a basis of fixed property,[39] a further spatialization. Here enters Euclid, whose geometry reflects the needs of the early agricultural systems and which established science on the wrong track by taking space as the primary concept.

In attempting a typology of the egalitarian society, Morton Fried declared that it had no regular division of labor (and thus no political power accrued therefrom) and that "Almost all of these societies are founded upon hunting and gathering and lack significant harvest periods when large reserves of food are stored."[40] Agricultural civilization changed all of this, introducing production via the development of surplus and specialization. Supported by surplus, the priest measured time, traced celestial movement, and predicted future events. Time, controlled by a powerful elite, was used directly to control the lives of great numbers of men and women.[41] The masters of the early calendars and their attendant lore "became a separate priestly caste,"[42] according to Lawrence Wright. A prime example was the very time-obsessed Mayans; G.J. Whitrow tells us that "of all ancient peoples, the Mayan priests developed the most elaborate and accurate astronomical calendar, and thereby gained enormous influence over the masses."[43]

Generally speaking, Henry Elmer Barnes is quite correct that formal time concepts came with the development of agriculture.[44] One is reminded here of the famous Old Testament curse of agriculture (Genesis 3:17-18) at the expulsion from Paradise, which announces work and domination. With the advance of farming culture the idea of time became more defined and conceptual, and differences in the interpretation of time constituted a demarcation line between a state of nature and one of civilization, between the educated classes and the masses.[45] It is recognized as a defining mode of the new Neolithic phenomena, as expressed by Nilsson's comment that "ancient civilized peoples appear in history with a fully-developed system of time-reckoning,"[46] and by Thompson's that "the form of the calendar is basic to the form of a civilization."[47]

The Babylonians gave the day 12 hours, the Hebrews gave the week 7 days, and the early notion of cyclical time, with its partial claim to a return to the beginnings, gradually succumbed to time as a linear progression. Time and domestication of nature advanced, at a price unrivalled. "The discovery of agriculture," as Eliade claimed, "provoked upheavals and spiritual breakdowns whose magnitude the modern mind finds it well-nigh impossible to conceive."[48] A world fell before this virulent partnership, but not without a vast struggle. So with Jacob Burkhardt we must approach history "as it were as a pathologist"; with Holderlin we still seek to know "How did it begin? Who brought the curse?"

Resuming the narrative, even up to Greek civilization did resistance flourish. In fact, even with Socrates and Plato and the primacy of systematic philosophy, was time at least held at bay, precisely because "forgetting" timeless beginnings was still regarded as the chief obstacle to wisdom or salvation.[49] J.B. Bury's classic *The Idea of Progress* pointed out the "widely-spread belief" in Greece that the human race had decidedly degenerated from an initial "golden age of simplicity"[50] — a longstanding bar to the progress of the idea of progress. Christianson found the anti-progress attitude later yet: "The Romans, no less than the Greeks and Babylonians, also clung to various notions of cyclical recurrence in time..."[51]

With Judaism and Christianity, however, time very clearly sharpened itself into a linear progression. Here was a radical departure, as the urgency of time seized upon humanity. Its standard features were outlined by Augustine, not coincidentally at one of the most catastrophic moments in history — the collapse of the ancient world and the fall of Rome.[52] Augustine definitely attacked cyclical time, portraying a unitary mankind that advances irreversibly through time; appearing at about 400 A.D., it is the first notable theory of history.

As if to emphasize the Christian stamp on triumphant linear time, one soon finds, in feudal Europe, the first instance of daily life ruled by a strict time-table: the monastery.[53] Run like a clock, organized and absolute, the monastery confined the individual in time just as its walls confined him in space. The Church was the first power to conjoin the measurement of time and a temporally ordered mode of life, a project it pursued vigorously. The invention of the striking and wheeled clock by Pope Sylvester II, in the year 1000, is thus quite fitting. The Benedictine order, in particular, has been seen by Coulton, Sombart, Mumford and others as perhaps the original founder of modern capitalism. The Benedictines, who ruled 40,000 monasteries at their height, helped crucially to yoke human endeavor to the regular, collective beat and rhythm of the machine, reminding us that the clock is not merely a means of keeping track of the hours, but of synchronizing human action.[55]

In the Middle Ages, specifically the 14th century, the march of time met a resistance unequalled in scope, quite possibly, since the Neolithic revolution of agriculture. This claim can be assessed by a comparison of very basic developments of time and social revolt, which seems to indicate a definite and profound collision of the two.

With the 1300s quantified, official time stakes its claim to the colonization of modern life; time then became fully abstracted into a uniform series of units, points and sections. The technology of the verge escapement early in the century produced the first modern mechanical clock, symbol of a qualitatively new era of confinement now dawning as temporal associations became completely separate from nature. Public clocks appear, and around 1345 the division of hours into sixty minutes and of minutes into sixty seconds became common,[56] among other new conventions and usages across Europe. The new exactitude carried a tighter synchronization forward, essential to a new level of domestication. Glasser remarked on the "loss of poetry and immediacy in personal experience" caused by time's new power, and reflected that this manifestation of time replaced the movement and radiance of the day by its utilization as a temporal unit.[57] Days, hours, and minutes became interchangeable like the standardized parts and work processes they prefigured.

These decisive and oppressive changes must have been at the heart of the great social revolts that coincided with them. Textile workers, peasants, and city poor shook the norms and barriers of society to the point of dissolution, in risings such as that of Flanders between 1323 and 1328, the *Jacquerie* of France in 1358, and the English revolt of 1381, to name only the three most prominent. The millenial character of revolutionary insurgence at this time, which in Bohemia and Germany existed even into the early 16th century, underlines the unmistakable time element and recalls earlier examples of longing for an original, unmediated condition. The mystical anarchism of the Free Spirit in England sought the state of nature, for example, as did the famous proverb stressed by the rebel John Ball: "When Adam delved and Eve span, who then was a gentleman?" Very instructive is a meditation of the radical mystic Suso, of Cologne, at about 1330:

> 'Whence have you come?' The image (appearing to Suso)
> answers 'I come from nowhere.' 'Tell me, what are you?'
> 'I am not.' 'What do you wish?' 'I do not wish' 'This is
> a miracle! Tell me, what is your name?' 'I am called
> Nameless Wildness.' 'Where does your insight lead to?'
> 'To untrammeled freedom.' 'Tell me, what do you call un-
> trammeled freedom?' 'When a man lives according to all
> his caprices without distinguishing between God and
> himself, and without looking before or after. . .'[58]

The desire "to hold all things in common," to abolish rank and hierarchy, and, even more so, Suso's explicitly anti-time utterance, reveal the most extreme desires of the 14th century social revolt and demonstrate its element of time refusal.[59]

This watershed in the late medieval period can also be understood via art, where the measured space of perspective followed the measured time of the clocks. Before the 14th century there was no attempt at perspective because the painter attempted to record things as they are, not as they look. After the 14th century, an acute time sense informs art; "Not so much a place as a moment is fixed for us, and a fleeting moment: a point of view in time more than in space,"[60] as Bronowski described it. Similarly, Yi-Fu Tuan pointed out that the landscape picture, which appeared only with the 15th century, represented a major re-ordering of time as well as space with its perspective.[61]

Motion is stressed by perspective's transformation of the similarity of space into a happening in time, which, returning to the theme of spatialization, shows in another way that a "quantum leap" in time had occurred. Movement again became a source of values following the defeat of the 14th century resistance to time; a new level of spatialization was involved, as seen most clearly in the emergence of the modern map, in the 15th century, and the ensuing age of the great voyages. Braudel's phrase, modern civilization's "war against empty space,"[62] is best understood in this light.

"The new valuation of Time, which then broke to the surface, actually became one of the most powerful agencies by which Western thought, at the end of the Middle Ages, was transformed..."[63] was Kantorowicz's way of expressing the new, strengthened hegemony of time. If in this objective temporal order of official, legal, factual time only the spatial found the possibility of real expression, all thinking would be necessarily shifted, and also brought to heel. A good deal of this reorientation can be found in Le Goff's simple observation concerning the early 15th century, that "the first virtue of the humanist is a sense of time."[64]

How else could modernity be achieved but by the new dimensions reached by time and technology together, their distinctive and perfected mating? Lilley noted that "the most complex machines produced by the Middle Ages were mechanical clocks,"[65] just as Mumford saw that "the clock, not the steam engine, is the key machine of the modern industrial age."[66] Marx too found here the first basis of machine industry: "The clock is the first automatic machine applied to practical purposes, and the whole theory of production of regular motion was developed on it."[67] Another telling congruence is the fact that, in the mid-15th century, the first document known to have been printed on Gutenberg's press was a calendar (not a bible). And it is noteworthy that the end of the millenarian revolt, such as that of the Taborites of Bohemia in the 15th century and the Anabaptists of Munster in the early 16th century, coincided with the perfection and spread of the mechanical clock. In Peter Breughel's *The Triumph of Time* (1574), the many objects and ideas of the painting are dominated by the figure of a modern clock.

This triumph, as noted above, awakened a great spatial urge by way of compensation: circumnavigating the globe and the discovery, suddenly, of vast new lands, for example. But just as certain is its relationship to "the progressive disrealization of the world,"[68] in the words of Charles Newman, which began at this time. Extension, in the form of domination, obviously accentuated alienation from the world: a totally fitting accompaniment to the dawning of modern history.

Official time had become a barrier both palpable and all-pervasive, filtering and distorting what people said to each other. As of this time, it unmistakably imposed a new distance on human relations and restraint on emotional responses. A Renaissance hallmark, the search for rare manuscripts and classical antiquities, is one form of longing to withstand this powerful time. But the battle had been decided, and abstract time had become the milieu, the new framework of existence. When Ellul opined that "the whole structure of being" was now permeated by "mechanical abstraction and rigidity," he referred most centrally to the time dimension.

All this bloomed in the 1600s, from Bacon, who first proclaimed modernity's domination of nature, and Descartes' formulation regarding the *maitres et possesseurs de la nature*, which "predicted the imperialistic control of nature which characterizes modern science,"[69] including Galileo and the whole ensemble of the century's scientific revolution. Life and nature became mere quantity, the unique lost its strength, and soon the Newtonian image of the world as a clock-like mechanism prevailed. Equivalence — with uniform time as its real model — came to rule, in a development that made "the dissimilar comparable by reducing it to abstract quantities."[70]

The poet Ciro di Pers understood that the clock made time scarce and life short. To him, it

> Speeds on the course of the fleeing century.
> And to make it open up,
> Knocks every hour at the tomb.[71]

Later in the 17th century, Milton's *Paradise Lost* sides with victorious time, to the point of denigrating the timeless, paradisical state:

> with labour I must earn
> My bread; what harm?
> Idleness had been worse.[72]

Well before the beginnings of industrial capitalism, then, had time substantially subdued and synchronized life. Advancing technology can be said to have been borne by the earlier breakthroughs of time. "It was the beginning of modern time that made the speed of technology possible,"[73] concluded Octavio Paz. E.P. Thompson's widely-known "Time, Work-Discipline, and Industrial Capitalism"[74] described the industrialization of time, but, more fundamentally, it was time that did the industrializing, the great daily life struggles of the late 18th and early 19th centuries against the factory system[75] notwithstanding.

In terms of the modern era, again one can discern in social revolts the definite aspect of time refusal, however inchoate. In the very late 18th century, for instance, the context of two revolutions, one must judge, helped Kant see that space and time are not part of the empirical world but part of our acquired intersubjective faculties. It is a non-revolutionary twist that a new, short-lived, calendar was introduced by the French Revolution — not resistance to time, but its renewal under new management![76] Walter Benjamin wrote of actual time refusal vis-à-vis the July revolution of 1830, noting the fact that in early fighting "the clocks in towers were being fired on simultaneously and independently from several places in Paris." He quoted an eyewitness the following verse:

Who would have believed! We are told that new Joshuas
at the foot of every tower, as though irritated with time
itself, fired at the dials in order to stop the day.[77]
Not that moments of insurgence are the only occasions of sensitivity to time's tyranny. According to Poulet, no one felt more grievously
the metamorphosis of time into something quite infernal than did
Baudelaire, who wrote of the malcontents "who have refused redemption by work," who wanted "to possess immediately, on this earth,
a Paradise"; these he termed "Slaves martyred by Time,"[78] a notion
echoed by Rimbaud's denunciation of the scandal of an existence in
time. These two poets suffered in the long, dark night of capital's mid-
and late-19th century ascendancy, though it could be argued that their
awareness of time was made clearest via their active participation,
respectively, in the 1848 revolution and the Commune of 1871.

Samuel Butler's utopian *Erewhon* portrayed workers who destroyed
their machines lest their machines destroy them. Its opening theme
derives from the incident of wearing a watch, and later a visitor's watch
is rather forcibly retired to a museum of bygone evils. Very much in
this spirit, and from the same era, are these lines of Robert Louis
Stevenson:

You may dally as long as you like by the roadside. It is
almost as if the millenium were arrived, when we shall
throw our clocks and watches over the housetop, and
remember time and seasons no more. Not to keep hours
for a lifetime is, I was going to say, to live forever. You
have no idea, unless you have tried it, how endlessly long
is a summer's day, that you measure only by hunger, and
bring an end to only when you are drowsy.[79]

Referrring to such phenomena as huge political rallies, Benjamin's
"The Work of Art in the Age of Mechanical Reproduction" made the
point that "Mass reproduction is aided especially by the reproduction
of masses. . ."[80] But one could go much further and say simply that
mass reproduction *is* the reproduction of masses, or the mass-man.
Mass production itself with its standardized, interchangeable parts and
wage-labor to match constitutes a fascism of everyday life long
predating the fascist rallies Benjamin had in mind. And, as described
above, it was time, several hundred years before that, which provided
the categorical paradigm to mass production, in the form of uniform
but discrete quanta ordering life.

Stewart Ewen held that during the 19th and early 20th centuries,
"the industrial definition of social time and space stood at the core
of social unrest,"[81] and this is certainly true; however, the breadth of

the time and space "issue" requires a rather broad historical perspective to allow for a comprehension of modernity's unfolding mass age. That the years immmediately preceding World War I expressed a rising radical challenge requiring the fearful carnage of the war to divert and destroy it is a thesis I have argued elswhere.[82] The depth of this challenge can best be plumbed in terms of the refusal of time. The contemporary tension between the domains of being and of time was first elucidated by Bergson in the pre-war period in his protest against the fragmentary and repressive character of mechanistic time.[83] With his distrust of science, Bergson argued that a qualitative sense of time, of lived experience or *durée*, requires a resistance to formalized, spatialized time. Though limited, his outlook announced the renewal of a developing opposition to a tyranny that had come to inform so many elements of subjugation.

Most of this century's anti-time impulse was rather fully articulated in the quickening movement just prior to the war. Cubism's urgent re-examination of appearances belongs here, of course; by smashing visual perspective, which had prevailed since the early Renaissance, the Cubists sought to apprehend reality as it was, not as it looked at a moment in time. It is this which enabled John Berger to judge that "the Cubist formula presupposed. . . for the first time in history, man living unalienated from nature."[84] Einstein and Minkowski also bespoke the time revolt context with the well-know scrapping of the Newtonian universe based on absolute time and space. In music, Arnold Schönberg liberated dissonance from the prevailing false positivity's restraints, and Stravinsky explicitly attacked temporal limitations in a variety of new ways, as did Proust, Joyce,[85] and others in literature. All modes of expression, according to Donald Lowe, "rejected the linear perspective of visuality and Archimedean reason, in that crucial decade of 1905-1915!"[86]

In the 1920s Heidegger emphasized time as the central concept for contemporary metaphysics and as forming the essential structure of subjectivity. But the devastating impact of the war had deeply altered the sense of possibilities within social reality. *Being and Time* (1927), in fact, far from questioning time, surrendered to it completely as the only vantage that allows understanding of being. Related, in the parallel provided by Adorno, is "the trick of military command, which dressed up imperative in the guise of a predicative sentence. . . Heidegger, too, cracks the whip when he italicizes the auxiliary verb in the sentence, 'Death *is*.'"[87]

Indeed, for almost forty years after World War I the anti-time spirit was essentially suppressed. By the 1930s one could still find signs of it in, say, the Surrealist movement, or novels of Aldous Huxley,[88] but predominant was the renewed rush of technology and domination, as reflected by Katayev's Five-Year-Plan novel *Time, Forward!* or the bestial deformation expressed in the literally millenarian symbol, the Thousand Year Reich.

Nearer to our contemporary situation, a restive awareness of time began to re-emerge as a new round of contestation neared. In the mid-1950s the scientist N.J. Berrill interrupted a fairly dispassionate book to comment on the predominant desire in society "to get from nowhere to nowhere in nothing flat," observing, "And still a minute can embrace eternity and a month be empty of meaning." Still more startling, he cried out that "For a long time I have felt trapped in time, like a prisoner searching desperately for some avenue of escape."[89] Perhaps an unlikely quarter from which to hear such an articulation, but another man of science made a similar statement forty years before, just as World War I was about to quell insurgence for decades; Wittgenstein noted, "Only a man who lives not in time but in the present is happy."[90]

Children, of course, live in a now and want their gratification now, if we are looking for subjects for the idea that only the present can be total. Alienation in time, the beginning of time as an alien "thing," begins in early infancy, as early as the maternity ward, though Joost Meerloo is correct that "With every trauma in life, every new separation, the awareness of time grows."[91] Raoul Vaneigem supplied the conscious element, outlining perfectly the function of schooling: "The child's days escape adult time; their time is swollen by subjectivity, passion, dreams haunted by reality. Outside, the educators look on, waiting, watch in hand, till the child joins and fits the cycle of the hours."[92] The levels of conditioning reflect, of course, the dimensions of a world so emptied, so exquisitely alienated that time has completely robbed us of the present. "Every passing second drags me from the moment that was to the moment that will be. Every second spirits me away from myself; now never exists."[93]

The repetitious, routine nature of industrial life is the obvious product of time and technology.[94] An important aspect of time-less hunter-gatherer life was the unique, sporadic quality of its activities, rather than the repetitive;[95] numbers and time apply to the quantitive, not the qualitative. In this regard Richard Schlegel judged that if events were always novel, not only would order and routine be impossible, but so would notions of time itself.[96]

In Beckett's play, *Waiting for Godot,* the two main characters receive a visitor, after which one of them sighs, "Well, at least it helped to pass the time." The other replies, "Nonsense, time would have passed anyway."[97] In this prosaic exchange the basic horror of modern life is plumbed. The meta-presence of time is by this time felt as a heavily oppressive force, standing over its subjects quite autonomously. Very apropos is this summing up by George Morgan: "A fretful busyness to 'kill time' and restless movement from novelty to novelty bury an ever-present sense of futility and vacuousness. In the midst of his endless achievements, modern man is losing the substance of human life."[98]

Loren Eisely once described "a feeling of inexplicable terror," as if he and his companion, who were examining a skull, were in the path of "a torrent that was sweeping everything to destruction." Understanding Eisely's sensation completely, his friend paraphrased him as saying, "to know time is to fear it, and to know civilized time is to be terror-stricken."[99] Given the history of time and our present plight in it, it would be hard to image a more prescient bit of communication.

In the 1960s Robert Lowell gave succinct expression to the extremity of the alienation of time:

> I am learning to live in history.
> What is history? What you cannot touch.[100]

Fortunately, also in the '60s may others were beginning the *un*learning of how to live in history, as evidenced by the shedding of wristwatches, the use of psychedelic drugs, and, paradoxically perhaps, by the popular single-word slogan of the French insurrectionaries of May 1968 — "Quick!" The element of time refusal in the revolt of the 60s was strong and there are signs — such as the revolt against work — that it continues to deepen even as it contends with extreme new spatializations of time.

Since Marcuse wrote of "the alliance between time and the order of repression,"[101] and Norman O. Brown on the sense of time or history as a function of repression,[102] the vividness of the connection has powerfully grown.

Christopher Lasch, in the late '70s, noticed that "A profound shift in our sense of time has transformed work habits, values, and the definition of success."[103] And if work is being refused as a key component of time, it is also becoming obvious how consumption gobbles up time alive. Today's perfect spatial symbol of the latter is the Pac-Man video game figure, which literally eats up space to kill time.[104]

As with Aldous Huxley's Mr. Propter, millions have come to find time "a thing intrinsically nightmarish."[105] A fixation with age and the pro-longevity movement, as discussed by Lasch and others, are two signs of its torment. Adorno once said, "As the subjects live less, death grows more precipitous, more terrifying."[106] There seems to be a new generation among the young virtually every three or four years, as time, growing more palpable, has accelerated since the '60s. Science has provided a popular reflection of time resistance in at least two phenomena; the widespread appeal of anti-time concepts more or less loosely derived from physical theory, such as black holes, time warps, spacetime singularities and the like, and the comforting appeal of the "deep time" of the so-called geological romances, such as John McPhee's *Basin and Range* (1981)

When Benjamin assayed that "The concept of the historical progress of mankind cannot be sundered from the concept of its progression through a homogenous time,"[107] he called for a critique of both, little realizing how resonant this call might someday become. Still less, of course, could Goethe's dictum that "No man can judge history but one who has himself experienced history"[108] have been foreseen to apply in such a wholesale way as it does now, with time the most real and onerous dimension. The project of annulling time and history will have to be developed as the only hope of human liberation.

Of course, there is no dearth of the wise who continue to assert that consciousness itself is impossible without time and its spatialization,[109] overlooking somehow an overwhelmingly massive period of humanity's existence. Some concluding words from William Morris's *News from Nowhere* are a fitting hope in reply to such sages of domination: "in spite of all the infallible maxims of your day there is yet a time of rest in store for the world, when mastery has changed into fellowship."[110]

LANGUAGE: ORIGIN AND MEANING

Fairly recent anthropology (e.g. Sahlins, R.B. Lee) has virtually obliterated the long-dominant conception which defined prehistoric humanity in terms of scarcity and brutalization. As if the implications of this are already becoming widely understood, there seems to be a growing sense of that vast epoch as one of wholeness and grace. Our time on earth, characterized by the very opposite of those qualities, is in the deepest need of a reversal of the dialectic that stripped that wholeness from our life as a species.

Being alive in nature, before our abstraction from it, must have involved a perception and contact that we can scarcely comprehend from our levels of anguish and alienation. The communication with all of existence must have been an exquisite play of all the senses, reflecting the numberless, nameless varieties of pleasure and emotion once accessible within us.

To Levy-Bruhl, Durkheim and others, the cardinal and qualitative difference between the "primitive mind" and ours is the primitive's lack of detachment in the moment of experience; "the savage mind totalizes,"[1] as Lévi-Strauss put it. Of course we have long been instructed that this original unity was destined to crumble, that alienation is the province of being human: consciousness depends on it.

In much the same sense as objectified time has been held to be essential to consciousness — Hegel called it "the necessary alienation" — so has language, and equally falsely. Language may be properly considered the fundamental ideology, perhaps as deep a separation from the natural world as self-existent time. And if timelessness resolves the split between spontaneity and consciousness, languagelessness may be equally necessary.

Adorno, in *Minima Moralia*, wrote: "To happiness the same applies as to truth: one does not have it, but is in it."[2] This could stand as an excellent description of humankind as we existed before the emergence of time and language, before the division and distancing that exhausted authenticity.

Language is the subject of this exploration, understood in its virulent sense. A fragment from Nietzsche introduces its central perspective: "words dilute and brutalize; words depersonalize; words make the uncommon common."[3]

Although language can still be described by scholars in such phrases as "the most significant and colossal work that the human spirit has evolved,"[4] this characterization occurs now in a context of extremity in which we are forced to call the aggregate of the work of the "human spirit" into question. Similarly, if in Coward and Ellis' estimation, the "most significant feature of twentieth-century intellectual development" has been the light shed by linguistics upon social reality,[5] this focus hints at how fundamental our scrutiny must yet become in order to comprehend maimed modern life. It may sound positivist to assert that language must somehow embody all the "advances" of society, but in civilization it seems that all meaning is ultimately linguistic; the question of the meaning of language, considered in its totality, has become the unavoidable next step.

Earlier writers could define consciousness in a facile way as that which can be verbalized, or even argue that wordless thought is impossible (despite the counter-examples of chess-playing or composing music). But in our present straits, we have to consider anew the meaning of the birth and character of language rather than assume it to be merely a neutral, if not benign, inevitable presence. The philosophers are now forced to recognize the question with intensified interest; Gadamer, for example: "Admittedly, the nature of language is one of the most mysterious questions that exists for man to ponder on."[6]

Because language is the symbolization of thought, and symbols are the basic units of culture, speech is a cultural phenomenon fundamental to what civilization is. And because at the level of symbols and structure there are neither primitive nor developed languages, it may be justifiable to begin by locating the basic qualities of language, specifically to consider the congruence of language and ideology, in a basic sense.

Ideology, alienation's armored way of seeing, is a domination embedded in systematic false consciousness. It is easier still to begin to locate language in these terms if one takes up another definition common to both ideology and language: namely, that each is a system of distorted communication between two poles and predicated upon symbolization.

Like ideology, language creates false separations and objectifications through its symbolizing power. This falsification is made possible by concealing, and ultimately vitiating, the participation of the subject in the physical world. Modern languages, for example, employ the word "mind" to describe a thing dwelling independently in our bodies, as compared with the Sanskrit word, which means "working within," involving an active embrace of sensation, perception and cognition. The logic of ideology, from active to passive, from unity to separation, is similarly reflected in the decay of the verb form in general. It is noteworthy that the much freer and sensuous hunter-gatherer cultures gave way to the Neolithic imposition of civilization, work and property at the same time that verbs declined to approximately half of all words of a language; in modern English, verbs account for less than 10% of words.[7]

Though language, in its definitive features, seems to be complete from its inception, its progress is marked by a steadily debasing process. The carving up of nature, its reduction into concepts and equivalences, occurs along lines laid down by the patterns of language.[8] And the more the machinery of language, again paralleling ideology, subjects existence to itself, the more blind its role in reproducing a society of subjugation.

Navajo has been termed an "excessively literal" language, from the characteristic bias of our time for the more general and abstract. In a much earlier time, we are reminded, the direct and concrete held sway; there existed a "plethora of terms for the touched and seen."[9] Toynbee noted the "amazing wealth of inflexions" in early languages and the later tendency toward simplification of language through the abandonment of inflexions.[10] Cassirer saw the "astounding variety of terms for a particular action" among American Indian tribes and understood that such terms bear to each other a relation of juxtaposition rather than of subordination.[11] But it is worth repeating once more that while very early on a sumptuous prodigality of symbols obtained, it was a closure of symbols, of abstract conventions, even at that stage, which might be thought of as adolescent ideology.

Considered as the paradigm of ideology, language must also be recognized as the determinant organizer of cognition. As the pioneer linguist Sapir noted, humans are very much at the mercy of language concerning what constitutes "social reality." Another seminal anthropological linguist, Whorf, took this further to propose that language determines one's entire way of life, including one's thinking and all other forms of mental activity. To use language is to limit oneself to the modes of perception already inherent in that language. The fact that language is only form and yet molds everything goes to the core of what ideology is.[12]

It is reality revealed only ideologically, as a stratum separate from us. In this way language creates, and debases the world. "Human speech conceals far more than it confides; it blurs much more than it defines; it distances more than it connects,"[13] was George Steiner's conclusion.

More concretely, the essence of learning a language is learning a system, a model, that shapes and controls speaking. It is easier still to see ideology on this level, where due to the essential arbitrariness of the phonological, syntactic, and semantic rules of each, every human language must be learned. The unnatural is imposed, as a necessary moment of reproducing an unnatural world.

Even in the most primitive languages, words rarely bear a recognizable similarity to what they denote; they are purely conventional.[14] Of course this is part of the tendency to see reality symbolically, which Cioran referred to as the "sticky symbolic net" of language, an infinite regression which cuts us off from the world.[15] The arbitrary, self-contained nature of language's symbolic organization creates growing areas of false certainty where wonder, multiplicity and non-equivalence should prevail. Barthes' depiction of language as "absolutely terrorist" is much to the point here; he saw that its systematic nature "in order to be complete needs only to be valid, and not to be true."[16] Language effects the original split between wisdom and method.

Along these lines, in terms of structure, it is evident that "freedom of speech" does not exist; grammar is the invisible "thought control" of our invisible prison. With language we have already accommodated ourselves to a world of unfreedom.

Reification, the tendency to take the conceptual as the perceived and to treat concepts as tangible, is as basic to language as it is to ideology. Language represents the mind's reification of its experience, that is, an analysis into parts which, as concepts, can be manipulated as if they were objects. Horkheimer pointed out that ideology consists more in what people are like — their mental constrictedness, their complete dependence on associations provided for them — than in what they believe. In a statement that seems as pertinent to language as to ideology, he added that people experience everything only within the conventional framework of concepts.[17]

It has been asserted that reification is necessary to mental functioning, that the formation of concepts which can themselves be mistaken for living properties and relationships does away with the otherwise almost intolerable burden of relating one experience to another.

Cassirer said of this distancing from experience, "Physical reality seems to reduce in proportion as man's symbolic activity advances."[18] Representation and uniformity begin with language, reminding us of Heidegger's insistence that something extraordinarily important has been forgotten by civilization.

Civilization is often thought of not as a forgetting but as a remembering, wherein language enables accumulated knowledge to be transmitted forward, allowing us to profit from others' experiences as though they were our own. Perhaps what is forgotten is simply that others' experiences are *not* our own, that the civilizing process is thus a vicarious and inauthentic one. When language, for good reason, is held to be virtually coterminous with life, we are dealing with another way of saying that life has moved progressively farther from directly lived experience.

Language, like ideology, mediates the here and now, attacking direct, spontaneous connections. A descriptive example was provided by a mother objecting to the pressure to learn to read: "Once a child is literate, there is no turning back. Walk through an art museum. Watch the literate adults read the title cards before viewing the paintings to be sure that they know what to see. Or watch them read the cards and ignore the paintings entirely . . . As the primers point out, reading opens doors. But once those doors are open it is very difficult to see the world without looking through them."[19]

The process of transforming all direct experience into the supreme symbolic expression, language, monopolizes life. Like ideology, language conceals and justifies, compelling us to suspend our doubts about its claim to validity. It is at the root of civilization, the dynamic code of civilization's alienated nature. As the paradigm of ideology, language stands behind all of the massive legitimation necessary to hold civilization together. It remains for us to clarify what forms of nascent domination engendered this justification, made language necessary as a basic means of repression.

It should be clear, first of all, that the arbitrary and decisive association of a particular sound with a particular thing is hardly inevitable or accidental. Language is an invention for the reason that cognitive processes must precede their expression in language. To assert that humanity is only human because of language generally neglects the corollary that being human is the precondition of inventing language.[20]

The question is how did words first come to be accepted as signs at all? How did the first symbol originate? Contemporary linguists seem to find this "such a serious problem that one may despair of finding a way out of its difficulties."[21] Among the more than ten thousand works on the origin of language, even the most recent admit that the theoretical discrepancies are staggering. The question of when language began has also brought forth extremely diverse opinions.[22] There is no cultural phenomenon that is more momentous, but no other development offers fewer facts as to its beginnings. Not surprisingly, Bernard Campbell is far from alone in his judgement that "We simply do not know, and never will, how or when language began."[23]

Many of the theories that have been put forth as to the origin of language are trivial: they explain nothing about the qualitive, intentional changes introduced by language. The "ding-dong" theory maintains that there is somehow an innate connection between sound and meaning; the "pooh-pooh" theory holds that language at first consisted of ejaculations of surprise, fear, pleasure, pain, etc.; the "ta-ta" theory posits the imitation of bodily movements as the genesis of language, and so on among "explanations" that only beg the question. The hypothesis that the requirements of hunting made language necessary, on the other hand, is easily refuted; animals hunt together without language, and it is often necessary for humans to remain silent in order to hunt.

Somewhat closer to the mark, I believe, is the approach of contemporary linguist E.H. Sturtevant: since all intentions and emotions are involuntarily expressed by gesture, look, or sound, voluntary communication, such as language, must have been invented for the purpose of lying or deceiving.[24] In a more circumspect vein, the philosopher Caws insisted that "truth . . . is a comparative latecomer on the linguistic scene, and it is certainly a mistake to suppose that language was invented for the purpose of telling it."[25]

But it is in the specific social context of our exploration, the terms and choices of concrete activities and relationships, that more understanding of the genesis of language must be sought. Olivia Vlahos judged that the "power of words" must have appeared very early; "Surely . . . not long after man had begun to fashion tools shaped to a special pattern."[26] The flaking or chipping of stone tools, during the million or two years of Paleolithic life, however, seems much more apt to have been shared by direct, intimate demonstration than by spoken directions.

Nevertheless, the proposition that language arose with the beginnings of technology — that is, in the sense of division of labor and its concomitants, such as a standardizing of things and events and the effective power of specialists over others — is at the heart of the matter, in my view. It would seem very difficult to disengage the division of labor — "the source of civilization,"[27] in Durkheim's phrase — from language at any stage, perhaps least of all the beginning. Division of labor necessitates a relatively complex control of group action; in effect it demands that the whole community be organized and directed. This happens through the breakdown of functions previously performed by everybody, into a progressively greater differentiation of tasks, and hence of roles and distinctions.

Whereas Vlahos felt that speech arose quite early, in relation to simple stone tools and their reproduction, Julian Jaynes has raised perhaps a more interesting question which is assumed in his contrary opinion that language showed up much later. He asks, how it is, if humanity had speech for a couple of million years, that there was virtually no development of technology?[28] Jaynes's question implies a utilitarian value inhering in language, a supposed release of latent potentialities of a positive nature.[29] But given the destructive dynamic of the division of labor, referred to above, it may be that while language and technology are indeed linked, they were both successfully resisted for thousands of generations.

At its origins language had to meet the requirements of a problem that existed outside language. In light of the congruence of language and ideology, it is also evident that as soon as a human spoke, he or she was separated. This rupture is the moment of dissolution of the original unity between humanity and nature; it coincides with the initiation of division of labor. Marx recognized that the rise of ideological consciousness was established by the division of labor; language was for him the primary paradigm of "productive labor." Every step in the advancement of civilization has meant added labor, however, and the fundamentally alien reality of productive labor/work is realized and advanced via language. Ideology receives its substance from division of labor, and, inseparably, its form from language.

Engels, valorizing labor even more explicitly than Marx, explained the origin of language from and with labor, the "mastery of nature." He expressed the essential connection by the phrase, "first labor, after it and then with it speech."[30] To put it more critically, the artificial communication which is language was and is the voice of the artificial separation which is (division of) labor.[31] (In the usual, repressive parlance, this is phrased positively, of course, in terms of the invaluable nature of language in organizing "individual responsibilities.")

Language was elaborated for the suppression of feelings; as the code of civilization it expresses the sublimation of Eros, the repression of instinct, which is the core of civilization. Freud, in the one paragraph he devoted to the origin of language, connected original speech to sexual bonding as the instrumentality by which work was made acceptable as "an equivalence and substitute for sexual activity."[32] This transference from a free sexuality to work is original sublimation, and Freud saw language constituted in the establishing of the link between mating calls and work processes.

The neo-Freudian Lacan carries this analysis further, asserting that the unconscious is formed by the primary repression of acquisition of language. For Lacan the unconscious is thus "structured like a language" and functions linguistically, not instinctively or symbolically in the traditional Freudian sense.[33]

To look at the problem of origin on a figurative plane, it is interesting to consider the myth of the Tower of Babel. The story of the confounding of language, like that other story in Genesis, the Fall from the grace of the Garden, is an attempt to come to terms with the origin of evil. The splintering of an "original language" into mutually unintelligible tongues may best be understood as the emergence of symbolic language, the eclipse of an earlier state of more total and authentic communication.

In numerous traditions of paradise, for example, animals can talk and humans can understand them.[34]

I have argued elsewhere[35] that the Fall can be understood as a fall into time. Likewise, the failure of the Tower of Babel suggests, as Russell Fraser put it, "the isolation of man in historical time."[36] But the Fall also has a meaning in terms of the origin of language. Benjamin found in it the mediation which is language and the "origin of abstraction, too, as a faculty of language-mind."[37] "The fall is into language,"[38] according to Norman O. Brown.

Another part of Genesis provides Biblical commentary on an essential of language, names,[39] and on the notion that naming is an act of domination. I refer to the creation myth, which includes "and whatsoever Adam called every living creature, that was the name thereof." This bears directly on the necessary linguistic component of the domination of nature: man became master of things only because he first named them, in the formulation of Dufrenne.[40] As Spengler had it, "To name anything by a name is to win power over it."[41]

The beginning of humankind's separation from and conquest of the world is thus located in the naming of the world. *Logos* itself as god is involved in the first naming, which represents the domination the deity. The well-known passage is contained in the Gospel of John: "In the beginning was the Word, and the Word was with God, and the Word was God."

Returning to the question of the origin of language in real terms, we also come back to the notion that the problem of language is the problem of civilization. The anthropologist Lizot noted that the hunter-gatherer mode exhibited that lack of technology and division of labor that Jaynes felt must have bespoken an absence of language: "(Primitive people's) contempt for work and their disinterest in technological progress per se are beyond question."[42] Furthermore, "the bulk of recent studies," in Lee's words of 1981, shows the hunter-gatherers to have been "well nourished and to have (had) abundant leisure time."[43]

Early humanity was not deterred from language by the pressures of constant worries about survival; the time for reflection and linguistic development was available but this path was apparently refused for many thousands of years. Nor did the conclusive victory of agriculture, civilization's cornerstone, take place (in the form of the Neolithic revolution) because of food shortage or population pressures. In fact, as Lewis Binford has concluded, "The question to be asked is not why agriculture and food-storage techniques were not developed everywhere, but why they were developed at all."[44]

The dominance of agriculture, including property ownership, law, cities, mathematics, surplus, permanent hierarchy and specialization, and writing, to mention a few of its elements, was no inevitable step in human "progress"; neither was language itself. The reality of pre-Neolithic life demonstrates the degradation or defeat involved in what has been generally seen as an enormous step forward, an admirable transcending of nature, etc. In this light, many of the insights of Horkheimer and Adorno in the *Dialectic of Enlightenment* (such as the linking of progress in instrumental control with regression in affective experience) are made equivocal by their false conclusion that "Men have always had to choose between their subjugation to nature or the subjugation of nature to the Self."[45]

"Nowhere is civilization so perfectly mirrored as in speech,"[46] as Pei commented, and in some very significant ways language has not only reflected but determined shifts in human life. The deep, powerful break that was announced by the birth of language prefigured and overshadowed the arrival of civilization and history, a mere 10,000 years ago. In the reach of language, "the whole of History stands unified and complete in the manner of a Natural Order,"[47] says Barthes.

Mythology, which, as Cassirer noted, "is from its very beginning potential religion,"[48] can be understood as a function of language, subject to its requirements like any ideological product. The nineteenth-century linguist Müller described mythology as a "disease of language" in just this sense; language deforms thought by its inability to describe things directly. "Mythology is inevitable, it is natural, it is an inherent necessity of language . . . (It is) the dark shadow which language throws upon thought, and which can never disappear till language becomes entirely commensurate with thought, which it never will."[49]

It is little wonder, then, that the old dream of a *lingua Adamica*, a "real" language consisting not of conventional signs but expressing the direct, unmediated meaning of things, has been an integral part of humanity's longing for a lost primeval state. As remarked upon above, the Tower of Babel is one of the enduring significations of this yearning to truly commune with each other and nature.

In that earlier (but long enduring) condition nature and society formed a coherent whole, interconnected by the closest bonds. The step from participation in the totality of nature to religion involved a detaching of forces and beings into outward, inverted existences. This separation took the form of deities, and the religious practitioner, the shaman, was the first specialist.

The decisive mediations of mythology and religion are not, however, the only profound cultural developments underlying our modern estrangement. Also in the Upper Paleolithic era, as the species Neanderthal gave way to Cro-Magnon (and the brain actually shrank in size), art was born. In the celebrated cave paintings of roughly 30,000 years ago is found a wide assortment of abstract signs; the symbolism of late Paleolithic art slowly stiffens into the much more stylized forms of the Neolithic agriculturalists. During this period, which is either synonymous with the beginnings of language or registers its first real dominance, a mounting unrest surfaced. John Pfeiffer described this in terms of the erosion of the egalitarian hunter-gather traditions, as Cro-Magnon established its hegemony.[50] Whereas there was "no trace of rank" until the Upper Paleolithic, the emerging division of labor and its immediate social consequences demanded a disciplining of those resisting the gradual approach of civilization. As a formalizing, indoctrinating device, the dramatic power of art fulfilled this need for cultural coherence and the continuity of authority. Language, myth, religion and art thus advanced as deeply "political" conditions of social life, by which the artificial media of symbolic forms replaced the directly-lived quality of life before division of labor. From this point on, humanity could no longer see reality face to face; the logic of domination drew a veil over play, freedom, affluence.

At the close of the Paleolithic Age, as a decreased proportion of verbs in the language reflected the decline of unique and freely chosen acts in consequence of division of labor, language still possessed no tenses.[51] Although the creation of a symbolic world was the condition for the existence of time, no fixed differentiations had developed before hunter-gatherer life was displaced by Neolithic farming. But when every verb form shows a tense, language is "demanding lip service to time even when time is furthest of our thoughts."[52] From this point one can ask whether time exists apart from grammar. Once the structure of speech incorporates time and is thereby animated by it at every expression, division of labor has conclusively destroyed an earlier reality. With Derrida, one can accurately refer to "language as the origin of history."[53] Language itself is a repression, and along its progress repression gathers — as ideology, as work — so as to generate historical time. Without language all of history would disappear.

Pre-history is pre-writing; writing of some sort is the signal that civilization has begun. "One gets the impression," Freud wrote in *The Future of an Illusion*, "that civilization is something which was imposed on a resisting majority by a minority which understood how to obtain possession of the means of power and coercion."[54] If the matter of time and language can seem problematic, writing as a stage of language makes its appearance contributing to subjugation in rather naked fashion. Freud could have legitimately pointed to written language as the lever by which civilization was imposed and consolidated.

By about 10,000 B.C. extensive division of labor had produced the kind of social control reflected by cities and temples. The earliest writings are records of taxes, laws, terms of labor servitude. This objectified domination thus originated from the practical needs of political economy. An increased use of letters and tablets soon enabled those in charge to reach new heights of power and conquest, as exemplified in the new form of government commanded by Hammurabi of Babylon. As Lévi-Strauss put it, writing "seems to favor rather the exploitation than the enlightenment of mankind . . . Writing, on this its first appearance in our midst, had allied itself with falsehood."[55]

Language at this juncture becomes the representation of representation, in hieroglyphic and ideographic writing and then in phonetic-alphabetic writing. The progress of symbolization, from the symbolizing of words, to that of syllables, and finally to letters in an alphabet, imposed an increasingly irresistible sense of order and control. And in the reification that writing permits, language is no longer tied to a speaking subject or community of discourse, but creates an autonomous field from which every subject can be absent.[56]

In the contemporary world, the avant-garde of art has, most

noticeably, performed at least the gestures of refusal of the prison of language. Since Mallarmé, a good deal of modernist poetry and prose has moved against the taken-for-grantedness of normal speech. To the question "Who is speaking?" Mallarmé answered, "Language is speaking."[57] After this reply, and especially since the explosive period around World War I when Joyce, Stein and others attempted a new syntax as well as a new vocabulary, the restraints and distortions of language have been assaulted wholesale in literature. Russian futurists, Dada (e.g. Hugo Ball's effort in the 1920s to create "poetry without words"), Artaud, the Surrealists and lettristes were among the more exotic elements of a general resistance to language.[58]

The Symbolist poets, and many who could be called their descendants, held that defiance of society also includes defiance of its language. But inadequacy in the former arena precluded success in the latter, bringing one to ask whether avant-garde strivings can be anything more than abstract, hermetic gestures. Language, which at any given moment embodies the ideology of a particular culture, must be ended in order to abolish both categories of estrangement; a project of some considerable social dimensions, let us say. That literary texts (e.g. *Finnegan's Wake*, the poetry of e.e. cummings) break the rules of language seems mainly to have the paradoxical effect of evoking the rules themselves. By permitting the free play of ideas about language, society treats these ideas as mere play.

The massive amount of lies — official, commercial and otherwise — is perhaps in itself sufficient to explain why Johnny Can't Read or Write, why illiteracy is increasing in the metropole. In any case, it is not only that "the pressure on language has gotten very great,"[59] according to Canetti, but that "unlearning" has come "to be a force in almost every field of thought,"[60] in Robert Harbison's estimation.

Today "incredible" and "awesome" are applied to the most commonly trivial and boring, and it is no accident that powerful or shocking words barely exist anymore. The deterioration of language mirrors a more general estrangement; it has become almost totally external to us. From Kafka to Pinter silence itself is a fitting voice of our times. "Few books are forgivable. Black on the canvas, silence on the screen, an empty white sheet of paper, are perhaps feasible,[61] as R.D. Laing put it so well. Meanwhile, the structuralists — Lévi-Strauss, Barthes,

Foucault, Lacan, Derrida — have been almost entirely occupied with the duplicity of language in their endless exegetical burrowings into it. They have virtually renounced the project of extracting meaning from language.

I am writing (obviously) enclosed in language, aware that language reifies the resistance to reification. As T.S. Eliot's Sweeney explains, "I've gotta use words when I talk to you." One can imagine replacing the imprisonment of time with a brilliant present — only by imagining a world without division of labor, without that divorce from nature from which all ideology and authority accrue. We couldn't live in this world without language and that is just how profoundly we must transform this world.

Words bespeak a sadness; they are used to soak up the emptiness of unbridled time. We have all had the desire to go further, deeper than words, the feeling of wanting only to be done with all the talk, knowing that being allowed to live coherently erases the need to formulate coherence.

There is a profound truth to the notion that "lovers need no words." The point is that we must have a world of lovers, a world of the face-to-face, in which even names can be forgotten, a world which knows that enchantment is the opposite of ignorance. Only a politics that undoes language and time and is thus visionary to the point of voluptuousness has any meaning.

NUMBER: ITS ORIGIN AND EVOLUTION

The wrenching and demoralizing character of the crisis we find ourselves in, above all, the growing emptiness of spirit and artificiality of matter, lead us more and more to question the most commonplace of "givens." Time and language begin to arouse suspicions; number, too, no longer seems "neutral." The glare of alienation in technological civilization is too painfully bright to hide its essence now, and mathematics is the schema of technology.

It is also the language of science—how deep we must go, how far back to reveal the "reason" for damaged life? The tangled skein of unnecessary suffering, the strands of domination, are unavoidably being unreeled, by the pressure of an unrelenting present.

When we ask, to what sorts of questions is the answer a number, and try to focus on the meaning or the reasons for the emergence of the quantitative, we are once again looking at a decisive moment of our estrangement from natural being.

Number, like language, is always saying what it cannot say. As the root of a certain kind of logic or method, mathematics is not merely a tool but a goal of scientific knowledge: to be perfectly exact, perfectly self-consistent, and perfectly general. Never mind that the world is inexact, interrelated, and specific, that no one has ever seen leaves, trees, clouds, animals that are any two the same, just as no two moments are identical.[1] As Dingle said, "All that can come from the ultimate scientific analysis of the material world is a set of numbers,"[2] reflecting upon the primacy of the concept of identity in math and its offspring, science.

A little further on I will attempt an "anthropology" of number and explore its social embeddedness. Horkheimer and Adorno point to the basis of the disease: "Even the deductive form of science reflects hierarchy and coercion. . .the whole logical order, dependency, progression, and union of [its] concepts is grounded in the corresponding conditions of social reality—that is, of the division of labor."[3]

If mathematical reality is the purely formal structure of normative or standardizing measure[4] (and later, science), the first thing to be measured at all was time.[5] The primal connection between time and number becomes immediately evident. Authority, first objectified as time, becomes rigidified by the gradually mathematized consciousness of time. Put slightly differently, time is a measure and exists as a reification or materiality thanks to the introduction of measure.

The importance of symbolization should also be noted, in passing, for a further interrelation consists of the fact that while the basic feature of all measurement is symbolic representation[6], the creation of a symbolic world is the condition of the existence of time.

To realize that representation begins with language, actualized in the creation of a reproducible formal structure, is already to apprehend the fundamental tie between language and number.[7] An impoverished present renders it easy to see, as language becomes more impoverished, that math is simply the most reduced and drained language. The ultimate step in formalizing a language is to transform it into mathematics; conversely, the closer language comes to the dense concretions of reality, the less abstract and exact it can be.

The symbolizing of life and meaning is at its most versatile in language, which, in Wittgenstein's later view, virtually constitutes the world. Further, language, based as it is on a symbolic faculty for conventional and arbitrary equivalences, finds in the symbolism of math its greatest refinement. Mathematics, as judged by Max Black, is "the grammar of all symbolic systems."[8]

The purpose of the mathematical aspect of language and concept is the more complete isolation of the concept from the senses. Math is the paradigm of abstract thought for the same reason that Levy termed pure mathematics "the method of isolation raised to a fine art."[9] Closely related are its character of "enormous generality,"[10] as discussed by Parsons, its refusal of limitations on said generality, as formulated by Whitehead.[11]

This abstracting process and its formal, general results provide a content that seems to be completely detached from the thinking individual; the user of a mathematical system and his/her values do not enter into the system. The Hegelian idea of the autonomy of alienated activity finds a perfect application with mathematics; it has its own laws of growth, its own dialectic,[12] and stands over the individual as a separate power. Self-existent time and the first distancing of humanity from nature, it must be preliminarily added, began to emerge when we first began to count. Domination of nature, and then, of humans is thus enabled.

In abstraction is the truth of Heyting's conclusion that "the characteristic of mathematical thought is that it does not convey truth about the external world."[13] Its essential attitude toward the whole colorful movement of life is summed up by, "Put this and that equal to that and this!"[14] Abstraction and equivalence or identity are inseparable; the suppression of the world's richness which is paramount in identity brought Adorno to call it 'the primal world of ideology."[15] The untruth of identity is simply that the concept does not exhaust the thing conceived.[16]

Mathematics is reified, ritualized thought, the virtual abandonment of thinking. Foucault found that "in the first gesture of the first mathematician one saw the constitution of an ideality that has been deployed throughout history and has been questioned only to be repeated and purified."[17]

Number is the most momentous idea in the history of human thought. Numbering or counting (and measurement, the process of assigning numbers to represent qualities) gradually consolidated plurality into quantification, and thereby produced the homogeneous and abstract character of number, which made mathematics possible. From its inception in elementary forms of counting (beginning with a binary division and proceeding to the use of fingers and toes as bases) to the Greek idealization of number, an increasingly abstract type of thinking developed, paralleling the maturation of the time concept. As William James put it, "the intellectual life of man consists almost wholly in his substitution of a conceptual order for the perceptual order in which his experience originally comes."[18]

Boas concluded that "counting does not become necessary until objects are considered in such generalized form that their individualities are entirely lost sight of."[19] In the growth of civilization we have learned to use increasingly abstract signs to point at increasingly abstract referents. On the other hand, prehistoric languages had a plethora of terms for the touched and felt, while very often having no number words beyond *one, two* and *many.*[20] Hunter-gatherer humanity had little if any need for numbers, which is the reason Hallpike declared that "we cannot expect to find that an operational grasp of quantification will be a cultural norm in many primitive societies."[21] Much earlier, and more crudely, Allier referred to "the repugnance felt by uncivilized men towards any genuine intellectual effort, more particularly towards arithmetic."[22]

In fact, on the long road toward abstraction, from an intuitive sense of amount to the use of different sets of number words for counting different kinds of things, along to fully abstract number, there was an immense resistance, as if the objectification involved was somehow seen for what it was. This seems less implausible in light of the striking, unitary beauty of tools of our ancestors half a million years ago, in which the immediate artistic and technical (for want of better words) touch is so evident, and by "recent studies which have demonstrated the existence, some 300,000 years ago, of mental ability equivalent to modern man,"[23] in the words of British archeologist Clive Gamble.

Based on observations of surviving tribal peoples, it is apparent, to provide another case in point, that hunter-gatherers possessed an enormous and intimate understanding of the nature and ecology of their local places, quite sufficient to have inaugurated agriculture perhaps hundreds of thousands of years before the Neolithic revolution.[24] But a new kind of relationship to nature was involved; one that was evidently refused for so many, many generations.

To us it has seemed a great advantage to abstract from the natural relationship of things, whereas in the vast Stone Age being was apprehended and valued as a whole, not in terms of separable attributes.[25] Today, as ever, when a large family sits down to dinner and it is noticed that someone is missing, this is not accomplished by counting. Or when a hut was built in prehistoric times, the number of required posts was not specified or counted, rather they were inherent to the idea of the hut, intrinisically involved in it.[26] (Even in early agriculture, the loss of a herd animal could be detected not by counting but by missing a particular face or characteristic features; it seems clear, however, as Bryan Morgan argues, that "man's first use for a number system" was certainly as a control of domesticated flock animals,[27] as wild creatures became products to be harvested.) In distancing and separation lies the heart of mathematics: the discursive reduction of patterns, states and relationships which we initially perceived as wholes.[28]

In the birth of categories aimed at control of what is free and unordered, crystallized by early counting, we see a new attitude toward the world. If naming is a distancing, a mastery, so too is number, which is impoverished naming. Though numbering is a corollary of language, it is the signature of a critical breakthrough of alienation. The root meanings of number are instructive: "quick to grasp or take" and "to take, especially to steal," also "taken, seized, hence...numb."[29] What is made an object of domination is thereby reified, becomes numb.

For hundreds of thousands of years hunter-gatherers enjoyed a direct, unimpaired access to the raw materials needed for survival. Work was not divided nor did private property exist. Dorothy Lee focused on a surviving example from Oceania, finding that none of the Trobrianders' activities are fitted into a linear, divisible line. "There is no job, no labor, no drudgery which finds its reward outside the act."[30] Equally important is the "prodigality," "the liberal customs for which hunters are properly famous," "their inclination to make a feast of everything on hand,"[31] according to Sahlins.

Sharing and counting or exchange are, of course, relative opposites. Where articles are made, animals killed or plants collected for domestic use and not for exchange, there is no demand for standardized numbers or measurements. Measuring and weighing possessions develops later, along with the measurement and definition of property rights and duties to authority. Isaac locates a decisive shift toward standardization of tools and language in the Upper Paleolithic period,[32] the last stage of hunter-gatherer humanity. Numbers and less abstract units of measurement derive, as noted above, from the equalization of differences. Earliest exchange, which is the same as earliest division of labor, was indeterminate and defied systematization; a table of equivalences cannot really be formulated.[33] As the predominance of the gift gave way to the progress of exchange and division of labor, the universal interchangeability of mathematics finds its concrete expression. What comes to be fixed as a principle of equal justice—the ideology of equivalent exchange—is only the practice of the domination of division of labor. Lack of a directly-lived existence, the loss of autonomy that accompany separation from nature are the concomitants of the effective power of specialists.

Mauss stated that any exchange can be defined only be defining all of the institutions of society.[34] Decades later Belshaw grasped division of labor as not merely a segment of society but the whole of it.[35] Likewise sweeping, but realistic, is the conclusion that a world without exchange or fractionalized endeavor would be a world without number.

Clastres, and Childe among others well before him, realized that people's ability to produce a surplus, the basis of exchange, does not necessarily mean that they decide to do so. Concerning the nonetheless persistent view that only mental/cultural deficiency accounts for the absence of surplus, "nothing is more mistaken,"[36] judged Clastres. For Sahlins, "Stone Age economics" was "intrinsically an anti-surplus system,"[37] using the term system extremely loosely. For long ages humans had no desire for the dubious compensations attendant on assuming a divided life, just as they had no interest in number. Piling up a surplus of anything was unknown, apparently, before Neanderthal times passed to the Cro-Magnon; extensive trade contacts were nonexistent in the earlier period, becoming common thereafter with Cro-Magnon society.[38]

Surplus was fully developed only with agriculture, and characteristically the chief technical advancement of Neolithic life was the perfection of the container: jars, bins, granaries and the like.[39]

This development also gives concrete form to a burgeoning tendency toward spatialization, the sublimation of an increasingly autonomous dimension of time into spatial forms. Abstraction, perhaps the first spatialization, was the first compensation for the deprivation caused by the sense of time. Spatialization was greatly refined with number and geometry. Ricoeur notes that 'Infinity is discovered . . . in the form of the idealization of magnitudes, of measures, of numbers, figures,"[40] to carry this still further. This quest for unrestricted spatiality is part and parcel of the abstract march of mathematics. So then is the feeling of being freed from the world, from finitude that Hannah Arendt described in mathematics.[41]

Mathematical principles and their component numbers and figures seem to exemplify a timelessness which is possibly their deepest character. Hermann Weyl, in attempting to sum up (no pun intended) the "life center of mathematics," termed it the science of the infinite.[42] How better to express an escape from reified time than by making it limitlessly subservient to space — in the form of math.

Spatialization—like math—rests upon separation; inherent in it are division and an organization of that division. The division of time into parts (which seems to have been the earliest counting or measuring) is itself spatial. Time has always been measured in such terms as the movement of the earth or moon, or the hands of a clock. The first time-indications were not numerical but concrete, as with all earliest counting. Yet, as we know, a number system, paralleling time, becomes a separate, invariable principle. The separations in social life —most fundamentally, division of labor—seem alone able to account for the growth of estranging conceptualization.

In fact, two critical mathematical inventions, zero and the place system, may serve as cultural evidence of division of labor. Zero and the place system, or position, emerged independently, "against considerable psychological resistance,"[43] in the Mayan and Hindu civilizations. Mayan division of labor, accompanied by enormous social stratification (not to mention a notorious obsession with time, and large-scale human sacrifice at the hands of a powerful priest class), is a vividly documented fact, while the division of labor reflected in the Indian caste system was "the most complex that the world had seen before the Industrial Revolution."[44]

The necessity of work (Marx) and the necessity of repression (Freud) amount to the same thing: civilization. These false commandments turned humanity away from nature and account for history as a "steadily lengthening chronicle of mass neurosis."[45] Freud credits scientific/mathematical achievement as the highest moment of civilization, and this seems valid as a function of its symbolic nature. "The neurotic process is the price we pay for our most precious human heritage, namely our ability to represent experience and communicate our thoughts by means of symbols."[46]

The triad of symbolization, work and repression finds its operating principle in division of labor. This is why so little progress was made in accepting numerical values until the huge increase in division of labor of the Neolithic revolution: from the gathering of food to its actual production. With that massive changeover mathematics became fully grounded and necessary. Indeed it became more a category of existence than a mere instrumentality.

The fifth century B.C. historian Herodotus attributed the origin of mathematics to the Egyptian king Sesostris (1300 B.C.), who needed to measure land for tax purposes.[47] Systematized math—in this case geometry, which literally means "land measuring"—did in fact arise from the requirements of political economy, though it predates Sesostris' Egypt by perhaps 2000 years. The food surplus of Neolithic civilization made possible the emergence of specialized classes of priests and administrators which by about 3200 B.C. had produced the alphabet, mathematics, writing and the calendar.[48] In Sumer the first mathematical computations appeared, between 3500 and 3000 B.C., in the form of inventories, deeds of sale, contracts, and the attendant unit prices, units purchased, interest payments, etc.[49] As Bernal points out, "mathematics, or at least arithmetic, came even before writing."[50] The number symbols are most probably older than any other elements of the most ancient forms of writing.[51]

At this point domination of nature and humanity are signaled not only by math and writing, but also by the walled, grain-stocked city, along with warfare and human slavery. "Social labor" (division of labor), the coerced coordination of several workers at once, is thwarted by the old, personal measures; lengths, weights, volumes must be standardized. In this standardization, one of the hallmarks of civilization, mathematical exactitude and specialized skill go hand in hand. Math and specialization, requiring each other, developed apace and math became itself a specialty. The great trade routes, expressing the triumph of division of labor, diffused the new, sophisticated techniques of counting, measurement and calculation.

In Babylon, merchant-mathematicians contrived a comprehensive arithmetic between 3000 and 2500 B.C., which system "was fully articulated as an abstract computational science by about 2000 B.C.[52] In succeeding centuries the Babylonians even invented a symbolic algebra, though Babylonian-Egyptian math has been generally regarded as extremely trial-and-error or empiricist compared to that of the much later Greeks.

To the Egyptians and Babylonians mathematical figures had concrete referents: algebra was an aid to commercial transactions, a rectangle was a piece of land of a particular shape. The Greeks, however, were explicit in asserting that geometry deals with abstractions, and this development reflects an extreme form of division of labor and social stratification. Unlike Egyptian or Babylonian society, in Greece, a large slave class performed all productive labor, technical as well as unskilled, such that the ruling class milieu that included mathematicians disdained practical pursuits or applications.

Pythagoras, more or less the founder of Greek mathematics (6th century, B.C.), expressed this rarefied, abstract bent in no uncertain terms. To him numbers were immutable and eternal. Directly anticipating Platonic idealism, he declared that numbers were the intelligible key to the universe. Usually encapsulated as "everything is number," the Pythagorean philosophy held that numbers exist in a literal sense and are quite literally all that does exist.[53]

This form of mathematical philosophy, with the extremity of its search for harmony and order, may be seen as a deep fear of contradiction or chaos, an oblique acknowledgement of the massive and perhaps unstable repression underlying Greek society. An artificial intellectual life that rested so completely on the surplus created by slaves was at pains to deny the senses, the emotions and the real world. Greek sculpture is another example, in its abstract, ideological conformations, devoid of feelings or their histories.[54] Its figures are standardized idealizations; the parallel with a highly exaggerated cult of mathematics is manifest.

The independent existence of ideas, which is Plato's fundamental premise, is directly derived from Pythagoras, just as his whole theory of ideas flows from the special character of mathematics. Geometry is properly an exercise of disembodied intellect, Plato taught, in character with his view that reality is a world of form from which matter, in every important respect, is banished. Philosophical idealism was thus established out of this world-denying impoverishment, based on the primacy of quantitative thinking. As C.I. Lewis observed, "from Plato to the present day, all the major epistemological theories have been dominated by, or formulated in the light of, accompanying conceptions of mathematics."[55]

It is no less accidental that Plato wrote, "Let only geometers enter," over the door to his Academy, than that his totalitarian *Republic* insists that years of mathematical training are necessary to correctly approach the most important political and ethical questions.[56] Consistently, he denied that a stateless society ever existed, identifying such a concept with that of a "state of swine."[57]

Systematized by Euclid in the third century B.C., about a century after Plato, mathematics reached an apogee not to be matched for almost two millenia; the patron saint of intellect for the slave-based and feudal societies that followed was not Plato, but Aristotle, who criticized the former's Pythagorean reduction of science to mathematics.[58]

The long non-development of math, which lasted virtually until the end of the Renaissance, remains something of a mystery. But growing trade began to revive the art of the quantitative by the twelfth and thirteenth centuries.[59] The impersonal order of the counting house in the new mercantile capitalism exemplified a renewed concentration on abstract measurement. Mumford stresses the mathematical prerequisite to later mechanization and standardization; in the rising merchant world, "counting numbers began here and in the end numbers alone counted."[60]

Division of labor is the familiar counterpart of trade. As Crombie noted, "from the early 12th century there was a tendency to increasing specialization."[61] Thus the connection between division of labor and math, discussed earlier in this essay, is also once more apparent: "the whole history of European science from the 12th to the 17th century can be regarded as a gradual penetration of mathematics."[62]

Decisive changes concerning time also announced a growing tendency toward re-establishment of the Greek primacy of mathematics. By the fourteenth century, public use of mechanical clocks introduced abstract time as the new medium of social life. Town clocks came to symbolize a "methodical expenditure of hours" to match the "methodical accountancy of money,"[63] as time became a succession of precious, mathematically isolated instants. In the steadily more sophisticated measurement of time, as in the intensely geometric Gothic style of architecture, could be seen the growing importance of quantification.

By the late fifteenth century an increasing interest in the ideas of Plato was underway[64] and in the Renaissance God acquired mathematical properties. The growth of maritime commerce and colonization after 1500 demanded unprecedented accuracy in navigation and artillery. Sarton compared the greedy victories of the Conquistadores to those of the mathematicians, whose "conquests were spiritual ones, conquests of pure reason, the scope of which was infinite."[65]

But the Renaissance conviction that mathematics should be applicable to all the arts (not to mention such earlier and atypical forerunners as Roger Bacon's 13th century contribution toward a strictly mathematical optics), was a mild prelude to the magnitude of number's triumph in the seventeenth century.

Though they were soon eclipsed by other advances of the 1600's, Johannes Kepler and Francis Bacon revealed its two most important and closely related aspects early in the century. Kepler, who completed the Copernican transition to the heliocentric model, saw the real world as composed of quantitative differences only; its differences are strictly those of number.[66] Bacon, in *The New Atlantis* (c. 1620) depicted an idealized scientific community, the main object of which was domination of nature; as Jaspers put it, "Mastery of nature... 'knowledge is power,' has been the watchword since Bacon."[67]

The century of Galileo and Descartes—pre-eminent among those who deepened all the previous forms of quantitative alienation and thus sketched a technological future—began with a qualitative leap in the division of labor. Franz Borkenau provided the key as to why a profound change in the Western world-view took place in the seventeenth century, a movement to a fundamentally mathematical-mechanistic outlook. According to Borkenau, a great extension of division of labor, occurring from about 1600, introduced the novel notion of abstract work.[68] This reification of human activity proved pivotal.

Along with degradation of work, the clock is the basis of modern life, equally "scientific" in its reduction of life to a measurability, via objective, commodified units of time. The increasingly accurate and ubiquitous clock reached a real domination in the seventeenth century, as, correspondingly, "the champions of the new sciences manifested an avid interest in horological matters."[69]

Thus it seems fitting to introduce Galileo in terms of just this strong interest in the measurement of time; his invention of the first mechanical clock based on the principle of the pendulum was likewise a fitting capstone to his long career. As increasingly objectified or reified time reflects, at perhaps the deepest level, an increasingly alienated social world, Galileo's principal aim was the reduction of the world to an object of mathematical dissection.

Writing a few years before World War II and Auschwitz, Husserl located the roots of the contemporary crisis in this objectifying reduction and identified Galileo as its main progenitor. The life-world has been "devalued" by science precisely insofar as the "mathematization of nature" initiated by Galileo has proceeded[70]—clearly no small indictment.

For Galileo as with Kepler, mathematics was the "root grammar of the new philosophical discourse that constituted modern scientific method."[71] He enunciated the principle, "to measure what is measurable and try to render what is not so yet."[72] Thus he resurrected the Pythagorean-Platonic substitution of a world of abstract mathematical relations for the real world and its method of absolute renunciation of the senses' claim to know reality. Observing this turning away from quality to quantity, this plunge into a shadow-world of abstractions, Husserl concluded that modern, mathematical science prevents us from knowing life as it is. And the rise of science has fueled ever more specialized knowledge, that stunting and imprisoning progression so well-known by now.

Collingwood called Galileo "the true father of modern science" for the success of his dictum that the book of nature "is written in mathematical language" and its corollary that therefore "mathematics is the language of science."[73] Due to this separation from nature, Gillispie evaluated, "After Galileo, science could no longer be humane."[74]

It seems very fitting that the mathematician who synthesized geometry and algebra to form analytic geometry (1637) and who, with Pascal, is credited with inventing calculus,[75] should have shaped Galilean mathematicism into a new system of thinking. The thesis that the world is organized in such a way that there is a total break between people and the natural world, contrived as a total and triumphant world-view, is the basis for Descartes' renown as the founder of modern philophy. The foundation of his new system, the famous, "cogito, ergo sum," is the assigning of scientific certainty to the separation between mind and the rest of reality.[76]

This dualism provided an alienated means for seeing only a completely objectified nature. In the *Discourse on Method...*, Descartes declared that the aim of science is "to make us as masters and possessors of nature."[77] Though he was a devout Christian, Descartes renewed the distancing from life that an already fading God could no longer effectively legitimize. As Christianity weakened, a new central ideology of estrangement came forth, this one guaranteeing order and domination based on mathematical precision.

To Descartes the material universe was a machine and nothing more, just as animals "indeede are nothing else but engines, or matter sett into a continual and orderly motion."[78] He saw the cosmos itself as a giant clockwork just when the illusion that time is a separate, autnomous process was taking hold. Also as living, animate nature died, dead, inanimate money became endowed with life, as capital and the market assumed the attributes of organic process and cycles.[79] Lastly, Descartes' mathematical vision eliminated any messy, chaotic or alive elements and ushered in an attendant mechanical world-view that was coincidental with a tendency toward central government controls and concentration of power in the form of the modern nation-state. "The rationalization of administration and of the natural order was occurring simultaneously,"[80] in the words of Merchant. The total order of math and its mechanical philosophy of reality proved irresistible; by the time of Descartes' death in 1650 it had become virtually the official frame-work of thought throughout Europe.

Leibniz, a near-contemporary, refined and extended the work of Descartes; the "pre-established harmony" he saw in existence is likewise Pythagorean in lineage. This mathematical harmony, which Leibniz illustrated by reference to two independent clocks, recalls his dictum, "There is nothing that evades number."[81] Responsible also for the more well-known phrase, "Time is money,"[82] Leibniz, like Galileo and Descartes, was deeply interested in the design of clocks.

In the binary arithmetic he devised, an image of creation was evoked; he imagined that one represented God and zero the void, that unity and zero expressed all numbers and all creation.[83] He sought to mechanize thought by means of a formal calculus, a project which he too sanguinely expected would be completed in five years. This undertaking was to provide all the answers, including those to questions of morality and metaphysics. Despite this ill-fated effort, Leibniz was perhaps the first to base a theory of math on the fact that it is a universal symbolic language; he was certainly the "first great modern thinker to have a clear insight into the true character of mathematical symbolism."[84]

Furthering the quantitative model of reality was the English royalist Hobbes, who reduced the human soul, will, brain, and appetites to matter in mechanical motion, thus contributing directly to the current conception of thinking as the "output" of the brain as computer.

The complete objectification of time, so much with us today, was achieved by Isaac Newton, who mapped the workings of the Galilean-Cartesian clockwork universe. Product of the severely repressed Puritan outlook, which focused on sublimating sexual energy into brutalizing labor, Newton spoke of absolute time, "flowing equably without regard to anything external."[85] Born in 1642, the year of Galileo's death, Newton capped the Scientific Revolution of the seventeenth century by developing a complete mathematical formulation of nature as a perfect machine, a perfect clock.

Whitehead judged that "the history of seventeenth-century science reads as though it were some vivid dream of Plato or Pythagoras,"[86] noting the astonishingly refined mode of its quantitative thought. Again the correspondence with a jump in division of labor is worth pointing out; as Hill described mid-seventeenth century England, ". . .significant specialization began to set in. The last polymaths were dying out. . ."[87] The songs and dances of the peasants slowly died, and in a rather literal mathematization, the common lands were enclosed and divided.

Knowledge of nature was part of philosophy until this time; the two parted company as the concept of mastery of nature achieved its definitive modern form. Number, which first issued from dissociation from the natural world, ended up describing and dominating it.

Fontenelle's *Preface on the Utility of Mathematics and Physics* (1702) celebrated the centrality of quantification to the entire range of human sensibilities, thereby aiding the eighteenth century consolidation of the breakthroughs of the preceding era. And whereas Descartes had asserted that animals could not feel pain because they are soulless, and that man is not exactly a machine because he has a soul, LeMettrie, in 1747, went the whole way and made man completely mechanical in his *L'Homme Machine.*

Bach's immense accomplishments in the first half of the eighteenth century also throw light on the spirit of math unleashed a century earlier and helped shape culture to that spirit. In reference to the rather abstract music of Bach, it has been said that he "spoke in mathematics to God."[88] At this time the individual voice lost its independence and tone was no longer understood as sung but as a mechanical conception. Bach, treating music as a sort of math, moved it out of the stage of vocal polyphony to that of instrumental harmony, based always upon a single, autonomous tone fixed by instruments, instead of somewhat variable with human voices.[89]

Later in the century Kant stated that in any particular theory there is only as much real science as there is mathematics, and devoted a considerable part of his *Critique of Pure Reason* to an analysis of the ultimate principles of geometry and arithmetic.[90]

Descartes and Leibniz strove to establish a mathematical science method as the paradigmatic way of knowing, and saw the possibility of a singular universal language, on the model of numerical symbols, that could contain the whole of philosophy. The eighteenth century Enlightenment thinkers acually worked at realizing this latter project. Condillac, Rousseau and others were also characteristically concerned with origins—such as the origin of language; their goal of grasping human understanding by taking language to its ultimate, mathematized symbolic level made them incapable of seeing that the origin of all symbolizing is alienation.

Symmetrical plowing is almost as old as agriculture itself, a means of imposing order on an otherwise irregular world. But as the landscape of cultivation became distinguished by linear forms of an increasingly mathematical regularity—including the popularity of formal gardens—another eighteenth-century mark of math's ascendancy can be gauged.

With the early 1800s, however, the Romantic poets and artists, among others, protested the new vision of nature as a machine. Blake, Goethe and John Constable, for example, accused science of turning the world into a clockwork, with the Industrial Revolution providing ample evidence of its power to violate organic life.

The debasing of work among textile workers, which caused the furious uprisings of the English Luddites during the second decade of the nineteenth century, was epitomized by such automated and cheapened products as those of the Jacquard loom. This French device not only represented the mechanization of life and work unleashed by seventeenth century shifts, but directly inspired the first attempts at the modern computer. The designs of Charles Babbage, unlike the "logic machines" of Leibniz and Descartes, involved both memory and calculating units under the control of programs via punched cards. The aims of the mathematical Babbage and the inventor-industrialist J.M. Jacquard can be said to rest on the same rationalist reduction of human activity to the machine as was then beginning to boom with industrialism. Quite in character, then, were the emphasis in Babbage's mathematical work on the need for improved notation to further the processes of symbolization, his *Principles of Economy*, which contributed to the foundations of modern management—and his contemporary fame as a crusader against London "nuisances," such as street musicians![91]

Paralleling the full onslaught of industrial capitalism and the hugely accelerated division of labor that it brought was a marked advance in mathematical development. According to Whitehead, "During the nineteenth century pure mathematics made almost as much progress as during the preceding centuries from Pythagoras onwards."[92]

The non-Euclidean geometries of Bolyai, Lobachevski, Riemann and Klein must be mentioned, as well as the modern algebra of Boole, generally regarded as the basis of symbolic logic. Boolean algebra made possible a new level of formulized thought, as its founder pondered "the human mind...an instrument of conquest and dominion over the powers of surrounding Nature,"[93] in an unthinking mirroring of the mastery mathematized capitalism was gaining in the mid-1800s. (Although the specialist is rarely faulted by the dominant culture for his "pure" creativity, Adorno adroitly observed that "The mathematician's resolute unconsciousness testifies to the connection between division of labor and "purity.")[94]

If math is impoverished language, it can also be seen as the mature form of that sterile coercion known as formal logic. Bertrand Russell, in fact, determined that mathematics and logic had become one.[95] Discarding unreliable, everyday language, Russell, Frege and others believed that in the further degradation and reduction of language lay the real hope for "progress in philosophy."[96]

The goal of establishing logic on mathematical grounds was related to an even more ambitious effort by the end of the nineteenth century, that of establishing the foundations of math itself. As capitalism proceeded to redefine reality in its own image and became desirous of securing its foundations, the "logic" stage of math in the late 19th and early 20th centuries, fresh from new triumphs, sought the same. David Hilbert's theory of formalism, one such attempt to banish contradiction or error, explicitly aimed at safeguarding "the state power of mathematics for all time from all 'rebellions.'"[97]

Meanwhile, number seemed to be doing quite well without the philosophical underpinnings. Lord Kelvin's late nineteenth century pronouncement that we don't really know anything unless we can measure it[98] bespoke an exalted confidence, just as Frederick Taylor's Scientific Management was about to lead the quantification edge of industrial management further in the direction of subjugating the individual to the lifeless Newtonian categories of time and space.

Speaking of the latter, Capra has claimed that the theories of relativity and quantum physics, developed between 1905 and the late 1920s, "shattered all the principal concepts of the Cartesian world view and Newtonian mechanics."[99] But relativity theory is certainly mathematical formalism, and Einstein sought a unified field theory by geometrizing physics, such that success would have enabled him to have said, like Descartes, that his entire physics was nothing other than geometry. That measuring time and space (or "space-time") is a relative matter hardly removes measurement as its core element. At the heart of quantum theory, similarly, is Heisenberg's Uncertainty Principle, which does not throw out quantification but rather expresses the limitations of classical physics in sophisticated mathematical ways. As Gillispie succinctly had it, Cartesian-Newtonian physical theory "was an application of Euclidean geometry to space, general relativity a spatialization of Riemann's curvilinear geometry, and quantum mechanics a naturalization of statistical probability."[100] More succinctly still: "Nature, before and after the quantum theory, is that which is to be comprehended mathematically."[101]

During these first three decades of the 20th century, moreover, the great attempts by Russell & Whitehead, Hilbert, et al., to provide a completely unproblematic basis for the whole edifice of math, referred to above, went forward with considerable optimism. But in 1931 Kurt Gödel dashed these bright hopes with his Incompleteness Theorem, which demonstrated that any symbolic system can be either complete or fully consistent, but not both. Gödel's devastating mathematical proof of this not only showed the limits of axiomatic number systems, but rules out enclosing nature by any closed, consistent language. If there are theorems or assertions within a system of thought which can neither be proved or disproved internally, if it is impossible to give a proof of consistency within the language used, as Gödel and immediate successors like Tarski and Church convincingly argued, "any system of knowledge about the world is, and must remain, fundamentally incomplete, eternally subject to revision."[102]

Morris Kline's *Mathematics: The Loss of Certainty* related the "calamities" that have befallen the once seemingly inviolable "majesty of mathematics,"[103] chiefly dating from Gödel. Math, like language, used to describe the world and itself, fails in its totalizing quest, in the same way that capitalism cannot provide itself with unassailable grounding. Further, with Gödel's Theorem mathematics was not only "recognized to be much more abstract and formal than had been traditionally supposed,"[104] but it also became clear that "the resources of the human mind have not been, and cannot be, fully formalized."[105]

But who could deny that, in practice, quantity has been mastering us, with or without definitively shoring up its theoretical basis? Human helplessness seems to be directly proportional to mathematical technology's domination over nature, or as Adorno phrased it, "the subjection of outer nature is successful only in the measure of the repression of inner nature."[106] And certainly understanding is diminished by number's hallmark, division of labor. Raymond Firth accidently exemplified the stupidity of advanced specialization, in a passing comment on a crucial topic: "the proposition that symbols are instruments of knowledge raises epistemological issues which anthropologists are not trained to handle."[107] The connection with a more common degradation is made by Singh, in the context of an ever more refined division of labor and a more and more technicised social life, noting that "automation of computation immediately paved the way for automatizing industrial operations."[108]

The heightened tedium of computerized office work is today's very visible manifestation of mathematized, mechanized labor, with its neo-Taylorist quantification via electronic display screens, announcing the "information explosion" or "information society." Information work is now the chief economic activity and information the distinctive commodity,[109] in large part echoing the main concept of Shannon's information theory of the late 1940s, in which "the production and the transmission of information could be defined quantitatively."[110]

From knowledge, to information, to data, the mathematizing trajectory moves away from meaning—paralleled exactly in the realm of "ideas" (those bereft of goals or content, that is) by the ascendency of structuralism. The "global communications revolution" is another telling phenomenon, by which a meaningless "input" is to be instantly available everywhere among people who live, as never before, in isolation.[111]

Into this spiritual vacuum the computer boldly steps. In 1950 Turing said, in answer to the question 'can machines think?', "I believe that at the end of the century the use of words and general educated opinion will have altered so much that one will be able to speak of machines thinking without expecting to be contradicted."[112] Note that his reply had nothing to do with the state of machines but wholly that of humans. As pressures build for life to become more quantified and machine-like, so does the drive to make machines more life-like.

By the mid-60s, in fact, a few prominent voices already announced that the distinction between human and machine was about to be superseded—and saw this as positive. Mazlish provided an especially unequivocal commentary: "Man is on the threshhold of breaking past the discontinuity between himself and machines...We cannot think any longer of man without a machine...Moreover, this change...is essential to our harmonious acceptance of an industrialized world."[113]

By the late 1980's thinking sufficiently impersonates the machine that Artificial Intelligence experts, like Minsky, can matter-of-factly speak of the symbol-manipulating brain as "a computer made of meat."[114] Cognitive psychology, echoing Hobbes, has become almost based on the computational model of thought in the decades since Turing's 1950 prediction.[115]

Heidegger felt that there is an inherent tendency for Western thinking to merge into the mathematical sciences, and saw science as "incapable of awakening, and in fact emasculating, the spirit of genuine inquiry."[116] We find ourselves, in an age when the fruits of science threaten to end human life altogether, when a dying capitalism seems capable of taking everything with it, more apt to want to discover the ultimate origins of the nightmare.

When the world and its thought (Levi-Strauss and Chomsky come immediately to mind) reach a condition that is increasingly mathematized and empty (where computers are widely touted as capable of feelings and even of life itself),[117] the beginnings of this bleak journey, including the origins of the number concept, demand comprehension. It may be that this inquiry is essential to save us and our humanness.

THE CASE AGAINST ART

Art is always about "something hidden." But does it help us connect with that hidden something? I think it moves us away from it.

During the first million or so years as reflective beings humans seem to have created no art. As Jameson put it, art had no place in that "unfallen social reality" because there was no need for it. Though tools were fashioned with an astonishing economy of effort and perfection of form, the old cliche about the aesthetic impulse as one of the irreducible components of the human mind is invalid.

The oldest enduring works of art are hand-prints, produced by pressure or blown pigment — a dramatic token of direct impress on nature. Later in the Upper Paleolithic era, about 30,000 years ago, commenced the rather sudden appearance of the cave art associated with names like Altamira and Lascaux. These images of animals possess an often breathtaking vibrancy and naturalism, though current sculpure, such as the widely-found "venus" statuettes of women, was quite stylized. Perhaps this indicates that domestication of people was to precede domestication of nature. Significantly, the "sympathetic magic" or hunting theory of earliest art is now waning in the light of evidence that nature was bountiful rather than threatening.

The veritable explosion of art at this time bespeaks an anxiety not felt before: in Worringer's words, "creation in order to subdue the torment of perception." Here is the appearance of the symbolic, as a moment of discontent. It was a social anxiety; people felt something precious slipping away. The rapid development of ritual or ceremony parallels the birth of art, and we are reminded of the earliest ritual re-enactments of the moment of "the beginning," the primordial paradise of the timeless present. Pictorial representation roused the belief in controlling loss, the belief in coercion itself.

And we see the earliest evidence of symbolic division, as with the half-human, half-beast stone faces at El Juyo. The world is divided into opposing forces, by which binary distinction the contrast of culture and nature begins and a productionist, hierarchical society is perhaps already prefigured.

The perceptual order itself, as a unity, starts to break down in reflection of an increasingly complex social order. A hierarchy of senses, with the visual steadily more separate from the others and seeking its completion in artificial images such as cave paintings, moves to replace the full simultaneity of sensual gratification. Lévi-Strauss discovered, to his amazement, a tribal people that had been able to see Venus in daytime; but not only were our faculties once so very acute, they were also not ordered and separate. Part of training sight to appreciate the objects of culture was the accompanying repression of immediacy in an intellectual sense: reality was removed in favor of merely aesthetic experience. Art anesthetizes the sense organs and removes the natural world from their purview. This reproduces culture, which can never compensate for the disability.

Not surprisingly, the first signs of a departure from those egalitarian principles that characterized hunter-gatherer life show up now. The shamanistic origin of visual art and music has been often remarked, the point here being that the artist-shaman was the first specialist. It seems likely that the ideas of surplus and commodity appeared with the shaman, whose orchestration of symbolic activity portended further alienation and stratification.

Art, like language, is a system of symbolic exchange that introduces exchange itself. It is also a necessary device for holding together a community based on the first symptoms of unequal life. Tolstoy's statement that "art is a means of union among men, joining them together in the same feeling," elucidates art's contribution to social cohesion at the dawn of culture. Socializing ritual required art; art works originated in the service of ritual; the ritual production of art and the artistic production of ritual are the same. "Music," wrote Seu-ma-tsen, "is what unifies."

As the need for solidarity accelerated, so did the need for ceremony; art also played a role in its mnemonic function. Art, with myth closely following, served as the semblance of real memory. In the recesses of the caves, earliest indoctrination proceeded via the paintings and other symbols, intended to inscribe rules in depersonalized, collective memory. Nietzsche saw the training of memory, especially the memory of obligations, as the beginning of civilized morality. Once the symbolic process of art developed it dominated memory as well as perception, putting its stamp on all mental functions. Cultural memory meant that one person's action could be compared with that of another, including portrayed ancestors, and future behavior anticipated and controlled. Memories became externalized, akin to property but not even the property of the subject.

Art turns the subject into object, into symbol. The shaman's role was to objectify reality; this happened to outer nature and to subjectivity alike because alienated life demanded it. Art provided the medium of conceptual transformation by which the individual was separated from nature and dominated, at the deepest level, socially. Art's ability to symbolize and direct human emotion accomplished both ends. What we were led to accept as necessity, in order to keep ourselves oriented in nature and society, was at base the invention of the symbolic world, the Fall of Man.

The world must be mediated by art (and human communication by language, and being by time) due to division of labor, as seen in the nature of ritual. The real object, its particularity, does not appear in ritual; instead, an abstract one is used, so that the terms of ceremonial expression are open to substitution. The conventions needed in division of labor, with its standardization and loss of the unique, are those of ritual, of symbolization. The process is at base identical, based on equivalence. Production of goods, as the hunter-gatherer mode is gradually liquidated in favor of agriculture (historical production) and religion (full symbolic production), is also ritual production.

The agent, again, is the shaman-artist, enroute to priesthood, leader by reason of mastering his own immediate desires via the symbol. All that is spontaneous, organic and instinctive is to be neutered by art and myth.

Recently the painter Eric Fischl presented at the Whitney Museum a couple in the act of sexual intercourse. A video camera recorded their actions and projected them on a TV monitor before the two. The man's eyes were riveted to the image on the screen, which was clearly more exciting than the act itself. The evocative cave pictures, volatile in the dramatic, lamp-lit depths, began the transfer exemplified in Fischl's tableau, in which even the most primal acts can become secondary to their representation. Conditioned self-distancing from real existence has been a goal of art from the beginning. Similarly, the category of audience, of supervised consumption, is nothing new, as art has striven to make life itself an object of contemplation.

As the Paleolithic Age gave way to the Neolithic arrival of agriculture and civilization — production, private property, written language, government and religion — culture could be seen more fully as spiritual decline via division of labor, though global specialization and a mechanistic technology did not prevail until the late Iron Age.

The vivid representation of late hunter-gatherer art was replaced by a formalistic, geometrical style, reducing pictures of animals and humans to symbolic shapes. This narrow stylization reveals the artist shutting himself off from the wealth of empirical reality and creating the symbolic universe. The aridity of linear precision is one of the hallmarks of this turning point, calling to mind the Yoruba, who associate line with civilization: "This country has become civilized," literally means, in Yoruba, "this earth has lines upon its face." The inflexible forms of truly alienated society are everywhere apparent; Gordon Childe, for example, referring to this spirit, points out that the pots of a Neolithic village are all alike. Relatedly, warfare in the form of combat scenes makes its first appearance in art.

The work of art was in no sense autonomous at this time; it served society in a direct sense, an instrument of the needs of the new collectivity. There had been no worship-cults during the Paleolithic, but now religion held sway, and it is worth remembering that for thousands of years art's function will be to depict the gods. Meanwhile, what Glück stressed about African tribal architecture was true in all other cultures as well: sacred buildings came to life on the model of those of the secular ruler. And though not even the first signed works show up before the late Greek period, it is not inappropriate to turn here to art's realization, some of its general features.

Art not only creates the symbols of and for a society, it is a basic part of the symbolic matrix of estranged social life. Oscar Wilde said that art does not imitate life, but vice versa; which is to say that life follows symbolism, not forgetting that it is (deformed) life that produces symbolism. Every art form, according to T.S. Eliot, is "an attack upon the inarticulate." Upon the unsymbolized, he should have said.

Both painter and poet have always wanted to reach the silence behind and within art and language, leaving the question of whether the individual, in adopting these modes of expression, didn't settle for far too little. Though Bergson tried to approach the goal of thought without symbols, such a breakthrough seems impossible outside our active undoing of all the layers of alienation. In the extremity of revolutionary situations, immediate communication has bloomed, if briefly.

The primary function of art is to objectify feeling, by which one's own motivations and identity are transformed into symbol and metaphor. All art, as symbolization, is rooted in the creation of substitutes, surrogates for something else; by its very nature therefore, it is falsification. Under the guise of "enriching the quality of human experience," we accept vicarious, symbolic descriptions of how we should feel, trained to need such public images of sentiment that ritual art and myth provide for our psychic security.

Life in civilization is lived almost wholly in a medium of symbols. Not only scientific or technological activity but aesthetic form are canons of symbolization, often expressed quite unspiritually. It is widely averred, for example, that a limited number of mathematical figures account for the efficacy of art. There is Cezanne's famous dictum to "treat nature by the cylinder, the sphere and the cone," and Kandinsky's judgment that "the impact of the acute angle of a triangle on a circle produces an effect no less powerful than the finger of God touching the finger of Adam in Michelangelo." The sense of a symbol, as Charles Pierce concluded, is its translation into another symbol, thus an endless reproduction, with the real always displaced.

Though art is not fundamentally concerned with beauty, its inability to rival nature sensuously has evoked many unfavorable comparisons. "Moonlight is sculpture," wrote Hawthorne; Shelley praised the "unpremeditated art" of the skylark; Verlaine pronounced the sea more beautiful than all the cathedrals. And so on, with sunsets, snowflakes, flowers, etc., beyond the symbolic products of art. Jean Arp, in fact, termed "the most perfect picture" nothing more than " warty, threadbare approximation, a dry porridge."

Why then would one respond positively to art? As compensation and palliative, because our relationship to nature and life is so deficient and disallows an authentic one. As Motherlant put it, "One gives to one's art what one has not been capable of giving to one's existence." It is true for artist and audience alike; art, like religion, arises from unsatisfied desire.

Art should be considered a religious activity and category also in the sense of Nietzsche's aphorism, "We have Art in order not to perish of Truth." Its consolation explains the widespread preference for metaphor over a direct relationship to the genuine article. If pleasure were somehow released from every restraint, the result would be the antithesis of art. In dominated life freedom does not exist outside art, however, and so even a tiny, deformed fraction of the riches of being is welcomed. "I create in order not to cry," revealed Klee.

This separate realm of contrived life is both important and in complicity with the actual nightmare that prevails. In its institutionalized separation it corresponds to religion and ideology in general, where its elements are not, and cannot be, actualized; the work of art is a selection of possibilities unrealized except in symbolic terms. Arising from the sense of loss referred to above, it conforms to religion not only by reason of its confinement to an ideal sphere and its absence of any dissenting consequences, but it can hence be no more than thoroughly neutralized critique at best.

Frequently compared to play, art and culture — like religion — have more often worked as generators of guilt and oppression. Perhaps the ludic function of art, as well as its common claim to transcendance, should be estimated as one might reassess the meaning of Versailles: by contemplating the misery of the workers who perished draining its marshes.

Clive Bell pointed to the intention of art to transport us from the plane of daily struggle "to a world of aesthetic exaltation," paralleling the aim of religion. Malraux offered another tribute to the conservative office of art when he wrote that without art works civilization would crumble "within fifty years". . . becoming "enslaved to instincts and to elementary dreams."

Hegel determined that art and religion also have "this in common, namely, having entirely universal matters as content." This feature of generality, of meaning without concrete reference, serves to introduce the notion that ambiguity is a distinctive sign of art.

Usually depicted positively, as a revelation of truth free of the contingencies of time and place, the impossibility of such a formulation only illuminates another moment of falseness about art. Kierkegaard found the defining trait of the aesthetic outlook to be its hospitable reconciliation of all points of view and its evasion of choice. This can be seen in the perpetual compromise that at once valorizes art only to repudiate its intent and content with "Well, after all, it is only art."

Today culture is commodity and art perhaps the star commodity. The situation is understood inadequately as the product of a centralized culture industry, à la Horkheimer and Adorno. We witness, rather, a mass diffusion of culture dependent on participation for its strength, not forgetting that the critique must be of culture itself, not of its alleged control.

Daily life has become aestheticized by a saturation of images and music, largely through the electronic media, the representation of representation. Image and sound, in their ever-presence, have become a void, ever more absent of meaning for the individual. Meanwhile, the distance between artist and spectator has diminished, a narrowing that only highlights the absolute distance between aesthetic experience and what is real. This perfectly duplicates the spectacle at large: separate and manipulating, perpetual aesthetic experience and a demonstration of political power.

Reacting against the increasing mechanization of life, avant-garde movements have not, however, resisted the spectacular nature of art any more than orthodox tendencies have. In fact, one could argue that Aestheticism, or "art for art's sake," is more radical than an attempt to engage alienation with its own devices. The late 19th century *art pour l'art* development was a self-reflective rejection of the world, as opposed to the avant-garde effort to somehow organize life around art.

A valid moment of doubt lies behind Aestheticism, the realization that division of labor has diminished experience and turned art into just another specialization: art shed its illusory ambitions and became its own content.

The avant-garde has generally staked out wider claims, projecting a leading role denied it by modern capitalism. It is best understood as a social institution peculiar to technological society that so strongly prizes novelty; it is predicated on the progressivist notion that reality must be constantly updated. But avant-garde culture cannot compete with the modern world's capacity to shock and transgress (and not just symbolically). Its demise is another datum that the myth of progress is itself bankrupt.

Dada was one of the last two major avant-garde movements, its negative image greatly enhanced by the sense of general historical collapse radiated by World War I. Its partisans claimed, at times, to be against all "isms," including the idea of art. But painting cannot negate painting, nor can sculpture invalidate sculpture, keeping in mind that all symbolic culture is the co-opting of perception, expression and communication. In fact, Dada was a quest for new artistic modes, its attack on the rigidities and irrelevancies of bourgeois art a factor in the advance of art; Hans Richter's memoirs referred to "the regeneration of visual art that Dada had begun." If World War I almost killed art, the Dadaists reformed it.

Surrealism is the last school to assert the political mission of art. Before trailing off into Trotskyism and/or art-world fame, the Surrealists upheld chance and the primitive as ways to unlock "the Marvelous" which society imprisons in the unconscious. The false judgment that would have re-introduced art into everyday life and thereby transfigured it certainly misunderstood the relationship of art to repressive society. The real barrier is not between art and social reality, which are one, but between desire and the existing world. The Surrealists' aim of inventing a new symbolism and mythology upheld those categories and mistrusted unmediated sensuality. Concerning the latter, Breton held that "enjoyment is a science; the exercise of the senses demands a personal initiation and therefore you need art."

Modernist abstraction resumed the trend begun by Aestheticism, in that it expressed the conviction that only by a drastic restriction of its field of vision could art survive. With the least strain of embellishment possible in a formal language, art became increasingly self-referential, in its search for a "purity" that was hostile to narrative. Guaranteed not to represent anything, modern painting is consciously nothing more than a flat surface with paint on it.

But the strategy of trying to empty art of symbolic value, the insistence on the work of art as an object in its own right in a world of objects, proved a virtually self-annihilating method. This "radical physicality," based on aversion to authority though it was, never amounted to more, in its objectiveness, than simple commodity status. The sterile grids of Mondrian and the repeated all-black squares of Reinhardt echo this acquiescence no less than hideous 20th century architecture in general. Modernist self-liquidation was parodied by Rauschenberg's 1953 *Erased Drawing*, exhibited after his month-long erasure of a de Kooning drawing. The very concept of art, Duchamp's showing of a urinal in a 1917 exhibition notwithstanding, became an open question in the '50s and has grown steadily undefinable since.

Pop Art demonstrated that the boundaries between art and mass media (e.g. ads and comics) are dissolving. Its perfunctory and mass-produced look is that of the whole society and the detached, blank quality of a Warhol and his products sum it up. Banal, morally weightless, depersonalized images, cynically manipulated by a fashion-conscious marketing strategem: the nothingness of modern art and its world revealed.

The proliferation of art styles and approaches in the '60s — Conceptual, Minimalist, Performance, etc. — and the accelerated obsolescence of most art brought the "postmodern" era, a displacement of the formal "purism" of modernism by an eclectic mix from past stylistic achievements. This is basically a tired, spiritless recycling of used-up fragments, announcing that the development of art is at an end. Against the global devaluing of the symbolic, moreover, it is incapable of generating new symbols and scarcely even makes an effort to do so.

Occasional critics, like Thomas Lawson, bemoan art's current inability "to stimulate the growth of a really troubling doubt," little noticing that a quite noticeable movement of doubt threatens to throw over art itself. Such "critics" cannot grasp that art must remain alienation and as such must be superseded, that art is disappearing because the immemorial separation between nature and art is a death sentence for the world that must be voided.

Deconstruction, for its part, announced the project of decoding Literature and indeed the "texts," or systems of signification, throughout all culture. But this attempt to reveal supposedly hidden ideology is stymied by its refusal to consider origins or historical causation, an aversion it inherited from structuralism/poststructuralism. Derrida, Deconstruction's seminal figure, deals with language as a solipsism, consigned to self-interpretation; he engages not in critical activity but in writing about writing. Rather than a de-constructing of impacted reality, this approach is merely a self-contained academicism, in which Literature, like modern painting before it, never departs from concern with its own surface.

Meanwhile, since Piero Manzoni canned his own feces and sold them in a gallery and Chris Burden had himself shot in the arm, and crucified to a Volkswagen, we see in art ever more fitting parables of its end, such as the self-portraits drawn by Anastasi — with his eyes closed. "Serious" music is long dead and popular music deteriorates; poetry nears collapse and retreats from view; drama, which moved from the Absurd to Silence, is dying; and the novel is eclipsed by non-fiction as the only way to write seriously.

In a jaded, enervated age, when it seems to speak is to say less, art is certainly less. Baudelaire was obliged to claim a poet's dignity in a society which had no more dignity to hand out. A century and more later how inescapable is the truth of that condition and how much more threadbare the consolation or station of "timeless" art.

Adorno began his last book thusly: "Today it goes without saying that nothing concerning art goes without saying, much less without thinking. Everything about art has become problematic: its inner life, its relation to society, even its right to exist." But *Aesthetic Theory* affirms art, just as Marcuse's last work did, testifying to despair and to the difficulty of assailing the hermetically sealed ideology of culture. And although other "radicals," such as Habermas, counsel that the desire to abolish symbolic mediation is irrational, it is becoming clearer that when we really experiment with our hearts and hands the sphere of art is shown to be pitiable. In the transfiguration we must enact the symbolic will be left behind and art refused in favor of the real. Play, creativity, self-expression and authentic experience will recommence at that moment.

AGRICULTURE

Agriculture, the indispensable basis of civilization, was originally encountered as time, language, number and art emerged. As the materialization of alienation, agriculture is the triumph of estrangement and the definite divide between culture and nature and humans from each other.

Agriculture is the birth of production, complete with its essential features and deformation of life and consciousness. The land itself becomes an instrument of production and the planet's species its objects. Wild or tame, weeds or crops speak of that duality that cripples the soul of our being, ushering in, relatively quickly, the despotism, war and impoverishment of high civilization over the great length of that earlier oneness with nature. The forced march of civilization, which Adorno recognized in the "assumption of an irrational catastrophe at the beginning of history," which Freud felt as "something imposed on a resisting majority," of which Stanley Diamond found only "conscripts, not volunteers," was dictated by agriculture. And Mircea Eliade was correct to assess its coming as having "provoked upheavals and spiritual breakdowns" whose magnitude the modern mind cannot imagine.

"To level off, to standardize the human landscape, to efface its irregularities and banish its surprises," these words of E.M. Cioran apply perfectly to the logic of agriculture, the end of life as mainly sensuous activity, the embodiment and generator of separated life. Artificiality and work have steadily increased since its inception and are known as culture: in domesticating animals and plants man necessarily domesticated himself.

Historical time, like agriculture, is not inherent in social reality but an imposition on it. The dimension of time or history is a function of repression, whose foundation is production or agriculture. Hunter-gatherer life was anti-time in its simultaneous and spontaneous openness; farming life generates a sense of time by its successive-task narrowness, its directed routine. As the non-closure and variety of Paleolithic living gave way to the literal enclosure of agriculture, time assumed power and came to take on the character of an enclosed space. Formalized temporal reference points— ceremonies with fixed dates, the naming of days, etc.—are crucial to the ordering of the world of production; as a schedule of production, the calendar is integral to civilization. Conversely, not only would industrial society be impossible without time schedules, the end of agriculture (basis of all production) would be the end of historical time.

Representation begins with language, a means of reining in desire. By displacing autonomous images with verbal symbols, life is reduced and brought under strict control; all direct, unmediated experience is subsumed by that supreme mode of symbolic expression, language. Language cuts up and organizes reality, as Benjamin Whorf put it, and this segmentation of nature, an aspect of grammar, sets the stage for agriculture. Julian Jaynes, in fact, concluded that the new linguistic mentality led very directly to agriculture. Unquestionably, the crystallization of language into writing, called forth mainly by the need for record-keeping of agricultural transactions, is the signal that civilization has begun.

In the non-commodified, egalitarian hunter-gatherer ethos, the basis of which (as has so often been remarked) was sharing, number was not wanted. There was no ground for the urge to quantify, no reason to divide what was whole. Not until the domestication of animals and plants did this cultural concept fully emerge. Two of number's seminal figures testify clearly to its alliance with separateness and property: Pythagoras, center of a highly influential religious cult of number, and Euclid, father of mathematics and science, whose geometry originated to measure fields for reasons of ownership, taxation and slave labor. One of civilization's early forms, chiefdomship, entails a linear rank order in which each member is assigned an exact numerical place. Soon, following the anti-natural linearity of plow culture, the inflexible 90-degree gridiron plan of even earliest cities appeared. Their insistent regularity constitutes in itself a repressive ideology. Culture, now numberized, becomes more firmly bounded and lifeless.

Art, too, in its relationship to agriculture, highlights both institutions. It begins as a means to interpret and subdue reality, to rationalize nature, and conforms to the great turning point which is agriculture in its basic features. The pre-Neolithic cave paintings, for example, are vivid and bold, a dynamic exaltation of animal grace and freedom. The Neolithic art of farmers and pastoralists, however, stiffens into stylized forms; Franz Borkenau typified its pottery as a "narrow, timid botching of materials and forms." With agriculture, art lost its variety and became standardized into geometrical designs that tended to degenerate into dull, repetitive patterns, a perfect reflection of standardized, confined, rule-patterned life. And where there had been no representation in Paleolithic art of men killing men, an obsession with depicting confrontation between people advanced with the Neolithic period, scenes of battles becoming common.

Time, language, number, art and all the rest of culture, which predates and leads to agriculture, rests on symbolization. Just as autonomy preceded domestication and self-domestication, the rational and the social precede the symbolic.

Food production, it is eternally and gratefully acknowledged, "permitted the cultural potentiality of the human species to develop." But what is this tendency toward the symbolic, toward the elaboration and imposition of arbitrary forms? It is a growing capacity for objectification, by which what is living becomes reified, thing-like. Symbols are more than the basic units of culture; they are screening devices to distance us from our experiences. They classify and reduce, "to do away with," in Leakey and Lewin's remarkable phrase, "the otherwise almost intolerable burden of relating one experience to another."

Thus culture is governed by the imperative of reforming and subordinating nature. The artificial environment which is agriculture accomplished this pivotal mediation, with the symbolism of objects manipulated in the construction of relations of dominance. For it is not only external nature that is subjugated: the face-to-face quality of pre-agricultural life in itself severely limited domination, while culture extends and legitimates it.

It is likely that already during the Paleolithic era certain forms or names were attached to objects or ideas, in a symbolizing manner but in a shifting, impermanent, perhaps playful sense. The will to sameness and security found in agriculture means that the symbols became as static and constant as farming life. Regularization, rule patterning, and technological differentiation, under the sign of division of labor, interact to ground and advance symbolization. Agriculture completes the symbolic shift and the virus of alienation has overcome authentic, free life. It is the victory of cultural control; as anthropologist Marshall Sahlins puts it, "The amount of work per capita increases with the evolution of culture and the amount of leisure per capita decreases."

Today, the few surviving hunter-gatherers occupy the least "economically interesting" areas of the world where agriculture has not penetrated, such as the snows of the Inuit ("Eskimos") or desert of the Australian aborigines. And yet the refusal of farming drudgery, even in adverse settings, bears its own rewards. The Hazda of Tanzania, Filipino Tasaday, !Kung of Botswana, or the Kalahari Desert !Kung San ("Bushmen")—who were seen by Richard Lee as easily surviving a serious, several years' drought while neighboring farmers starved— also testify to Hole and Flannery's summary that "No group on earth has more leisure time than hunters and gatherers, who spend it primarily on games, conversation and relaxing." Service rightly attributed this condition to "the very simplicity of the technology and lack of control over the environment" of such groups. And yet simple Paleolithic methods were, in their own way, "advanced." Consider a basic cooking technique like steaming foods by heating stones in a covered pit; this is immemorially older than any pottery, kettles or baskets (in fact, is anti-container in its non-surplus, non-exchange orientation) and is the most nutritionally sound way to cook, far healthier than boiling food in water, for example. Or consider the fashioning of such stone tools as the long and exceptionally thin "laurel leaf" knives, delicately chipped but strong, which modern industrial techniques cannot duplicate.

The hunting and gathering lifestyle represents the most successful and enduring adaptation ever achieved by humankind. In occasional pre-agriculture phenomena like the intensive collection of food or the systematic hunting of a single species can be seen signs of impending breakdown of a pleasurable mode that remained so static for so long precisely because it was pleasurable. The "penury and day-long grind" of agriculture, in Clark's words, is the vehicle of culture, "rational" only in its perpetual disequilibrium and its logical progression toward ever-greater destruction, as will be outlined below.

Although the term hunter-gatherer should be reversed (and has been by not a few current anthropologists) because it is recognized that gathering constitutes by far the larger survival component, the nature of hunting provides salient contrast to domestication. The relationship of the hunter to the hunted animal, which is sovereign, free and even considered equal, is obviously qualitatively different from that of the farmer or herdsman to the enslaved chattels over which he rules absolutely.

Evidence of the urge to impose order or subjugate is found in the coercive rites and uncleanness taboos of incipient religion. The eventual subduing of the world that is agriculture has at least some of its basis where ambiguous behavior is ruled out, purity and defilement defined and enforced.

Lévi-Strauss defined religion as the anthropomorphism of nature; earlier spirituality was participatory with nature, not imposing cultural values or traits upon it. The sacred means that which is separated, and ritual and formalization, increasingly removed from the ongoing activities of daily life and in the control of such specialists as shamans and priests, are closely linked with hierarchy and institutionalized power. Religion emerges to ground and legitimize culture, by means of a "higher" order of reality; it is especially required, in this function of maintaining the solidarity of society, by the unnatural demands of agriculture.

In the Neolithic village of Catal Hüyük in Turkish Anatolia, one of every three rooms were used for ritual purposes. Plowing and sowing can be seen as ritual renunciations, according to Burkert, a form of systematic repression accompanied by a sacrificial element. Speaking of sacrifice, which is the killing of domesticated animals (or even humans) for ritual purposes, it is pervasive in agricultural societies and found only there.

Some of their major Neolithic religions often attempted a symbolic healing of the agricultural rupture with nature through the mythology of the earth mother, which needless to say does nothing to restore the lost unity. Fertility myths are also central: the Egyptian Osiris, the Greek Persephone, Baal of Canaanites, and the New Testament Jesus, gods whose death and resurrection testify to the perserverance of the soil, not to mention the human soul. The first temples signified the rise of cosmologies based on a model of the universe as an arena of domestication or barnyard, which in turn serves to justify the suppression of human autonomy. Whereas precivilized society was, as Redfield put it, "held together by largely undeclared but continually realized ethical conceptions, "religion developed as a way of creating citizens, placing the moral order under public management.

Domestication involved the initiation of production, vastly increased divisions of labor, and the completed foundations of social stratification. This amounted to an epochal mutation both in the character of human existence and its development, clouding the latter with ever more violence and work. Contrary to the myth of hunter-gatherers as violent and aggressive, by the way, recent evidence shows that existing non-farmers, such as the Mbuti ("pygmies") studied by Turnbull, apparently do what killing they do without any aggressive spirit, even with a sort of regret. Warfare and the formation of every civilization or state, on the other hand, are inseparably linked.

Primal peoples did not fight over areas in which separate groups might converge in their gathering and hunting. At least "territorial" struggles are not part of the ethnographic literature and they would seem even less likely to have occurred in pre-history when resources were greater and contact with civilization non-existent.

Indeed, these peoples had no conception of private property, and Rousseau's figurative judgment, that divided society was founded by the man who first sowed a piece of ground, saying "This land is mine," and found others to believe him, is essentially valid. "Mine and thine, the seeds of all mischief, have no place with them," reads Pietro's 1511 account of the natives encountered on the second voyage of Columbus. Centuries later, surviving Native Americans asked, "Sell the Earth? Why not sell the air, the clouds, the great sea?" Agriculture creates and elevates possessions; consider the *longing* root of *belongings*, as if they ever make up for the loss.

Work, as a distinct category of life, likewise did not exist until agriculture. The human capacity of being shackled to crops and herds, devolved rather quickly. Food production overcame the common absence or paucity of ritual and hierarchy in society and introduced civilized activities like the forced labor of temple-building. Here is the real "Cartesian split" between inner and outer reality, the separation whereby nature became merely something to be "worked." On this capacity for a sedentary and servile existence rests the entire superstructure of civilization with its increasing weight of repression.

Male violence toward women originated with agriculture, which transmuted women into beasts of burden and breeders of children. Before farming, the egalitarianism of foraging life "applied as fully to women as to men," judged Eleanor Leacock, owing to the autonomy of tasks and the fact that decisions were made by those who carried them out. In the absence of production and with no drudge work suitable for child labor such as weeding, women were not consigned to onerous chores or the constant supply of babies.

Along with the curse of perpetual work, via agriculture, in the expulsion from Eden, God told woman, "I will greatly multiply thy sorrow and thy conception: in sorrow thou shalt bring forth children; and that desire shall be to thy husband, and he shall rule over thee." Similarly, the first known codified laws, those of the Sumarian king, Ur-Namu, prescribed death to any woman satisfying desires outside of marriage. Thus Whyte referred to the ground women "lost relative to men when humans first abandoned a simple hunting and gathering way of life," and Simone de Beauvoir saw in the cultural equation of plow and phallus a fitting symbol of the oppression of women.

As wild animals are converted into sluggish meat-making machines, the concept of becoming "cultivated" is a virtue enforced on people, meaning the weeding out of freedom from one's nature, in the service of domestication and exploitation. As Rice points out, in Sumer, the first civilization, the earliest cities had factories with their characteristic high organization and refraction of skills. Civilization from this point exacts human labor and the mass production of food, buildings, war and authority.

To the Greeks, work was a curse and nothing else. The name for it—*ponos*—has the same root as the Latin *poena*, sorrow. The famous Old Testament curse on agriculture as the expulsion from Paradise (Genesis 3:17-18) reminds us of the origin of work. As Mumford put it, "Conformity, repetition, patience were the keys to this [Neolithic] culture...the patient capacity for work." In this monotony and passivity of tending and waiting is born, according to Paul Shepard, the peasant's "deep, latent resentments, crude mixtures of rectitude and heaviness, and absence of humor." One might also add a stoic insensitivity and lack of imagination inseparable from religious faith, sullenness, and suspicion among traits widely attributed to the domesticated life of farming.

Although food production by its nature includes a latent readiness for political domination and although civilizing culture was from the beginning its own propaganda machine, the changeover involved a monumental struggle. Fredy Perlman's *Against Leviathan! Against His-Story!*

is unrivaled on this, vastly enriching Toynbee's attention to the "internal" and "external proletariats," discontents within and without civilization. Nonetheless, along the axis from digging stick farming to plow agriculture to fully differentiated irrigation systems, an almost total genocide of gatherers and hunters was necessarily effected.

The formation and storage of surpluses are part of the domesticating will to control and make static, an aspect of the tendency to symbolize. A bulwark against the flow of nature, surplus takes the forms of herd animals and granaries. Stored grain was the earliest medium of equivalence, the oldest form of capital. Only with the appearance of wealth in the shape of storable grains do the gradations of labor and social classes proceed. While there were certainly wild grains before all this (and wild wheat, by the way, is 24 percent protein compared to 12 percent for domesticated wheat) the bias of culture makes every difference. Civilization and its cities rested as much on granaries as on symbolization.

The mystery of agriculture's origin seems even more impenetrable in light of the recent reversal of long-standing notions that the previous era was one of hostility to nature and an absence of leisure. "One could no longer assume," wrote Arme, "that early man domesticated plants and animals to escape drudgery and starvation. If anything, the contrary appeared true, and the advent of farming saw the end of innocence." For a long time, the question was "why wasn't agriculture adopted much earlier in human evolution?" More recently, we know that agriculture, in Cohen's words, "is not easier than hunting and gathering and does not provide a higher quality, more palatable, or more secure food base." Thus the consensus question now is, "why was it adopted at all?"

Many theories have been advanced, none convincingly. Childe and others argue that population increase pushed human societies into more intimate contact with other species, leading to domestication and the need to produce in order to feed the additional people. But it has been shown rather conclusively that population increase did not precede agriculture but was caused by it. "I don't see any evidence anywhere in the world," concluded Flannery, "that suggests that population pressure was responsible for the beginning of agriculture." Another theory has it that major climactic changes occurred at the end of the Pleistocene, about 11,000 years ago, which upset the old hunter- gatherer life-world and led directly to the cultivation of certain surviving staples. Recent dating methods have helped demolish this approach; no such climatic shift happened that could have forced the new mode into existence. Besides, there are scores of examples of agriculture being adopted—or refused— in every type of climate. Another major hypothesis is that agriculture was introduced via a chance discovery or invention as if it had never occurred to the species before a certain moment that, for example, food grows from sprouted seeds. It seems certain that Paleolithic humanity had a virtually inexhaustible knowledge of flora and fauna for many tens of thousands of years before the cultivation of plants began, which renders this theory especially weak.

Agreement with Carl Sauer's summation that, "Agriculture did not originate from a growing or chronic shortage of food" is sufficient, in fact, to dismiss virtually all originary theories that have been advanced. A remaining idea, presented by Hahn, Isaac and others, holds that food production began at base as a religious activity. This hypothesis comes closest to plausibility.

Sheep and goats, the first animals to be domesticated, are known to have been widely used in religious ceremonies, and to have been raised in enclosed meadows for sacrificial purposes. Before they were domesticated, moreover, sheep had no wool suitable for textile purposes. The main use of the hen in southeastern Asia and the eastern Mediterranean—the earliest centers of civilization—"seems to have been," according to Darby, "sacrificial or divinatory rather than alimentary." Sauer adds that the "egg laying and meat producing qualities" of tamed fowl "are relatively late consequences of their domestication." Wild cattle were fierce and dangerous; neither the docility of oxen nor the modified meat texture of such castrates could have been foreseen. Cattle were not milked until centuries after their initial captivity, and representations indicate that their first known harnessing was to wagons in religious processions.

Plants, next to be controlled, exhibit similar backgrounds so far as is known. Consider the New World examples of squash and pumpkin, used originally as ceremonial rattles. Johannessen discussed the religious and mystical motives connected with the domestication of maize, Mexico's most important crop and center of its native Neolithic religion. Likewise Anderson investigated the selection and development of distinctive types of various cultivated plants because of their magical significance. The shamans, I should add, were well- placed in positions of power to introduce agriculture via the taming and planting involved in ritual and religion, sketchily referred to above.

Though the religious explanation of the origins of agriculture has been somewhat overlooked, it brings us, in my opinion, to the very doorstep of the real explanation of the birth of production: that non-rational, cultural force of alienation which spread, in the forms of time, language, number and art, to ultimately colonize material and psychic life in agriculture. "Religion" is too narrow a conceptualization of this infection and its growth. Domination is too weighty, too all-encompassing, to have been solely conveyed by the pathology that is religion.

But the cultural values of control and uniformity that are part of religion are certainly part of agriculture, and from the beginning. Noting that strains of corn cross-pollinate very easily, Anderson studied the very primitive agriculturalists of Assam, the Naga tribe, and their variety of corn that exhibited no differences from plant to plant. True to culture, showing that it is complete from the beginning of production, the Naga kept their varieties so pure "only by a fanatical adherence to an ideal type." This exemplifies the marriage of culture and production in domestication, and its inevitable progeny, repression and work.

The scrupulous tending of strains of plants finds its parallel in the domesticating of animals, which also defies natural selection and re- establishes the controllable organic world at a debased, artificial level. Like plants, animals are mere things to be manipulated; a cow, for instance, is seen as a kind of machine for converting grass into milk. Transmuted from a state of freedom to that of helpless parasites, these animals become completely dependent on man for survival. In domestic mammals, as a rule, the size of the brain becomes relatively smaller as specimens are produced that devote more energy to growth and less to activity. Placid, infantilized, typified perhaps by the sheep, most domesticated of herd animals; the remarkable intelligence of wild sheep is completely lost in their tamed counterparts. The social relationships among domestic animals are reduced to the crudest essentials. Non-reproductive parts of the life cycle are minimized, courtship is curtailed, and the animal's very capacity to recognize its own species is impaired.

Farming also created the potential for rapid environmental destruction and the domination over nature soon began to turn the green mantle that covered the birthplaces of civilization into barren and lifeless areas. "Vast regions have changed their aspect completely," estimates Zeuner, "always to quasi-drier condition, since the beginnings of the Neolithic." Deserts now occupy most of the areas where the high civilizations once flourished, and there is much historical evidence that these early formations inevitably ruined their environments.

Throughout the Mediterranean Basin and in the adjoining Near East and Asia, agriculture turned lush and hospitable lands into depleted, dry, and rocky terrain. In *Critias*, Plato described Attica as "a skeleton wasted by disease," referring to the deforestation of Greece and contrasting it to its earlier richness. Grazing by goats and sheep, the first domesticated ruminants, was a major factor in the denuding of Greece, Lebanon, and North Africa, and the desertification of the Roman and Mesopotamian empires.

Another, more immediate impact of agriculture, brought to light increasingly in recent years, involved the physical well-being of its subjects. Lee and Devore's researches show that "the diet of gathering peoples was far better than that of cultivators, that starvation is rare, that their health status was generally superior, and that there is a lower incidence of chronic disease." Conversely, Farb summarized, "Production provides an inferior diet based on a limited number of foods, is much less reliable because of blights and the vagaries of weather, and is much more costly in terms of human labor expended.''

The new field of paleopathology has reached even more emphatic conclusions, stressing, as does Angel, the "sharp decline in growth and nutrition" caused by the changeover from food gathering to food production. Earlier conclusions about life span have also been revised. Although eyewitness Spanish accounts of the sixteenth century tell of Florida Indian fathers seeing their fifth generation before passing away, it was long believed that primitive people died in their 30's and 40's. Robson, Boyden and others have dispelled the confusion of longevity with life expectancy and discovered that current hunter-gatherers, barring injury and severe infection, often outlive their civilized contemporaries. During the industrial age only fairly recently did life span lengthen for the species, and it now widely recognized that in Paleolithic times humans were long-lived animals, once certain risks were passed. DeVries is correct in his judgment that duration of life dropped sharply upon contact with civilization.

Tuberculosis and diarrheal disease had to await the rise of farming, measles and bubonic plague the appearance of large cities,'' wrote Jared Diamond. Malaria, probably the single greatest killer of humanity, and nearly all other infectious diseases are the heritage of agriculture. Nutritional and degenerative diseases in general appear with the reign of domestication and culture. Cancer, coronary thrombosis, anemia, dental caries, and mental disorders are but a few of the hallmarks of agriculture; previously women gave birth with no difficulty and little or no pain.

People were far more alive in all their senses. !Kung San, reported R. H. Post, have heard a single-engined plane while it was still 70 miles away, and many of them can see four moons of Jupiter with the naked eye. The summary judgment of Harris and Ross, as to "an overall decline in the quality—and probably in the length—of human life among farmers as compared with earlier hunter-gatherer groups," is understated.

One of the most persistent and universal ideas is that there was once a Golden Age of innocence before history began. Hesiod, for instance, referred to the "life-sustaining soil, which yielded its copious fruits unbribed by toil.'' Eden was clearly the home of the hunter-gatherers and the yearning expressed by the historical images of paradise must have been that of disillusioned tillers of the soil for a lost life of freedom and relative ease.

The history of civilization shows the increasing displacement of nature from human experience, characterized in part by a narrowing of food choices. According to Rooney, prehistoric peoples found sustenance in over 1500 species of wild plants, whereas, "All civilizations,"

Wenke reminds us, "have been based on the cultivation of one or more of just six plant species: wheat, barley, millet, rice, maize, and potatoes."

It is a striking truth that over the centuries "the number of different edible foods which are actually eaten," Pyke points out, "has steadily dwindled." The world's population now depends for most of its subsistence on only about 20 genera of plants while their natural strains are replaced by artificial hybrids and the genetic pool of these plants becomes far less varied.

The diversity of food tends to disappear or flatten out as the proportion of manufactured foods increases. Today the very same articles of diet are distributed worldwide so that an Inuit Eskimo and an African native may soon be eating powdered milk manufactured in Wisconsin or frozen fish sticks from a single factory in Sweden. A few big multinationals such as Unilever, the world's biggest food production company, preside over a highly integrated service system in which the object is not to nourish or even to feed, but to force an ever-increasing consumption of fabricated, processed products upon the world.

When Descartes enunciated the principle that the fullest exploitation of matter to *any* use is the whole duty of man, our separation from nature was virtually complete and the stage was set for the Industrial Revolution. Three hundred and fifty years later this spirit lingers in the person of Jean Vorst, Curator of France's Museum of Natural History, who pronounces that our species, "because of intellect," can no longer re-cross a certain threshold of civilization and once again become part of a natural habitat. He further states, expressing perfectly the original and perservering imperialism of agriculture, "As the earth in its primitive state is not adopted to our expansion, man must shackle it to fulfill human destiny."

The early factories literally mimicked the agricultural model, indicating again that at base all mass production is farming. The natural world is to be broken and forced to work. One thinks of the mid-American prairies where settlers had to yoke six oxen to plow in order to cut through the soil for the first time. Or a scene from the 1870s in *The Octopus* by Frank Norris, in which gang-plows were driven like "a great column of field artillery" across the San Joaquin Valley, cutting 175 furrows at once.

Today the organic, what is left of it, is fully mechanized under the aegis of a few petrochemical corporations. Their artificial fertilizers, pesticides, herbicides and near-monopoly of the world's seed stock define a total environment that integrates food production from planting to consumption. Although Lévi-Strauss is right that "Civilization manufactures monoculture like sugar beet," only since World War II has a completely synthetic orientation begun to dominate.

Agriculture takes more organic matter out of the soil than it puts back, and soil erosion is basic to the monoculture of annuals. Regarding the latter, some are promoted with devastating results to the land; along with cotton and soybeans, corn, which in its present domesticated state is totally dependent on agriculture for its existence, is especially bad. J. Russell Smith called it "the killer of continents...and one of the worst enemies of the human future." The erosion cost of one bushel of Iowa corn is two bushels of topsoil, highlighting the more general large-scale industrial destruction of farmland. The continuous tillage of huge monocultures, with massive use of chemicals and no application of manure or humus, obviously raised soil deterioration and soil loss to much higher levels.

The dominant agricultural mode has it that soil needs massive infusions of chemicals, supervised by technicians whose overriding goal is to maximize production. Artificial fertilizers and all the rest from this outlook eliminate the need for the complex life of the soil and indeed convert it into a mere instrument of production. The promise of technology is total control, a completely contrived environment that simply supersedes the natural balance of the biosphere.

But more and more energy is expended to purchase great monocultural yields that are beginning to decline, never mind the toxic contamination of the soil, groundwater and food. The U.S. Department of Agriculture says that cropland erosion is occurring in this country at a rate of two billion tons of soil a year. The National Academy of Sciences estimates that over one third of topsoil is already gone forever. The ecological imbalance caused by monocropping and synthetic fertilizers causes enormous increases in pests and crop diseases; since World War II, crop loss due to insects has actually doubled. Technology responds, of course, with spiralling applications of more synthetic fertilizers, and weed and pest killers, accelerating the crime against nature.

Another post-war phenomenon was the Green Revolution, billed as the salvation of the impoverished Third World by American capital and technology. But rather than feeding the hungry, the Green Revolution drove millions of poor people from farmlands in Asia, Latin America and Africa as victims of the program that fosters large corporate farms. It amounted to an enormous technological colonization creating dependency on capital-intensive agribusiness, destroying older agrarian communalism, requiring massive fossil fuel consumption and assaulting nature on an unprecedented scale.

Desertification, or loss of soil due to agriculture, has been steadily increasing. Each year, a total area equivalent to more than two Belgiums is being converted to desert worldwide. The fate of the world's tropical rainforests is a factor in the acceleration of this desiccation: half of them have been erased in the past thirty years. In Botswana, the last wilderness region of Africa has disappeared like much of the Amazon jungle and almost half of the rainforests of Central America, primarily to raise cattle for the hamburger markets in the U.S. and Europe. The few areas safe from deforestation are where agriculture doesn't want to go; the destruction of the land is proceeding in the U.S. over a greater land area than was encompassed by the original 13 colonies, just as it is at the heart of the severe African famine of the mid-1980s and the extinction of one species of wild animal and plant after another.

Returning to animals, one is reminded of the words of Genesis in which God said to Noah, "And the fear of you and the dread of you shall be upon every fowl of the air, upon all that moveth upon the earth, and upon all the fishes of the sea; into your hands are they delivered." When newly discovered territory was first visited by the advance guard of production, as a wide descriptive literature shows, the wild mammals and birds showed no fear whatsoever of the explorers. The agriculturalized mentality, however, so aptly foretold in the biblical passage, projects an exaggerated belief in the *fierceness* of wild creatures, which follows from progressive estrangement and loss of contact with the animal world plus the need to maintain dominance over it.

The fate of domestic animals is defined by the fact that agricultural technologists continually look to factories as models of how to refine their own production systems. Nature is banished from these systems as, increasingly, farm animals are kept largely immobile throughout their deformed lives, maintained in high-density, wholly artificial environments. Billions of chickens, pigs, and veal calves, for example, no longer even see the light of day much less roam the fields, fields growing more silent as more and more pastures are plowed up to grow feed for these hideously confined beings.

The high-tech chickens, whose beak ends have been clipped off to reduce death due to stress-caused fighting, often exist four or even five to a 12" by 18" cage and are periodically deprived of food and water for up to ten days to regulate their egg-laying cycles. Pigs live on concrete floors with no bedding; foot-rot, tail-biting and cannibalism are endemic because of physical conditions and stress. Sows nurse their piglets separated by metal grates, mother and offspring barred from natural contact. Veal calves are often raised in darkness, chained to stalls so narrow as to disallow turning around or other normal posture adjustment. These animals are generally under regimens of constant medication due to the tortures involved and their heightened susceptibility to diseases: automated animal production relies upon hormones and antibiotics. Such systematic cruelty, not to mention the kind of food that results, brings to mind the fact that captivity itself and every form of enslavement has agriculture as its progenitor or model.

Food has been one of our most direct contacts with the natural environment, but we are rendered increasingly dependent on a technological production system in which finally even our senses have become redundant; taste, once vital for judging a food's value or safety, is no longer experienced, but rather certified by a label. Overall, the healthfulness of what we consume declines and land once cultivated for food now produces coffee, tobacco, grains for alcohol, marijuana, and other drugs creating the context for famine. Even the non-processed foods like fruits and vegetables are now grown to be tasteless and uniform because the demands of handling, transport and storage, not nutrition or pleasure, are the highest considerations.

Total war borrowed from agriculture to defoliate millions of acres in Southeast Asia during the Vietnam War, but the plundering of the biosphere proceeds even more lethally in its daily, global forms. Food as a function of production has also failed miserably on the most obvious level: half of the world, as everyone knows, suffers from malnourishment ranging to starvation itself.

Meanwhile, the "diseases of civilization," as discussed by Eaton and Konner in the January 31, 1985 *New England Journal of Medicine* and contrasted with the healthful pre-farming diets, underline the joyless, sickly world of chronic maladjustment we inhabit as prey of the manufacturers of medicine, cosmetics, and fabricated food. Domestication reaches new heights of the pathological in genetic food engineering, with new types of animals in the offing as well as contrived microorganisms and plants. Logically, humanity itself will also become a domesticate of this order as the world of production processes us as much as it degrades and deforms every other natural system.

The project of subduing nature, begun and carried through by agriculture, has assumed gigantic proportions. The "success" of civilization's progress, a success earlier humanity never wanted, tastes more and more like ashes. James Serpell summed it up this way: "In short we appear to have reached the end of the line. We cannot expand; we seem unable to intensify production without wreaking further havoc, and the planet is fast becoming a wasteland." Lee and Devore noted how fast all of this has come to pass and how, to "interplanetary archeologists of the future," the probable fate of civilization would look: "...a very long and stable period of small-scale hunting and gathering was followed by an apparently instantaneous efflorescence of technology...leading rapidly to extinction. 'Stratigraphically' the origin of agriculture and thermonuclear destruction will appear as essentially simultaneous."

Physiologist Jared Diamond termed the initiation of agriculture "a catastrophe from which we have never recovered." Agriculture has been and remains a "catastrophe" at all levels, the one which underpins the entire and spiritual culture of alienation now destroying us. Liberation is impossible without its dissolution.

INDUSTRIALISM AND DOMESTICATION

The modern definitions of division of labor, progress, ideology, and the workers' movement were inscribed by the coming of industrial capitalism and the factory system. The dynamics of what Hobsbawm termed "the most fundamental transformation of human life" in written history—specifically the reasons why it happened—explain the legacy and value of these institutions. Not surprisingly, much at the core of Marx's thought can also be evaluated against the reality of the Industrial Revolution.

Eighteenth-century England, where it all began, had long since seen the demise of feudalism. Capitalist social relations, however, had been unable to establish a definitive hegemony. Gwyn Williams(*Artisans and Sans-Culottes*) found it hard to find a single year free from popular uprisings; "England was preeminently the country of the eighteenth-century mob," he wrote. Peter Laslett (*The World We Have Lost*) surveyed the scene at the beginning of the century, noting the general consciousness that working people were openly regarded as a proletariat, and the fact, as "everyone was quite well aware," that violence posed a constant threat to the social order.

Laslett further noted that enclosure, or the fencing off of lands previously pastured, ploughed, and harvested cooperatively, commenced at this time and "destroyed communality altogether in English rural life." Neither was there, by 1750, a significant land-owning peasantry; the great majority on the land were either tenant-farmers or agricultural wage laborers. T.S. Ashton, who wrote a classic economic history of 18th century England, identified a crucial key to this development by his observation that "Enclosure was desirable if only because rights of common led to irregularity of work," as was widely believed. Britain in 1750, in any case, engendered a number of foreign visitors' accounts that its common people were much "given to riot," according to historian E.J. Hobsbawm.

The organization of manufacture prevailing then was the domestic, or "putting out," system, in which workers crafted goods in their own homes, and the capitalists were mainly merchants who supplied the raw materials and then marketed the finished products. At first these craftsmen generally owned their own tools, but later came to rent them. In either case, the relationship to the "means of production" afforded great strategic strength. Unsupervised, working for several masters, and with their time their own, a degree of independence was maintained. "Luddism," as E.P. Thompson (*Making of the English Working Class*) reminds us, "was the work of skilled men in small workshops." The Luddites (c. 1810–1820), though they belong toward the end of the period surveyed here, were perhaps the machine-breakers par excellence—textile knitters, weavers, and spinners who exemplify both the relative autonomy and anti-employer sentiment of the free craftsman.

Scores of commentators have discussed the independence of such domestic workers as the handloom weavers; Muggeridge's report on Lancashire craftsmen (from Exell, *Brief History of the Weavers of the Country of Gloucester*), for example, notes that this kind of work "gratifies that innate love of independence...by leaving the workman entirely a master of his own time, and the sole guide of his actions." These workers treasured their versatility, and their right to execute individual designs of their own choosing rather than the standardization of the new factory employment (which began to emerge in earnest about 1770). Witt Bowden (*Industrial Society in England Towards the End of the Eighteenth Century*) noted that earlier processes of production had indeed often "afforded the workers genuine opportunities for the expression of their personalities in their work," and that in these pre-specialization times craftsmen could pursue "artistic conceptions" in many cases.

A non-working class observer (Malachy Postlewayt, c. 1750), in fact, expressed the view that the high quality of English manufactures was to be attributed to the frequent "relaxation of the people in their own way." Others discerned in the workers' control over time a distinct threat to authority as well as to profits; Ashton wrote how "very serious was the almost universal practice of working a short week," adding a minister's alarm that "It is not those who are absolutely idle that injure the public so much as those who work but half their time." If anything, Ashton understated the case when he concluded that "...leisure, at times of their own choice, stood high on the workers' scale of preferences."

William Temple's admonition (1739) that the only way to insure temperance and industry on the part of laborers was to make it necessary that they work all the time physically possible "in order to procure the common necessaries of life," was a frequent expression of ruling-class frustration. Temple's experience with the turbulent weavers of Gloucestershire had thus led him to agree with Arthur Young's "everyone but an idiot knows that the lower classes must be kept poor or they will never be industrious" dictum.

Among the craftsmen of cloth, the insistence on their own methods—including, at times, the ingenious sabotage of finished goods—was matched by another weapon, that of embezzlement of the raw materials assigned to them. As Ashton reports, "A survey of the measures passed to suppress embezzlement and delay in returning materials shows a progressive increase in penalties." But throughout the 18th century, according to Wadsworth and Mann (*The Cotton Trade and Industrial Lancashire, 1600-1780*), "the execution of the anti-embezzlement acts...lagged behind their letter." Their effectiveness was limited by the "resentment of the spinners and workpeople," which prosecutors incurred and by the difficulty of detection without regular inspection. James' *History of the Worsted Manufacture* echoes this finding: "Justices of the Peace...until compelled by mandamus, refused to entertain charges against or convict upon proper evidence, embezzlers or false reelers."

Wadsworth and Mann perceived in the embezzlement issue the relationship between the prevailing "work ethic" and the prevailing mode of production: *The fact is simply that a great many...have never seen eye to eye with their employers on the rights and sanctity of ownership. The home worker of the eighteenth century, living away from the restraints of the factory and workshop and the employer's eye, had every inducement [to try] to defeat the hard bargain the employer had driven.*

The independent craftsman was a threatening adversary to the employing class, and he clung strongly to his prerogatives: his well-known propensity, for instance, to reject "the higher material standard of the factory towns," in Thompson's phrase, to gather his own fruits, vegetables and flowers, to largely escape the developing industrial blight and pollution, to gather freely with his neighboring workers at the dinner hour. Thompson noted a good example of the nature of the domestic worker in "the Yorkshire reputation for bluntness and independence" which could be traced to what local historian Frank Peel saw as "men who doffed their caps to no one, and recognized no right in either squire or parson to question or meddle with them."

Turning to some of the specifics of pre-factory system revolt in England, Ashton provides a good introduction:*Following the harvest failure of 1709 the keelmen of the Tyne took to rioting. When the price of food rose sharply in 1727 the tin-miners of Cornwall plundered granaries at Falmouth, and the coal-miners of Somerset broke down the turnpikes on the road to Bristol. Ten years later the Cornish tinners assembled again at Falmouth to prevent the exportation of corn, and in the following season there was rioting at Tiverton. The famine of 1739– 40 led to a "rebellion" in Northumberland and Durham in which women seem to have taken a leading part: ships were boarded, warehouses broken open, and the guild at Newcastle was reduced to ruins. At the same time attacks on corn dealers were reported from North and South Wales. The years 1748 and 1753 saw similar happenings in several parts of the country; and in 1756–7 there was hardly a county from which no report reached the Home Office of the pulling down of corn mills or Quaker meeting-houses, or the rough handling of bakers and grain dealers. In spite of drastic penalties the same thing occurred in each of the later dearths of the century: in 1762, 1765–7, 1774, 1783, 1789, 1795, and 1800.*

This readiness for direct action informs the strife in textiles, the industry so important to England and to capitalist evolution, where, for example, "discontent was the prevalent attitude of the operatives engaged in the wool industries for centuries," said Burnley in his *Historys of Wool and Woolcombing*. Popular ballads give ample evidence to this, as does the case of rioting London weavers, who panicked the government in 1675. Lipson's *History of the Woollen and Worsted Industries* provides many instances of the robustness of domestic textile workers' struggles, including that of a 1728 weavers' strike which was intended to have been pacified by a meeting of strike leaders and employers; a "mob" of weavers "burst into the room in which the negotiations were taking place, dragged back the clothiers as they endeavored to escape from the windows, and forced them to concede all their demands." Or these additional accounts by Lipson: *The Wiltshire weavers were equally noted for their turbulent character and the rude violence with which they proclaimed the wrongs under which they smarted. In 1738 they assembled together in a riotous manner from the villages round Bradford and Trowbridge, and made an attack upon the house of a clothier who had reduced the price of weaving. They smashed open the doors, consumed or spoiled the provisions in the cellar, drank all the wine they could, set the casks running, and ended up by destroying great quantities of raw materials and utensils. In addition to this exploit they extorted a promise from all the clothiers in Melksham that they would pay fifteen pence a yard for weaving.... Another great tumult occurred at Bradford (Wiltshire) in 1752. Thirty weavers had been committed to prison; the next day above a thousand weavers assembled, armed with bludgeons and firearms, beat the guard, broke open the prison, and rescued their companions.*

Similarly, J.P. Kay was driven from Leeds in 1745 and from Bury in 1753, as outbreaks of violence flared in many districts in response to his invention, the flying shuttle for mechanizing weaving.

Wadsworth and Mann found the Manchester Constables Accounts to have reported "great Riots, Tumults, and Disorders" in the late 1740's, and that "After 1750 food riots and industrial disputes grow more frequent," with outbreaks in Lancashire (the area of their study) virtually every year. These historians further recount "unrest and violence in all parts of the country" in the middle to late 1750's, with Manchester and Liverpool frequently in alarm and "panic among the propertied classes."

After sporadic risings, such as Manchester, 1762, the years 1764–68 saw rioting in almost every county in the country; as the King put it in 1766, "a spirit of the most daring insurrection has in divers parts broke forth in violence of the most criminal nature." Although the smashing of stocking frames had been made a capital offense in 1727, in a vain attempt to stem worker violence, Hobsbawm counted 24 incidents of wages and prices being forcibly set by exactly this type of riotous destruction in 1766 alone.

Sporadic rioting occurred in 1769, such as the anti-spinning jenny outbursts which menaced the inventor Hargreaves and during which buildings were demolished at Oswaldthistle and Blackburn in order to smash the hated mechanization. A whole new wave began in 1772. Sailors in Liverpool, for example, responded to a wage decrease proposal in 1775 by "sacking the owners' houses, hoisting 'the bloody flag,' and bringing cannon ashore which they fired on the Exchange," according to Wadsworth and Mann.

The very widespread anti-machinery risings of 1779 saw the destruction of hundreds of weaving and spinning devices which were too large for domestic use. The rioters' sentiments were very widely shared, as evidenced by arrest records that included miners, nailmakers, laborers, joiners—a fair sample of the entire industrial population. The workers' complaint averred that the smaller machines are "in the Hands of the Poor and the larger 'Patent Machines' in the Hands of the Rich," and "that the work is better manufactured by small [textile machines] than by large ones."

This list, very incomplete as it is, could be easily extended into the many early 19th century outbreaks, all of which seem to have enjoyed great popular support. But perhaps a fitting entry on which to close this sample would be these lines from a public letter written by Gloucestershire shearmen in 1802: "We hear in Formed that you got Shear in mee sheens and if you Don't Pull them Down in a Forght Nights Time we will pull them Down for you Wee will you Damd infernold Dog.''

This brief look at the willfulness of the 18th century proletariat serves to introduce the conscious motivation behind the factory system. Sidney Pollard (*The Genesis of Modern Management*) recognized the capitalists' need of "breaking the social bonds which had held the peasants, the craftsmen and the town poor of the eighteenth century together in opposition to the new order." Pollard saw too the essential nature of the domestic system, that the masters "had to depend on the work performed in innumerable tiny domestic workshop units, unsupervised and unsupervisable. Such "incompatibility," he concluded, "was bound to set up tensions and to drive the merchants to seek new ways of production, imposing their own managerial achievements and practices in the productive sector."

This underlying sense of the real inadequacy of existing powers of control was also firmly grasped by David Landes (*The Unbound Prometheus*): "One can understand why the thoughts of employers turned to workshops where the men would be brought together to labour under watchful overseers, and to machines that would solve the shortage of manpower while curbing the insolence and dishonesty of men." According to Wadsworth and Mann, in fact, many employers definitely felt that "the country would perish if the poor—that is, the working classes—were not brought under severe discipline to habits of industry and docile subordination."

Writing on the evolution of the "central workshop" or factory, historian N. S. B. Gras saw its installation strictly in terms of control of labor: "It was purely for purposes of discipline, so that the workers could be effectively controlled under the supervision of foremen." Factory work itself became the central weapon to force an enemy character into a safe, reliable mold following the full realization that they were dealing with a recalcitrant, hostile working class whose entire morale, habits of work, and culture had to be broken. Bowden described this with great clarity: "More directly as a result of the introduction of machinery and of large-scale organization was the subjection of the workers to a deadening mechanical and administrative routine."

Adam Smith, in his classic *Wealth of Nations*, well understood that the success of industrial capitalism lies with nothing so much as with the division of labor, that is, with ever-increasing specialization and the destruction of versatility in work. He also knew that the division of labor is as much about the production and allocation of commodities. And certainly the new order is also related to consumption as to the need to guarantee control of production; in fact, there are those who see its origin almost strictly in terms of market demand for mass production, but who do not see the conscious element here either.

In passing, Bishop Berkeley's query of 1755, "whether the creation of wants be not the likeliest way to produce industry in a people?" is eminently relevant. As Hobsbawm pointed out, the populace was definitely not originally attracted to standardized products; industrialization gradually enabled production "to expand its own markets, if not actually to create them." The lure of cheap, identical goods succeeded essentially due to the enforced absence of earlier pleasures. When independence and variety of pursuits were more possible, a different kind of leisure and consumption was the norm. This, of course, was in itself a target of the factory system, "the tendency, so deplored by economists, to work less when food was cheap," as Christopher Hill put it.

Exports, too, were an obvious support of the emerging regime, backed by the systematic and aggressive help of government, another artificial demand mechanism. But the domestic market was at least as important, stemming from the "predisposing condition" that specialization and discipline of labor makes for further "progress," as Max Weber observed.

Richard Arkwright (1732–1793) agreed completely with those who saw the need for consciously spurring consumption, "as to the necessity of arousing and satisfying new wants," in his phrase. But it is as the developer of cotton spinning machinery that he deserves a special word here; because he is generally regarded as the most prominent figure in the history of the textile industries and even as "the founder of the factory system." Arkwright is a clear illustration of the political and social character of the technology he did so much to advance. His concern with social control is very evident from his writings and correspondence, and Mantoux (*The Industrial Revolution in the Eighteenth Century*) discerned that "his most original achievement was the discipline he established in the mills."

Arkwright also saw the vital connection between work discipline and social stability: "Being obliged to be more regular in their attendance on their work, they became more orderly in their conduct." For his pioneering efforts, he received his share of appropriate response; Lipson relates that in 1767, with "the news of the riots in the neighborhood of Blackburn which had been provoked by Hargreaves' spinning jenny," he and his financial backer Smolley, "fearing to draw upon themselves the attention of the machine-wreckers, removed to Nottingham." Similarly, Arkwright's Birkacre mill was destroyed by workers in 1779. Lipson ably summarizes his managerial contribution: *In coordinating all the various parts of his vast industrial structures; in organising and disciplining large bodies of men, so that each man fitted into his niche and the whole acted with the mechanical precision of a trained army...in combining division of labour with effective supervision from a common centre...a new epoch was inaugurated.*

Andrew Ure's *Philosophy of Manufactures* is one of the major attempts at an exposition of the factory system, a work cited often by Marx in *Capital*. Its revealing preface speaks of tracing "the progression of the British system of industry, according to which every process peculiarly nice, and therefore liable to injury from the ignorance and waywardness of workmen, is withdrawn from handicraft control, and placed under the guidance of self-acting machinery." Examining the nature of the new system, we find, instead of domestic craft labor, "industrial labor... [which] imposes a regularity, routine, and monotony...which conflicts...with all the inclinations of a humanity as yet unconditioned into it," in the words of Hobsbawm. Factory production slowly supplanted that of the domestic system in the face of fierce opposition, and workers experienced the feeling of daily entering a prison to meet the new "strain and violence of work," as the Hammonds put it. Factories often resembled pauper work-houses or prisons, after which they had actually often been modeled; Weber saw a strong initial similarity between the modern factory and the Russian serf-labor workshops, wherein the means of production and the workers themselves were appropriated by the masters.

Hammonds' *Town Labourer* saw "the depreciation of human life" as the leading fact about the new system for the working classes: "The human material was used up rapidly; workmen were called old at forty." Possibly just as important was the novel, "inhuman" nature of its domination, as if all "were in the grasp of a great machine that threatened to destroy all sense of the dignity of human life." A famous characterization by J.P. Kay (1832) put the everyday subjugation in hard to forget terms: *Whilst the engine runs the people must work—men, women and children are yoked together with iron and steam. The animal machine—breakable in the best case, subject to a thousand sources of suffering—is chained fast to the iron machine, which knows no suffering and no weariness.*

Resistance to industrial labor displayed a great strength and persistence, reflecting the latent anti-capitalism of the domestic worker— "the despair of the masters"—in a time when a palpable aura of unfreedom clung to wage-labor. Lipson gives us the example of Ambrose Crowley, perhaps the very first factory owner and organizer (from

1691) who displayed an obsession with the problem of disciplining his workers to "an institution so alien in its assumptions about the way in which people should spend their lives."

Lewis Paul wrote from his London firm in 1742 that "I have not half my people come to work today and I have no fascination in the prospect that I have put myself in the power of such people." In 1757 Josiah Tucker noted that factory-type machinery is highly provocative to the populace who "never fail to break out into Riots and Insurrections whenever such things are proposed." As we have seen, and as Christopher Hill put it, "Machine-breaking was the logical reaction of free men...who saw the concentration of machinery in factories as the instrument of their enslavement."

A hosiery capitalist, in admitting defeat to the Committee on Woollen Manufacture, tells us much of the independent spirit that had to be broken: *I found the utmost distaste on the part of the men, to any regular hours or regular habits.... The men themselves were considerably dissatisfied, because they could not go in and out as they pleased, and go on just as they had been used to do...to such an extent as completely to disgust them with the whole system, and I was obliged to break it up.*

The famous early entrepreneurs, Boulton and Watt, were likewise dismayed to find that the miners they had to deal with were "strong, healthy and resolute men, setting the law at defiance; no officer dared to execute a warrant against them."

Wedgwood, the well-known pottery and china entrepreneur, had to fight "the open hostility of his workpeople" when he tried to develop division of labor in his workshops, according to Mantoux. And Jewitt's *The Wedgwoods*, exposing the social intent of industrial technology, tells us "It was machinery [which] ultimately forced the worker to accept the discipline of the factory."

Considering the depth of workers' antipathy to the new regimen, it comes as no surprise that Pollard should speak of "the large evidence which all points to the fact that continuous employment was precisely one of the most hated aspects of factory work." This was the case because the work itself, as an agent of pacification, was perceived "precisely" in its true nature. Pollard later provides the other side of the coin to the workers' hatred of the job; namely, the rulers' insistence on it for its own (disciplinary) sake: "Nothing strikes so modern a note in the social provisions of the factory villages as the attempts to provide continuous employment."

Returning to the specifics of resistance, Sir Frederic Eden, in his *State of the Poor* (1797), stated that the industrial laborers of Manchester "rarely work on Monday and that many of them keep holiday two or three days in the week." Thus Ure's tirades about the employees' "unworkful impulses," their "aversion to the control and continuity of factory labor," are reflected in such data as the fact that as late as 1800, spinners would be missing from the factories on Mondays and Tuesdays. Absenteeism, as well as turnover, then, was part of the syndrome of striving to maintain a maximum of personal liberty.

Max Weber spoke of the "immensely stubborn resistance" to the new work discipline, and a later social scientist, Reinhard Bendix, saw also that the drive to establish the management of labor on "an impersonal, systematic basis" was opposed "at every point." Ure, in a comment worth quoting at length, discusses the fight to master the workers in terms of Arkwright's career: *The main difficulty [he faced was] above all, in training human beings to renounce their desultory habits of work, and to identify themselves with the unvarying regularity of the complex automation. To devise and administer a successful code of factory discipline, suited to the necessities of factory diligence, was the Herculean enterprise, the noble achievement of Arkwright. Even at the present day, when the system is perfectly organized, and its labour lightened to the utmost, it is found nearly impossible to convert persons past the age of puberty, whether drawn from rural or from handicraft occupations, into useful factory hands.*

We also encounter in this selection from Ure the reason why early factory labor was so heavily comprised of the labor of children, women and paupers threatened with loss of the dole. Thompson quotes a witness before a Parliamentary investigative committee, that "all persons working on the power-loom are working there by force because they cannot exist any other way." Hundreds of thousands clung to the deeply declining fortunes of hand-loom weaving for decades, in a classic case of the primacy of human dignity, which Mathias (*The First Industrial Nation*) notes "defied the operation of simple economic incentives."

What Hill termed the English craftsmen's tradition "of self-help and self-respect" was a major source of that popular will which denied complete dominion by capital, the "proud awareness that voluntarily going into a factory was to surrender their birth-right."

Thompson demonstrates that the work rules "appeared as unnatural and hateful restraints" and that everything about factory life was an insult. "To stand at their command"—this was the most deeply resented indignity. For he felt himself, at heart, to be the real maker of the cloth...."

This spirit was why, for example, paper manufacturers preferred to train inexperienced labor for the new (post-1806) machine processes, rather than employ skilled hand paper-makers. And why Samuel Crompton, inventor of the spinning mule, lamented, relatively late in this period, *To this day, though it is more than thirty years since my first machine was shown to the public, I am hunted and watched with as much never-ceasing care as if I was the most notorious villain that ever disgraced the human form; and I do affirm that if I were to go to a smithy to get a common nail made, if opportunity offered to the bystanders, they would examine it most minutely to see if it was anything but a nail.*

The battle raged for decades, with victories still being won at least as late as that over a Bradford entrepreneur in 1882, who tried to secretly install a power-loom but was discovered by the domestic workers. "It was therefore immediately taken down, and placed in a cart under a convoy of constables, but the enraged weavers attacked and routed the constables, destroyed the loom, and dragged its roller and warp in triumph through Baildon." Little wonder that Ure wrote of the requirement of "a Napoleon nerve and ambition to subdue the refractory tempers of work-people."

Without idealizing the earlier period, or forgetting that it was certainly defined by capitalist relationships, it is also true, as Hill wrote, "What was lost by factories and enclosure was the independence, variety and freedom which small producers had enjoyed." Adam Smith admitted the "mental mutilation" due to the new division of labor, the destruction of both an earlier alertness of mind and a previous "vivacity of both pain and pleasure."

Robert Owen likewise discussed this transformation when he declared, in 1815, that "The general diffusion of manufactures throughout a country generates a new character...an essential change in the general character of the mass of the people." Less abstractly, the Hammonds harkened back to the early 19th century and heard the "lament that the games and happiness of life are disappearing," and that soon "the art of living had been degraded to its rudest forms."

In 1819 the reformer Francis Place, speaking of the population of industrial Lancashire, was pleased to note that "Until very lately it would have been very dangerous to have assembled 500 of them on any occasion....Now 100,000 people may be collected together and no riot ensue." It was as Thompson summarized: gradually, between 1780 and 1830, "the 'average' English working man became more disciplined, more subject to the productive time of the clock, more reserved and methodical, less violent and less spontaneous."

A rising at the end of this period, the "last Labourers' Revolt," of agricultural workers in 1830, says a good deal about the general change that had occurred. Similar to outbreaks of 1816 and 1822, much rural property had been destroyed and large parts of Kent and East Anglia were in the rebels' control. The Duke of Buckingham, reflecting the government's alarm, declared the whole country as having been taken over by the rioters. But despite several weeks' success, the movement collapsed at the first show of real force. Historian Pauline Gregg described the sudden relapse into apathy and despair; they were "unused to asserting themselves," their earlier tradition of vigor and initiative conquered by the generalized triumph of the new order.

Also concerning this year as marking a watershed, is Mantoux's remark about Arkwright, that "About 1830 he became the hero of political economy." Absurd, then, are the many who date the "age of revolution" as beginning at this time, such as the Tills' *Rebel Century*, 1830–1930. Only with the defeat of the workers could Arkwright, the architect of the factory system, be installed as the hero of the bourgeoisie; this defeat of authentic rebellion also gave birth to political ideology. Socialism, a caricature of the challenge that had existed, could have begun no other way.

The German businessman Harkort, wrote in 1844 of the "new form of serfdom," the diminution of the strength and intelligence of the workers that he saw. The American Colman witnessed (1845) nothing less than "Wretched, defrauded, oppressed, crushed human nature, lying in bleeding fragments all over the face of society." Amazing that another businessman of this time could, in his *Condition of the Working Class* glory that the "factory hands, eldest children of the industrial revolution, have from the beginning to the present day formed the nucleus of the Labour Movement." But Engels' statement at least contains no internal contradiction; the tamed, defeated factory operative has clearly been the mainstay of the labor movement and socialist ideology among the working class. As Rexford Tugwell admitted in his *Industrial Discipline and the Governmental Arts*: "When the factory came into existence...work became an indignity rather than a matter for pride....Organized labor has always consented to this entirely uncreative subjection."

Thus, "the character structure of the rebellious pre-industrial labourer or artisan was violently recast into that of the submissive industrial worker," in Thompson's words; by trade unionism, the fines, firings, beatings, factory rules, Methodism, the education system, the diversion known as ideology—the entire battery of institutions that have never achieved unchallenged success.

Thompson recognized the essentially "repressive and disabling" discipline of industrialization and yet, as if remembering that he is a Marxist historian, somehow finds the process good and inevitable. How could the Industrial Revolution have happened without this discipline, he asks, and in fact finds that in the production of "sober and disciplined" workers, "this growth in self-respect(!) and political consciousness" to have been the "one real gain" of the transformation of society.

If this appears as insanity to the healthy reader, it is wholly consistent with the philosophy of Marx. "Division of labor," said the young Marx, "increases with civilization." It is a fundamental law, just as its concomitant, the total victory of the capitalist system.

In Volume 1 of *Capital*, Marx described the inevitable and necessary "movement of the proletariat": *In the ordinary run of things, the worker can be left to the action of the natural laws of production, i.e. to his dependence on capital, a dependence springing from, guaranteed, and perpetuated by the very mechanism of production.*

Until, as he says elsewhere, on the day of the Revolution the proletariat will have been "disciplined, united, and organized by the very mechanism of production." Then they will have achieved that state whereby they can totally transform the world; "completely deprived of any self-activity" or "real life content," as the young Marx prescribed.

To back-track for a moment, consider the conservative historian Ashton's puzzlement at such workers as *the west-country weavers who destroyed tenter frames, or of the colliers who frequently smashed the pit gear, and sometimes even set the mines on fire: they must have realized that their action would result in unemployment, but their immediate concern was to assert their strength and inflict loss on stubborn employers. There seems to have been little or no social theory in the minds of the rioters and very little class consciousness in the Marxist sense of the term.*

This orthodox professor would certainly have understood Marx's admonition to just such workers, "to direct their attacks, not against the material instruments of production, but against the mode in which they are used." Marx understood, after all, that "the way machinery is utilized is totally distinct from the machinery itself," as he wrote in 1846! Similarly, Engels destroyed the logic of the anarchists by showing that the well-known neutrality of technology necessitates subordination, authority and power. How else, he asks, could a factory exist? In fact, Marx and Engels explain worker resistance to "scientific socialism" largely in terms of the survival of artisan-type jobs; those who are the more beaten and subordinated resist it the least. It is historical fact that those closest to the category artisan ("underdeveloped") actually have felt the most capacity to abolish the wage system, precisely because they still exercise some control of work processes.

Throughout nearly all his writings, however, Marx managed to return to the idea that, in socialist society, individuals would develop fully in and through their work. But by the third volume of *Capital* his attitude had changed and the emphasis was upon the "realm of freedom" which "only begins, in fact, where that labor, which is determined by need and external purpose, ceases," lying "outside the sphere of material production proper." Thus Marx admits that *not even under socialism* will the degradation of labor be undone. (This is closely related to the Marxist notion of *revolutionary preservation*, in which the acquisitions and productivity of the capitalist economic system are not to be disturbed by proletarian revolution.) The free creation of life is hence banished, reduced to the marginalia of existence much like hobbies in class society. Despite his analysis of alienated labor, much of the explicit core of his philosophy is virtually a consecration of work as tyranny.

Durkheim, writing in the late 19th century, saw as the main social problem the need for a cohesive social integration. Much like Marx, who also desired the consolidation and maturation of capitalism, albeit for different reasons, Durkheim thought he found the key in the division of labor. In the need for coordination engendered by division of labor, he discerned the essential source of solidarity. Today this grotesque inversion of human values is recognized rather fully; the hostility to specialization and its always authoritarian expertise is strongly present. A look at the recent opinion polls, or decades of articles like *Fortune*'s "The Senseless War on Science" (March, 1971) will suffice.

The perennial struggle against integration by the dominant system now continues as a struggle for *dis*-integration, a more and more consciously nihilist effort. The progress of "progress" is left with few partisans, and its enemies with few illusions as to what is worth preserving.

WHO KILLED NED LUDD?

[*A papier-mache likeness of Ned Ludd is one of the*] *symbols of the days that have gone, a reminder of what the workers' attitude to the new ideas might be if the unions had not grown strong and efficient.*
Trade Union Congress magazine *Labour*, at the time of the Production Exhibition, 1956.

In England, the first industrial nation, and beginning in textiles, capital's first and foremost enterprise there, arose the widespread revolutionary movement (between 1810 and 1820) known as Luddism. The challenge of the Luddite risings—and their defeat—was of very great importance to the subsequent course of modern society. Machine-wrecking, a principal weapon, pre-dates this period, to be sure; Darvall accurately termed it "perennial" throughout the 18th century, in good times and bad. And it was certainly not confined to either textile workers or England. Farm workers, miners, millers, and many others joined in destroying machinery, often against what would generally be termed their own "economic interests." Similarly, as Fülop-Miller reminds us, there were the workers of Eurpen and Aix-la-Chapelle who destroyed the important Cockerill Works, the spinners of Schmollen and Crimmitschau who razed the mills of those towns, and countless others at the dawn of the Industrial Revolution.

Nevertheless, it was the English cloth workers—knitters, weavers, spinners, croppers, shearmen, and the like—who initiated a movement, which "in sheer insurrectionary fury has rarely been more widespread in English history," as Thompson wrote, in what is probably an understatement. Though generally characterized as a blind, unorganized, reactionary, limited, and ineffective upheaval, this "instinctive" revolt against the new economic order was very successful for a time and had revolutionary aims. It was strongest in the more developed areas, the central and northern parts of the country especially. *The Times* of February 11, 1812 described "the appearance of open warfare" in England. Vice-Lieutenant Wood wrote to Fitzwilliam in the government on June 17, 1812 that "except for the very spots which were occupied by Soldiers, the Country was virtually in the possession of the lawless."

91

The Luddites indeed were irresistible at several moments in the second decade of the century and developed a very high morale and self-consciousness. As Cole and Postgate put it, "Certainly there was no stopping the Luddites. Troops ran up and down helplessly, baffled by the silence and connivance of the workers." Further, an examination of newspaper accounts, letters and leaflets reveals insurrection as the stated intent; for example, "all Nobles and tyrants must be brought down," read part of a leaflet distributed in Leeds. Evidence of explicit general revolutionary preparations was widely available in both York-shire and Lancashire, for instance, as early as 1812.

An immense amount of property was destroyed, including vast numbers of textile frames which had been redesigned for the production of inferior goods. In fact, the movement took its name from young Ned Ludd, who, rather than do the prescribed shoddy work, took a sledge-hammer to the frames at hand. This insistence on either the control of the productive processes or the annihilation of them fired the popular imagination and brought the Luddites virtually unanimous support. Hobsbawm declared that there existed an "overwhelming sympathy for machine-wreckers in all parts of the population," a condition which by 1813, according to Churchill, "had exposed the complete absence of means of preserving public order." Frame-breaking had been made a capital offense in 1812 and increasing numbers of troops had to be dispatched, to a point exceeding the total Wellington had under his command against Napoleon. The army, however, was not only spread very thin, but was often found unreliable due to its own sympathies and the presence of many conscripted Luddites in the ranks. Likewise, the local magistrates and constabulary could not be counted upon, and a massive spy system proved ineffective against the real solidarity of the populace. As might be guessed the volunteer militia, as detailed under the Watch and Ward Act, served only to "arm the most powerfully disaffected," according to the Hammonds, and thus the modern professional police system had to be instituted, from the time of Peel.

Required against what Mathias termed "the attempt to destroy the new society," was a weapon much closer to the point of production, namely the furtherance of an acceptance of the fundamental order in the form of trade unionism. Though it is clear that the promotion of trade unionism was a consequence of Luddism as much as the creation of the modern police was, it must also be realized that there had existed a long-tolerated tradition of unionism among the textile workers and others prior to the Luddite risings. Hence, as Morton and Tate almost alone point out, the machine-wrecking of this period cannot be viewed as the despairing outburst of workers having no other outlet. Despite the Combination Acts, which were an unenforced ban on unions between 1799 and 1824, Luddism did not move into a vacuum but was successful for a time in opposition to the refusal of the extensive union apparatus to compromise capital. In fact, the choice between the two was available and the unions were thrown aside in favor of the direct self-organization of workers and their radical aims.

During the period in question it is quite clear that unionism was seen as fundamentally distinct from Luddism and promoted as such, in the hope of absorbing the Luddite autonomy. Contrary to the fact of the Combination Acts, unions were often held to be legal in the courts, for example; and when unionists were prosecuted they generally received light punishment or none whatever, whereas the Luddites were usually hanged. Some members of Parliament openly blamed the owners for the social distress, for not making full use of the trade union path of escape. This is not to say that union objectives and control were as clear or pronounced as they are today, but the indispensible role of unions vis-à-vis capital was becoming clear, illumined by the crisis at hand and the felt necessity for allies in the pacification of the workers. Members of Parliament in the Midlands counties urged Gravenor Henson, head of the Framework Knitters Union, to combat Luddism—as if this were needed. His method of promoting restraint was of course his tireless advocacy of the extension of union strength. The Framework Knitters Committee of the union, according to Church's study of Nottingham, "issued specific instructions to workmen not to damage frames." And the Nottingham Union, the major attempt at a general industrial union, likewise set itself against Luddism and never employed violence.

If unions were hardly the allies of the Luddites, it can only be said that they were the next stage after Luddism in the sense that unionism played the critical role in its defeat, through the divisions, confusion, and deflection of energies the unions engineered. It "replaced" Luddism in the same way that it rescued the manufacturers from the taunts of the children in the streets, from the direct power of the producers. Thus the full recognition of unions in the repeal laws in 1824 and 1825 of the Combination Acts "had a moderating effect upon popular discontent," in Darvall's words. The repeal efforts, led by Place and Hume, easily passed an unreformed Parliament, by the way, with much pro-repeal testimony from employers as well as unionists, with only a few reactionaries opposed. In fact, while the conservative arguments of Place and Hume included a prediction of fewer strikes post-repeal, many employers understood the cathartic, pacific role of strikes and were not much dismayed by the rash of strikes which attended repeal. The repeal Acts of course officially delimited unionism to its traditional marginal wages and hours concern, a legacy of which is the universal presence of "management's rights" clauses in collective bargaining contracts to the present period.

The mid-1830's campaign against unions by some employers only underlined in its way the central role of unions: the campaign was possible only because the unions had succeeded so well as against the radicality of the unmediated workers in the previous period. Hence, Lecky was completely accurate later in the century when he judged that "there can be little doubt that the largest, wealthiest and best-organized Trade Unions have done much to diminish labor conflicts," just as the Webbs also conceded in the 19th century that there existed much more labor revolt before unionism became the rule.

But to return to the Luddites, we find very few first-person accounts and a virtually secret tradition mainly because they projected themselves through their acts, seemingly unmediated by ideology. What was it really all about? Stearns, perhaps as close as the commentators come, wrote "The Luddites developed a doctrine based on the presumed virtues of manual methods." He all but calls them "backward-looking wretches" in his condescension, yet there is a grain of truth here certainly. The attack of the Luddites was not occasioned by the introduction of new machinery, however, as is commonly thought, for there is no evidence of such in 1811 and 1812 when Luddism proper began. Rather, the destruction was leveled at the new slip-shod methods which were ordered into effect on the extant machinery. Not an attack against production on economic grounds, it was above all the violent response of the textile workers (soon joined by others) to their attempted degradation in the form of inferior work; shoddy goods— the hastily-assembled "cut-ups," primarily—was the issue at hand. While Luddite offensives generally corresponded to periods of economic downturn, it was because employers often took advantage of these periods to introduce new production methods. But it was also true that not all periods of privation produced Luddism, as it was that Luddism appeared in areas not particularly depressed. Leicestershire, for instance, was the least hit by hard times and it was an area producing the finest quality woolen goods; Leicestershire was a strong center for Luddism.

To wonder what was so radical about a movement which seemed to demand "only" the cessation of fraudulent work, is to fail to perceive the inner truth of the valid assumption, made on every side, of the connection between frame-breaking and sedition. As if the fight by the producer for the integrity of his work-life can be made without call-ing the whole of capitalism into question. The demand for the cessa-tion of fraudulent work necessarily becomes a cataclysm, an all-or-nothing battle insofar as it is pursued; it leads directly to the heart of the capitalist relationship and its dynamic.

Another element of the Luddite phenomenon generally treated with condescension, by the method of ignoring it altogether, is the or-ganizational aspect. Luddites, as we all know, struck out wildly and blindly, while the unions provide the only organized form to the work-ers. But in fact, the Luddites organized themselves locally and even federally, including workers from all trades, with an amazing, sponta-neous coordination. Eschewing an alienating structure, their organi-zation was neither formal nor permanent. Their revolt tradition was without a center and existed largely as an "unspoken code"; theirs was a non-manipulative community, organization which trusted itself. All this, of course, was essential to the depth of Luddism, to the appeal at its roots. In practice, "no degree of activity by the magistrates or by large reinforcements of military deterred the Luddites. Every attack revealed planning and method," stated Thompson, who also gave credit to their "superb security and communications." An army offi-cer in Yorkshire understood their possession of "a most extraordinary degree of concert and organization." William Cobbett wrote, concern-ing a report to the government in 1812: "And this is the circumstance that will most puzzle the ministry. They can find no agitators. It is a movement of the people's own."

Coming to the rescue of the authorities, however, despite Cob-bett's frustrated comments, was the leadership of the Luddites. Theirs was not a completely egalitarian movement, though this element may have been closer to the mark than was their appreciation of how much was within their grasp and how narrowly it eluded them. Of course, it was from among the leaders that "political sophistication" issued most effectively in time, just as it was from them that union cadres developed in some cases.

In the "pre-political" days of the Luddites—developing in our "post-political" days, too—the people openly hated their rulers. They cheered Pitt's death in 1806 and, more so, Perceval's assassination in 1812. These celebrations at the demise of prime ministers bespoke the weakness of mediations between rulers and ruled, the lack of integra-tion between the two. The political enfranchisement of the workers was certainly less important than their industrial enfranchisement or integration, via unions; it proceeded the more slowly for this reason. Nevertheless, it is true that a strong weapon of pacification was the strenuous effort made to interest the population in legal activities, namely the drive to widen the electoral basis of Parliament. Cobbett, described by many as the most powerful pamphleteer in English history, induced many to join Hampden Clubs in pursuit of voting reform, and was also noted, in the words of Davis, for his "outspoken condemnation of the Luddites." The pernicious effects of this divisive reform campaign can be partially measured by comparing such robust earlier demonstrations of anti-government wrath as the Gordon Riots (1780) and the mobbing of the King in London (1795) with such massacres and fiascos as the Pentridge and Peterloo "risings," which coincided roughly with the defeat of Luddism just before 1820.

But to return, in conclusion, to more fundamental mechanisms, we again confront the problem of work and unionism. The latter, it must be agreed, was made permanent upon the effective divorce of the worker from control of the instruments of production—and unionism itself contributed most critically to this divorce, as we have seen. Some, certainly including the Marxists, see this defeat and its form, the victory of the factory system, as both an inevitable and desirable outcome, though even they must admit that in work execution resides a significant part of the direction of industrial operations even now. A century after Marx, Galbraith located the guarantee of the system of productivity over creativity in the unions' basic renunciation of any claims regarding work itself. But work, as all ideologists sense, is an area closed off to permanent falsification. Thus modern mediators ignore the unceasing universal Luddite contest over control of the productive processes, even as every form of "employee participation" is now promoted.

In the early trade union movement there existed a good deal of democracy. Widespread, for example, was the practice of designating delegates by rotation or by lot. But what cannot be legitimately democratized is the real defeat at the root of the unions' victory, which makes them the organization of complicity, a mockery of community. Form on this level cannot disguise unionism, the agent of acceptance and maintenance of a grotesque world.

The Marxian quantification elevates productivity as the *summum bonum*, as leftists likewise ignore the ending of the direct power of the producers and so manage, incredibly, to espouse unions as all that untutored workers can have. The opportunism and elitism of all the Internationals, indeed the history of leftism, sees its product finally in fascism, when accumulated confines bring their result. When fascism could successfully appeal to workers as the removal of inhibitions, as the "Socialism of Action," etc.—*as revolutionary*—it should be clear how much was buried with the Luddites.

There are those who already again fix the label of "age of transition" on today's growing crisis, hoping all will turn out nicely in another defeat for the luddites. We see today the same need to enforce work discipline as in the earlier period, perhaps even the same awareness by the population of the meaning of "progress." Quite possibly we now can recognize all our enemies the more clearly, so that this time the transition can be in the hands of the creators.

AXIS POINT OF AMERICAN INDUSTRIALISM

The 1820s constituted a watershed in U.S. life. By the end of that decade, about ten years after the last of the English Luddite risings had been suppressed, industrialism secured its decisive American victory; by the end of the 1830s all of its cardinal features were definitively present.

The many overt threats to the coherence of emerging industrial capitalism, the ensemble of forms of resistance to its hegemony, were blunted at this time and forced into the current of that participation so vital to modern domination. In terms of technology, work, politics, sexuality, culture, and the whole fabric of ordinary life, the struggles of an earlier, relative autonomy, which threatened both old and new forms of authority, fell short and a dialectic of domestication, so familiar to us today, broke through.

The reactions engendered in the face of the new dynamic in this epoch of its arrival seem, by the way, to offer some implicit parallels to present trends as technological civilization likely enters its terminal crisis: the answers of progress, now anything but new or promising, encounter a renewed legitimation challenge that can be informed, even inspired, by understanding the past.

American "industrial consciousness," which Samuel Reneck judged to have triumphed by 1830,[1] was in large measure and from the outset a virtual project of the State. In 1787, generals and government officials sponsored the first promotional effort, the Pennsylvania Society for the Encouragement of Manufactures and the Useful Arts. With Benjamin Franklin as the Society's official patron, capital was raised and a factory equipped, but arson put an end to this venture early in 1790.

Another benchmark of the period was Alexander Hamilton's *Report on the Subject of Manufactures*, drafted by his tirelessly pro-factory technology assistant secretary of the Treasury, Tench Coxe. It is noteworthy that Coxe received government appointments from both the Federalist Hamilton and his arch-rival Jefferson, Republican and career celebrator of the yeoman free-holder as the basis of independent values. While Hamilton pushed industrialization, arguing,[2] for example, that children were better off in mills than at home or in school, Jefferson is remembered as a constant foe of that evil, alien import, manufacturing.

To correct the record is to glimpse the primacy of technology over ideological rhetoric as well as to remember that no Enlightenment man was not also an enthusiast of science and technology. In fact, it is fitting that Jefferson, the American most closely associated with the Enlightenment, introduced and promoted the idea of interchangeability of parts, key to the modern factory, from France as early as 1785.[3]

Also to the point is Charles V. Hagnar's remark that in the 1790s "Thomas Jefferson,...a personal friend of my father...indoctrinated him with the manufacturing fever," and induced him to start a cotton mill.[4] As early as 1805, Jefferson, at least in private, complained that his earlier insistence on independent producers as the bedrock of national virtue was misunderstood, that his condemnation of industrialism was only meant to apply to the cities of Europe.[5]

Political foliage aside, it was becoming clear that mechanization was in no way impeded by government. The role of the State is tellingly reflected by the fact that the "armory system" now rivals the older "American system of manufactures" term as the more accurate to describe the new system of production methods.[6] It is along these lines that Cochran referred to the need for the federal authority to "keep up the pressure," around 1820, in order to soften local resistance to factories and their methods.[7]

In the 1820s a fully developed industrial lobby in Congress and the extensive use of the technology fair and exhibit—not to mention nationalist pro-development appeals such as that to anti-British sentiment after the War of 1812, and other non-political factors to be discussed below—contributed to the assured ascendancy of industrialization, by 1830.

Ranged against the efforts to achieve that ascendancy was an unmistakeable antipathy, observed in the references to its early manifestations in classic historical works. Norman Ware found that the Industrial Revolution "was repugnant to an astonishingly large section of the earlier American community,"[8] and Victor S. Clark noted the strong popular prejudice that existed "against factory industries as detrimental to the welfare of the working-people."[9]

Later, too, this aversion was still present, if declining, as a pivotal force. The July 4, 1830 oratory of pro-manufacture Whig Edward Everett contained a necessary reference to the "suffering, depravity, and brutalism"[10] of industrialism—in Europe—for the purpose of deflecting hostility from its American counterpart. Later in the 1830s the visiting English liberal Harriet Martineau, in her efforts to defend manufacturing, indicated that her difficulties were precisely her audiences' antagonism to the subject.[11]

Yet despite the "slow and painful"[12] nature of the changeover and especially the widespread evidence of deep-seated resistance (of which the foregoing citations are a minute sample), there lingers the notion of an enthusiastic embrace of mechanization in America by craftsmen as well as capitalists.[13] Fortunately, recent scholarship has been contributing to a better grasp of the struggles of the early-to-mid-nineteenth century, Merritt Roe Smith's excellent *Harpers Ferry Armory and the New Technology*,[14] for example. "The Harpers Ferry story diverges sharply from oft-repeated generalizations that 'most Americans accepted and welcomed technological change with uncritical enthusiasm,' "[15] Smith declares in his introduction.

Suffice it to interject here that no valid separation exists between anti-technology feelings and the more commonly recognized elements of contestation of classes that proceeded from the grounding of that technology; in practice the two strands were (and are) obviously intertwined. This reference to the "massive and irrefutable"[16] class opposition of early industrialism or to Taft and Ross' dictum that "the United "States has had the bloodiest and most violent labor history of any industrial nation,' "[17] finds its full meaning when we appraise both levels of anti-authoritarianism, especially in the watershed period of the 1820s.

In early 1819 the English visitor William Faux declared that "Labour is quite as costly as in England, whether done by slaves, or by hired whites, and it is also much more troublesome."[18] Later that year his travel journal further testified to the "very villainous" character of American workers, who "feel too free to work in earnest, or at all, above two or three days in a week."[19] Indeed, travelers seemed invariably to remark on "the independent manners of the laboring classes,"[20] in slightly softer language.

More specifically, dissent by skilled workers, as has often been noted, was the sharpest and most durable. Given the "astonishing versatility of the average native laborer,"[21] however, it is also true that a generalized climate of resistance confronted the impending debasement of work by the factory.

Those most clearly identified as artisans give us the clearest look at resistance, owing to the self-reliant culture that was a function of autonomous handicraft production. Bruce Laurie, on some Philadelphia textile craftsmen, illustrates the vibrant pre-industrial life in question, with its blasé attitude toward work: "On a muggy summer day in August 1828 Kensington's hand loom weavers announced a holiday from their daily toil. News of the affair circulated throughout the district and by mid-afternoon the hard-living frame tenders and their comrades turned the neighborhood avenues into a playground. Knots of lounging workers joked and exchanged gossip...The more athletic challenged one another to foot races and games...(and) quenched their thirst with frequent drams. The spree was a classic celebration of St.

Monday.''[22]

It was no accident that mass production—primarily textile factories—first appeared in New England, with its relative lack of strong craft traditions, rather than in say, Philadelphia, the center of American artisan skills.[23] Traditions of independent creativity obviously posed an obstacle to manufacturing innovation, causing Carl Russell Fish to assay that "craftsmen were the only actively dissatisfied class in the country.''[24]

The orthodox explanation of industrialism's triumph stresses the much higher U.S. wage levels, compared to Europe, and an alleged shortage of skilled workers. These are, as a rule, considered the primary factors that produced "an environment affording every suggestion and inducement to substitute machinery for men,'' and that nurtured that "inventiveness and mechanical intuition which are sometimes regarded as a national trait,'' in the descriptive phrases of Clark.[25]

But the preceding discussion should already be enough to indicate that it was the presence of work skills that challenged the new technology; not their absence. Research shows no dearth of skilled workers,[26] and there is abundant evidence that "the trend toward mechanization came more from cultural and managerial bias than from carefully calculated marginal costs.''[27]

Habakkuk's comparison of American and British antebellum technology and labor economics cites the "scarcity and belligerency of the available skilled labour"[28] and we must accent the latter quality, while realizing that scarcity can also mean the ability to make oneself scarce—namely, the oft-remarked high turnover rates.[29]

It was industrial discipline that was missing, especially among craftsmen. At mid-century Samuel Colt confided to a British engineering group that "uneducated laborers" made the best workers in his new mass-production arms factory because they had so little to unlearn;[30] skills—and the recalcitrance accompanying them—were hardly at a premium.

Strikes and unionization (though certainly not always linked) became common from 1823 forward,[31] and the modern labor movement showed particular vitality during the militant "great uprising" period of 1833-1837.[32]

However, especially by the 1830s, these struggles (largely for shorter hours, secondarily over wages) were essentially situated within the world of a standardizing, regimenting technology, predicated on the worker as a component of it. And although this distinction is not total, it was the "unorganized" workers who mounted the most extreme forms of opposition, luddite in many instances, contrary to the time-honored wisdom that luddism and America were strangers.

Gary Kulik's excellent scholarship on industrial Rhode Island determined that in Pawtucket alone more than five arson attempts were made against cotton mill properties, and that the deliberate burning of textile mills was far from uncommon throughout early nineteenth century New England, declining by the 1830s.[33] Jonathon Prude reached a similar conclusion: "Rumors abounded in antebellum New England that fires suffered by textile factories were often of 'incendiary origin.' "[34] The same reaction was felt in Philadelphia, albeit slightly later: "Several closely spaced mill burnings triggered cries of 'incendiarism' in the 1830s, a decade of intense industrial conflict."[35]

The hand sawyers who burned Oliver Evans' new steam mill at New Orleans in 1813[36] also practiced machine-wrecking by arson, like their Northeastern cousins, and shortly later Massachusetts rope makers attacked machine-made yarn, boasting that their handspun product was stronger.[37]

Sailors in New York often inflicted damage on vessels during strikes, according to Dulles, who noted "the seamen were not organized and were an especially obstreperous lot."[38]

Though its impact, as with resistance in general, declined after the 1820s, luddite-type violence continued. The unpopular superintendent of the Harpers Ferry Armory[39] was shot dead in his office in early 1830 by an angry craftsman named Ebenezer Cox. Though Cox was hung for his act, he was a folk hero among the Harpers Ferry workers, who hated Dunn's emphasis on supervision and factory-type discipline, and "never tired of citing Dunn's fate as a blunt reminder to superintendents of what could be expected if they became overzealous in executing their duties and impinged on the traditional freedoms of employees.[40]

Construction laborers, especially in railroad work, frequently destroyed property; Gutman provides an example from 1831 in which about three hundred of them punished a dishonest contractor by tearing up the track they built.[41] The destructive fury of Irish strikers on the Baltimore and Ohio Canal in 1834 occasioned the inaugural use of federal troops in a labor dispute, on orders of Andrew Jackson. And in the mid-1830s anti-railroad teamsters still waylaid trains and shot at their crews from ambush.[42]

In the Philadelphia handloom weavers' strike of 1842, striking artisans used machine breaking, intimidation, destruction of unwoven wool and finished cloth, house wrecking, and threats of even worse violence. During this riotous struggle, weavers marched on a water powered, mass-production mill to burn it; the attack was driven off, with two constables wounded.[43]

Returning to the New England textile mills and incendiary luddism, Prude describes the situation after 1840: "Managers were rarely directly challenged by their hands; and although mills continued to burn down, contemporaries did not as quickly assume that workers were setting the fires."[44]

Looking for social-political reasons for the culture of industrialism, one finds that official efforts to domesticate the ruled via the salutary effects of poor relief led Boston officials to put widows and orphans to work, beginning in 1735, in what amounted to a major experiment to inculcate habits of industry and routine. But even threats of denial of subsistence aid failed to establish industrial discipline over irregular work habits and independent attitudes.[45]

Artisanal—and agricultural—work was far more casual than that regimented by modern productionist models. Unlike that of the factory, for example, it could almost always be interrupted in favor of an encounter, an adventure, or simply a distraction. This easy entry to gaming, drinking, personal projects, hunting, extended and often raucous revelry on a great variety of occasions, among other interruptions, was a preserve of independence from authority in general.

On the other hand, the regulation and monotony that adhere to the work differentiation of industrial technology combat such casual, undomesticated tendencies. Division of labor embodies, as an implicit purpose, the control and domination of the work process and those tied to it. Adam Smith saw this, and so did Tocqueville, in the 1830s: "As the principle of the division of labor is ever more completely applied, the workman becomes weaker, more limited, and more dependent-...Thus, at the same time that industrial science constantly lowers the standing of the working class, it raises that of the masters."[46]

This subordination, including its obvious benefit, social control, was widely appreciated, especially but not exclusively, by the early industrialists. Manufacturers, with unruliness very visible to them, came quickly to identify technological progress with a more subdued populace. In 1816 Walton Felch, for instance, claimed that the "restless dispositions and insatiate prodigality" of working people were altered, by "manufacturing attendance," into patterns of regularity and calmness.[47] Another New England millowner, Smith Wilkinson, judged in 1835 that factory labor imposed a "restraining influence" on people who "are often very ignorant, and too often vicious."[48] The English visitor Harriet Martineau, introduced above, was of like mind in the early 1840s: "The factories are found to afford a safe and useful employment for much energy that would otherwise be wasted and misdirected." She determined that unlike the situation that had prevailed "before the introduction of manufactures...now the same society is eminently orderly...disorders have almost entirely disappeared."[49]

Eli Whitney provides another case in point of the social designs inhering in mechanization, namely that of his Mill Rock armory, which moved from craft shop to factory status during the period of the late 1790s to Whitney's death in 1825. Long associated with the birth of the "American System" of interchangeable parts production, he was thoroughly unpopular with his employees for regimentation he developed via increasing division of labor. His penchant for order and discipline was embodied in his view of Mill Rock as a "moral gymnasium," where "correct habits" of diligence and industry were inculcated through systematic control of all facets of the work day.[50]

Andrew Ure, the English ideologue of early industrial capitalism, summed up the control intentionality behind the new technology by typifying the factory as "a creation designed to restore order," while proclaiming that "when capital enlists science into her service, the refractory hand of labor will always be taught docility."[51]

As skill levels were forcibly reduced, the art of living was also purposefully degraded by the sheer number of hours involved in industrial work. Emerson, usually thought of in terms of a vague philosophy of human possibilities, applauded the suppression of potential enacted by the work hours of 1830s railroad-building: he observed the long, hard construction shifts as "safe vents for peccant humors; and this grim day's work of fifteen or sixteen hours, though deplored by all humanity of the neighborhood, is a better police than the sheriff and his deputies."[52] A hundred years later Simone Weil supplied a crucial part of the whole equation of industrialization: "No one would accept two daily hours of slavery. To be accepted, slavery must be of such a daily duration as to break something in a man."[53] Similar is Cochran's more recent (and more conservative) reference to the twelve-hour day, that it was "maintained in part to keep workers under control."[54]

Pioneer industrialist Samuel Slater wondered, in the 1830s, whether national institutions could survive "amongst a people whose energies are not kept constantly in play by the pursuit of some incessant productive employment."[55] Indeed, technological "progress" and the modern wage-slavery accompanying it offered a new stability to representative government, owing essentially to its magnified powers for suppressing the individual. Slater's biographer recognized that "to maintain good order and sound government, [modern industry] is more efficient than the sword or bayonet."[56]

A relentless assault on the worker's historic rights to free time, self-education, craftsmanship, and play was at the heart of the rise of the factory system; "increasingly, a feeling of degradation spread among factory hands," according to Rex Burns.[57] By the mid-1830s a common refrain in the working-class press was that the laborer had been debased "into a necessary piece of machinery."[58]

Assisted by sermons, a growing public school system, a new didactic popular literature, and other social institutions that sang the praises of industrial discipline, the factory had won its survival by 1830. From this point on, and with increasing visibility by the end of the 1830s, conditions worsened and pay decreased.[59] No longer was there a pressing need to lure first-time operatives into industrialized life and curry their favor with high wages and relatively light duties. Beginning before 1840, for example, the pace of work in textile mills was greatly speeded up, facilitated also by the first major immigration influx, that of impoverished Irish and French Canadians.[60]

Henry Clay asked, "Who has not been delighted with the clockwork movements of a large cotton factory?"[61] reminding us that concomitant with such regimentation was the spread of a new conception of time. Although certainly things did not always go "like clockwork" for the industrialists—"punctuality and absenteeism remained intractable problems for management" throughout the first half of the nineteenth century,[62] for example—a new, industrial time, against great resistance, made gradual headway.

In the task-oriented labors of artisans and farmers, work and play were freely mixed; a constant pace of unceasing labor was the ideal not of the mechanic but of the machine: more specifically, of the clock. The largely spontaneous games, fairs, festivals, and excursions gave way, along with working at one's own pace, to enslavement to the uniform, unremitting technological time of the factory whistle, centralized power, and unvarying routine.

For the Harpers Ferry armorers early in the century, the workshops opened at sunrise and closed at sunset but they were free to come and go as they pleased. They had long been accustomed to controlling the duration and scheduling of their tasks, and "the idea of a clocked day seemed not only repugnant but an outrageous insult to their self-respect and freedom."[63] Hence, the opposition to 1827 regulations that installed a clock and announced a ten-hour day was bitter and protracted.

For those already under the regimen of factory production, struggles against the alien time were necessarily of a lingering, rear-guard character by the late 1820s. An interesting illustration is that of Pawtucket, Rhode Island, a mill village whose denizens built a town clock by public subscription in 1828.[64] In their efforts to counter the monopoly of recording time which had been the mill owner's factory bell, one can see that by this time the whole level of contestation had degenerated: the issue was not industrial time itself but merely the democratization of its measurement.

The clock, favorite machine of the Enlightenment, is a master device in the depiction of American political economy by Thoreau and others. Its function is decisive because it links the industrial apparatus with consciousness.[65] It is fitting that clockmaking, along with gun manufacture, was a model of the new technology; the U.S. led the world in the production of inexpensive timepieces by the 1820s, a testimony to the encroaching industrial value system and the marked anxiety about the passage of time that was part of it.[66]

Though even in the first decades of the Republic there was a permanent operative class in at least three urban centers of the Mid-Atlantic seaboard,[67] industrialization began in earnest with New England cloth production twenty years after the Constitution was adopted. For example, forty-one new woolen mills were built in the U.S., chiefly along New England streams, between 1807 and 1813.[68] The textile industry selected the most economically deprived areas, and with cheery propaganda and, initially, relatively good working conditions, enticed women and children (who had no other options) into the mills. That they "came from families which could no longer support them at home,"[69] means that theirs was essentially forced labor. In 1797 Obadiah Brown, in a letter to a partner regarding the selection of a mill site, determined that "the inhabitants appear to be poor, their homes very much on the decline. I apprehend it might be a very good place for a Cotton Manufactory, Children appearing very plenty."[70] "In collecting our help," a Connecticut millowner said thirty years later, "we are obliged to employ poor families and generally those having the greatest number of children."[71]

New England factory cloth output increased from about 2.4 million yards in 1815 to approximately 13.9 million yards in 1820, and the shift of weaving from home to factory was virtually completed by 1824.[72] Despite arson, absenteeism, stealing, and sabotage persisting with particular emphasis into the 1830s,[73] the march of industrialization proceeded in textiles as elsewhere. If, as Inkeles and Smith[74] (among others) have contended, a prime element of modernity is the amount of time spent in factories, the 1820s was indeed a watershed.

"Certainly by 1825 the first stage of the industrialization of the United States was over,"[75] in Cochran's estimation. In 1820, factories were capitalized to $50,000,000; by 1840, to $250,000,000, and the number of people working in them had more than doubled.[76] Also by the 1820s the whole direction of specialized bureaucratic control, realized a generation later in such large corporations as the railroads, had already become clear.[77]

As the standardizing, quasi-military machine replaced the individual's tools, it provided authority with an invaluable, "objective" ally against "disorder." Not coincidentally did modern mass politics also labor to implant itself in the 1820s: political hegemony, as a necessary part of social power, had also failed to fully resolve the issue in its favor in the struggles of the early republic.[78] Conflict of all kinds was rampant, and a "terrible precariousness,"[79] in Page Smith's phrase, characterized the cohesion of national power. In fact, by the early 1820s a virtual breakdown of the legitimacy of traditional rule by informal elites was underway and a serious restructuring of American politics was required.

Part of the restructuring dealt with law, in a parallel to the social meaning of technology: "neutral" universal principles came to the fore to justify increased coercion. Modern bourgeois society was forced to rely on an increasingly objectified legal system, which reflected, at base, the progress of division of labor. It must, in David Grimsted's words, "elevate law because of what it is creating and what it has to destroy."[80] By the time of Jackson's ascendancy in the late 1820s, America had become largely a government of laws not men (though juries mitigated legality), despite the unpopularity of this development as seen, for example, in the widespread scorn of lawyers.[81]

Along with the need to mobilize the lower orders into industrial work, it was important to greatly increase political participation in the interests of legitimizing the whole. Although by the mid-1820s almost every state had extended the franchise to include all white males, the numbers of voters remained very low during the decade.[82] By this time newspapers had proliferated and were playing a key role in working toward the critical integration achieved with Jackson and new, mass political machinery.

In 1826, a workingman was chosen for the first time as a mayoral candidate in Baltimore, explicitly in order to attract workingmen's participation,[83] an early example of a necessary part of moving away from narrow based, old-style rule.

However, John Quincy Adams, who had become president in 1825, "failed to comprehend that voters needed at least the appearance of consultation and participation in making decisions."[84] A conservative and a nationalist, he was at least occasionally candid: as he told Tocqueville, there is "a great equality before the law, ... [which] ceases absolutely in the habits of life. There are upper classes and working classes."[85]

Following Adams, the election of Andrew Jackson in 1828 symbolized and accelerated a shift in American life. At the moment that mechanization was securing its domination of life and culture, the Jacksonian era signalled the arrival of professional politics and a crucial diversion of the remaining potentially dangerous energies. Embodying this domestication in his successful appeal to the "common man," the old general was in reality a plantation owner, land speculator, and lawyer, whose first case in 1788 defended the interests of Tennessee creditors against debtors.

He reversed the decline in executive strength that had plagued his three predecessors, essentially renewing state power by a direct appeal to the working classes for the first time in U.S. history. The mob at the 1829 White House inaugural, celebrated in history text-books with its smashing of china and trampling of the furniture, did in fact "symbolize a new power,"[86] in Curti's phrase—a power tamed and delivering itself to government.

Jackson's "public statements address a society divided into classes, invidiously distinguished and profoundly antagonistic."[87] And yet, employing the Jeffersonian argot, he regularly identified the class enemy in misleading terms as the money power, the moneyed aristocracy, etc.

By the presidential contest of 1832 the gentleman-leader had certainly been rendered an anachronism,[88] in large part via the use of class-oriented rhetoric. In Jackson's second term, after he had been overwhelmingly re-elected on the strength of his attacks on the Bank of the United States,[89] he vetoed the rechartering of the bank in the most popular act of his administration.

Although many conservatives feared that Jackson's policies and conduct would result in a "disastrous, perhaps a fatal," revolution,[90] that the Jacksonians "had raised up forces greater than they could control,"[91] the bank proved a safe target for the Jacksonian project of deflecting popular anger. As Fish noted, "hostility was merely keenest against banks; it existed against all corporations."[92]

Thus, the "Monster" Bank, which did reap outrageous profits and openly purchased members of Congress, was inveighed against as the incarnation of aristocracy, privilege, and the spirit of luxury, while, missing the essential point, Daniel Webster and others warned against such inflaming of the poor against the rich.[93] Needless to say, the growth of an enslaving technology was never attacked; rather, as Bray Hammond maintained, Jackson represented "a blow at an older set of capitalists by a newer, more numerous set."[94] And meanwhile, along with the phrase-making of this "frontier democrat," class distinctions widened, and tensions increased, minus the means to successfully overcome them.

In the mid-1830s various workers' parties also sprang up. Many were far from totally proletarian in composition, and few went much further than Jacksonian Democracy, in their denunciations of the "monopolists" and such demands as free public schools and equality of "opportunity." This political workerism only advanced the absorption of working people into the new political system and displayed, for the first time, the now familiar interchangeability of labor leader and politician.

But integration was not accomplished smoothly or automatically. For one thing, political insurrection was a legacy of the eighteenth century: from Bacon's Rebellion (1675) in Virginia, by 1760 there had been eighteen uprisings aimed at overthrowing colonial governments,[95] and more recently there had appeared Shays' Rebellion in Massachusetts (1786-1787), the Whiskey Rebellion in western Pennsylvania (1794), and Fries' Rebellion in eastern Pennsylvania (1798-99).

Twenty-five years after the Constitution was signed, extensive anti-Federalist rioting in Baltimore seemed to connect with this legacy, rather than to less authentic political alternatives to the old informal means of social control. Significantly, over the course of the summer 1812 upheavals, the composition of the mob shifted toward an exclusively proletarian, unpropertied make-up.[96]

Moving into the period under particular scrutiny, the depth of general contestation is somewhat reflected by a most unlikely revolt, that of a "vicious cadet mutiny" at West point in 1826. On Christmas morning in that year, "drunken and raging cadets endeavored to kill at least one of their superior officers and converted their barracks into a bastion which they proposed to defend, armed, against assault by relieving Regular Army troops on the Academy reservation.[97] The fury of this amazing turn of events, though detailed in much Board of Inquiry and courts-martial testimony, remains a little-known episode in U.S. history; it can be seen to have introduced a whole chapter of wholesale tumult, nonetheless.

By the late 1820s group violence had reached great prominence in American life, such that within a few years "many Americans had a strong sense of social disintegration."[98] The annual New York parade of artisans in November 1830 was another incident that told a great deal about the mounting unruliness. Printers, coopers, furniture-makers, and a great many other tradesmen assembled at the culmination of the procession, to hear speeches expressing the usual republican virtues. But on this day politicians mouthing the same old ritual phrases about political freedom and the dignity of labor were suddenly confronted by curses, scuffling and a defiant temper. "As the militia tried to quiet the militants, the dissatisfied crowd knocked out the supports of the scaffolding, causing the entire stage to crash to the ground,"[99] and bringing the ceremonies to an undignified end.

The public violence of the 1830s was more a prolonged aftershock, however, than a moment of revolutionary possibility. For the reasons given above, the triumph of industrial technology was a fact by the end of the 1820s and the ensuing aftermath, though major, could not be decisive.

But it is true that, by Hammett's reckoning, "A climate of disorder prevailed...which seemed to be moving the nation to the edge of disaster."[100] As Page Smith described urban life in the early 1830s, "What is hard to comprehend today is the constant ferment of social unrest and bitterness that manifested itself almost monthly in violent riots and civic disorders."[101] Gilje's research revealed "nearly 200 instances of riot between 1793 and 1829 in New York City alone,"[102] for example, and Weinbaum counted 116 in that city just in the period of 1821 to 1837.[103] Philadelphia, Baltimore, and Boston witnessed outbreaks on a similar scale, often directed at bankers and "monopolists."

Michael Chavalier wrote a chapter entitled "Symptoms of Revolution" against the backdrop of four days of rioting in Baltimore over exploitative practices of the Bank of Maryland in the summer of 1835.[104] Also in that year, disorders that caused Jackson to increasingly resort to the use of federal troops, occasioned William Ellery Channing's report from Boston: "The cry is, 'Property is insecure, law a rope of sand, and the mob sovereign.' "[105] Likewise, the Boston *Evening Journal* pondered the "disorganizing, anarchical spirit" of the times in an August 7, 1835 editorial.

February, 1836 saw hundreds of debtor farmers attack and burn offices of the Holland Land Company in western New York.[106] During 1836 and 1837 crowds in New York City broke into warehouses several times, furious over high food, rent, and fuel prices. The Workingmen's Party in New York, known as the Locofoco Party, has been linked with these "flour riots," but, interestingly, at the February 1837 outburst most closely tied to Locofoco speech-making, of fifty-three rioters arrested none was a party member.[107]

Despite the narrow chances for the ultimate success of 1830s uprisings, it is impossible to deny the existence of deep and bitter class feelings, of the notion that the promise of equality contained in the Declaration of Independence was mocked by reality. Serious disturbances continued: the 1838 "Buckshot War," in which Harrisburg was seized by an irate, armed crowd in a Pennsylvania senatorial election dispute, for example; the "Anti-rent" riots by New York tenants of the Van Rensselaer family in 1839; the "Dorr War" of 1842 (somewhat reminiscent of the independent "Indian Stream Republic" of 1832-35 in New Hampshire) in which thousands in Rhode Island approached civil war in a fight over rival state constitutions; and the sporadic anti-railroad riots in the Kensington section of Philadelphia from 1840 to 1842, were among major hostilities.

But ethnic, racial and religious disputes began fairly early in the decade to begin to supersede class-conscious struggles, though often disparate elements co-existed in the same occasions. This decline in consciousness was manifested in anti-Irish, anti-abolitionist, and anti-Catholic riots largely, and must be seen in the context of the earlier, principal defeat of working people by the factory system, in the 1820s. Cut off from the only terrain on which challenge could gain basic victories, could change life, the upheaval in the 1830s was destined to sour. Characteristically, the end of the 1830s saw both the professionalization of urban police forces and organized gang violence in place as permanent fixtures.

If by 1830 virtually every aspect of American life had undergone major alteration, the startling changes in drinking habits shed particular light on the industrialism behind this transformation. The "great alcoholic binge of the early nineteenth century,"[108] and its precipitous decline in the early 1830s, have much to say about how the culture of the new technology took shape.

Drinking, on the one hand, was a part of the pre-industrial blurring of the distinction between work and leisure. On up into the early decades of the century, small amounts of alcohol were commonly consumed throughout the day, at work and at home (sometimes the same place); reference has been made above to the frequent, spontaneous holidays of all kinds, and the wide-spread observance of "Blue Mondays" or three-day weekends, "which run pretty well into the week," according to one complaining New York employer.[109] Drinking was the universal accompaniment to these parties, celebrations, and extended weekends, as it was to the normal work-day.

The tavern or grog-shop, with its "unstructured, leisurely, and wholly unproductive, even anti-productive, character,"[110] was a social center well-suited to a non-mechanized age, and in fact became more than ever the workingman's club as modernization cut him off from other emotional outlets.[111]

But drunkenness—binge-drinking and solitary drinking, most importantly— was increasing by 1820; significantly, alcoholic delirium, or D.T.'s, first appeared in the U.S. during the 1820s.[112] Alcoholism is an obvious register of strains and alienation, of the inability of people to cope with the burden of daily life which a society places on them. Clearly, there is little healthy or resistant about the resort to such drinking practices.

Temperance reform was a part of the larger syndrome of social disciplining expressed in industrialization, as irregular drinking habits were an obstacle to a well-managed population. Not surprisingly, factory owners were in the forefront of such efforts, having to contend with troublesome wage-earners who had little taste for such dictums as "the steady arm of industry withers from drink."[113] Tyrell's examination of Worcester, Massachusetts also found that "the leading temperance reformers were those with a hand in the work of inventions and of innovations in factory and machine production."[114]

While at one point workers considered a daily liquor issue a nonnegotiable right and an emblem of their independence, increasing reliance on alcohol signified the debility that went along with their domination by machine culture. The Secretary of War estimated in 1829 that "three-quarters of the nation's laborers drank daily at least four ounces of distilled spirits,"[115] and in 1830 the average annual consumption of liquor exceeded five gallons, nearly triple the amount 150 years later.[116]

The anti-alcohol crusade began in earnest in 1826 with the formation of the American Temperance Society, and other local groups such as the Society in Lynn (Massachusetts) for the Promotion of Industry, Frugality and Temperance. In the same year Beecher wrote his *Six Sermons on Intemperance*, the leading statement of anti-drinking of the period, which pronounced tippling to be politically dangerous. In Gusfield's excellent summation, Beecher's writings "displayed the classic fear the creditor has of the debtor, the propertied of the propertyless, and the dominant of the subordinate—the fear of disobedience, renunciation, and rebellion."[117]

Temperance exertions in the 1820s revealed in their propaganda the tenuous influence that the respectable held over the laboring classes during the height of the battle to establish industrial values and a predictable work-force. As this battle was won, drinking suddenly leveled off at the end of the 1820s and began to plummet in the early 1830s toward an unprecedented low.[118] As working people became domesticated, the temperance movement shifted toward the goal of complete abstinence, and in the 1840s a "dry" campaign swept the nation.[119]

The other major reform movement, also arising in the mid-1820s, was for a public school system, and like the temperance campaign it was explicitly undertaken to "make the dangerous classes trustworthy."[120] The concept of mass schooling had arrived by the early Jacksonian period, when innovative forms of coercion were demanded by deteriorating restraints on social behavior, and auxiliary institutions came to the aid of the factory.

The "willingness of early nineteenth century school promoters to intervene directly and without invitation in the lives of the working class"[121] was a consequence of the notion that education was something the ruling orders did to the rest to make them orderly and tractable. Thus "the first compulsory schools were alien institutions set in hostile territory,"[122] as Katz put it, owing largely to the spirit of autonomy and egalitarianism that parents had instilled in their children. Faux noted, in 1819, the "prominent want of respect for rule and rulers," which he connected with a common refusal of "strict discipline" in schools;[123] Marryat's diary reported that students "learn precisely what they please and no more."[124]

Drunkenness and rioting occurred in schools as well as in the rest of society and educators interpreted the overall situation as announcing general subversion; in an 1833 address on education, John Armstrong declared, "When Revolution threatens the overthrow of our institutions, everything depends on the character of our people."[125]

Industrial morality—obedience, self-sacrifice, restraint, and order— constituted the most important goal of public education; character was of far greater importance than intellectual development.[126] The school system came into existence to shape behavior and attitudes and thus reinforce the emerging world. The belief that attendance should be universal and compulsory followed logically from assumptions about its importance.[127]

Moral instruction was also amplified by the churches during the 1820s and 1830s, an antidote to that tendency to "rejoice in casting off restraints and unsettling the foundations of social order,"[128] woefully recorded by the Reverend Charles Hall. Sunday School and the society for diffusion of religious tracts were two new ecclesiastical contributions to social control in this period.

The Jacksonian period is also synonymous with the "Age of the Asylum," a further development in the quest for civic docility. The regularity and efficiency of the factory was the model for the penitentiaries, insane asylums, orphanages, and reformatories that now appeared.[129] Embodying uniformity and regularity, the factory was indeed the model, as we have seen, for the whole of society.

Religious revivalism and millenarianism grew in strength after the mid-1820s, and one of the new denominations to appear was the Millerites (today's Seventh-day Adventists). On October 22, 1844 the group gathered to await what they predicted would be the end of the world. Their expectation was but the most literal manifestation of a feeling that began to pervade the country after 1830;[130] without unduly elevating the pre-industrial past, one can recognize the lament for a world that was indeed ended.

The early stages of industrial capitalism introduced a sharpened division between the worlds of work and home, male and female, and private and public life, with large extended families eroding toward small, isolated nuclear families.

Along with this process of increasing separation and isolation came a focused repression of personal feelings, stemming from new requirements for rationalized, predictable behavior. As planning and organization moved ahead via the progress of the machine model of the individual, the range of human sentiments became suspect, a target for suppression. For example, whereas in 1800 it was not considered "unmanly" for a man to weep openly, by the 1830s a proscription against any extreme emotional display, especially crying, was gaining strength.[131] Similarly, in child training this tendency became very pronounced; in the widely-distributed *Advice to Christian Parents* (1839), the Reverend John Hersey emphasized that "in every stage of domestic education, children should be disciplined to restrain their appetites and desires."[132]

The seventeenth century Puritans were hardly "puritanical" about sexual matters, and eighteenth century American society—especially in the latter part of the century—was characterized by very open sexuality;[133] during the seventeenth and eighteenth centuries, moreover, much emphasis was placed on the arousal, pleasure, and satisfaction of women. *Aristotle's Master Piece*, for example, was a very popular work of erotica and anatomy in the eighteenth and early nineteenth centuries, predicated on the sexual interest of women. There were at least one-hundred editions of the book prior to 1830— and no known complaints about it in any newspapers or periodicals.[134]

In 1831, the year that the last edition of *Aristotle's Master Piece* was published, J.N. Bolles' *Solitary Vice Considered* appeared, an anti-masturbation booklet of a type that would proliferate from the early 1830s on.[135] While the advice books on sex of the early part of the century could be quite explicit concerning women's sexual satisfaction, the trend was that "medical, biological, instructional, and popular literature contained countless defenses of extreme modern moderation and self-control."[136] The turning point, again, in this area as elsewhere, was the 1820s. By the 1840s the very idea of women's sexuality was becoming virtually erased. In the middle years of the century Dr. William Acton's *Functions and Disorders of the Reproductive Organs* was a popular standby; it summed up the official view on the subject thusly: "The majority of women (happily for them) are not very much troubled with sexual feelings of any kind. What men are habitually, women are only exceptionally."[137]

Among working and non-white women (not exclusive categories, obviously) this ideology had less impact than among those of higher station, for whom the relentless quelling of the recognition of "animal passions" caused vast physical and psychological damage.[138] The cult of female purity, or cult of the lady, or "true womanhood," emerged among the latter in the 1830s, stressing piety and domesticity.[139] This American woman was now exclusively a consumer of her husband's income, at a period when advertising developed on a scale and sophistication unique in the world.

Not surprisingly, national expansionist policy came into its own now, too. The hemispheric imperialism proclaimed in late 1823—the Monroe Doctrine— coincided with the beginnings of real Indian genocide, both occurring, of course, against the backdrop of a gathering industrial cancer. The Seminoles and Creeks were crushed at this time, an answer to the "especially menacing" specter of a combined Indian and runaway slave coalition: the First Seminole War was in large part undertaken "to secure Indian lands and therewith deny sanctuary to runaway slaves."[140]

From 1814 to 1824, Jackson had been "the moving force behind southern Indian removal,"[141] a policy inherited from Jefferson and one which he completed upon becoming president in 1828. Indian destruction, surely one of the major horror tales of the modern age, was more than an ugly stain on American politics and culture; indeed, Rogin's argument that its scope "defines for America the stage of primitive capitalist accumulation,"[142] is at least partly true. At the very least it presaged the further acquisitiveness that blossomed in the Manifest Destiny conquest spirit of the 1840s. But the more monstrous perhaps is its moral dimension, committed under Jackson's description of "extending the area of freedom."[143]

The Red Man, as Noble Savage, had to disappear; he was "savage", after all. The Dead Indian is obviously a more apt symbol for the trajectory of industrial capitalism, though the romantic use of the Indian reached its height at the moment of capital's victory, when, by the 1830s Nature truly became an evil to be subdued, while the machine was the fountainhead of all values that counted.

Nevertheless, voices and symbols of opposition survived. Johnny Appleseed (Jonathon Chapman), for instance, who was respected by the Indians during the first forty years of the century, and who represents riches of a wholly non-productionist, non-commodity type. There were such doubters of the period as Thoreau, Hawthorne, Poe, and Melville. Lee Clark Mitchell, among other contemporary scholars, has found, in letters, diaries, and essays, the record of a popular sense of deep foreboding about the conquest of the wilds by technological progress.[144] The victories of the dominant order have certainly never completely erased this alternative spirit of refusal, a spirit renewing itself today.

THE PRACTICAL MARX

Karl Marx is always approached as so many thoughts, so many words. But in this case, as for every other, there is a lurking question: What of real life? What connection is there between lived choices—one's willful lifetime—and the presentation of one's ideas?

Marx in his dealings with family and associates, his immediate relations to contemporary politics and to survival, the practical pattern and decisions of a life; this is perhaps worth a look. Despite my rejection of basic conceptions he formulated, I aim not at character assassination in lieu of tackling those ideas, but as a reminder to myself and others that our many compromises and accommodations with a grisly world are the real field of our effort to break free, more so than merely stating our ideas. It is in disregarding abstractions for a moment that we see our actual equality, in the prosaic courses of our common nightmare. A brief sketch of the "everyday" Marx, introducing the relationship between his private and public lives as a point of entry, may serve to underline this.

By 1843 Marx had become a husband and father, roles predating that of Great Thinker. In this capacity, he was to see three of his six children die, essentially of privation. Guido in 1850, Francesca in 1852, and Edgar in 1855 perished not because of poverty itself, so much as from his desire to maintain bourgeois appearances. David McLellan's *Marx: His Life and Thought*, generally accepted as the definitive biography, makes this point repeatedly.

Despite these fairly constant domestic deficiencies, Marx employed Helene Demuth as maid, from 1845 until his death in 1881, and a second servant was added as of 1857. Beyond any question of credibility, it was Demuth who bore Marx's illegitimate son Frederick in 1851. To save Marx from scandal, and a "difficult domestic conflict" according to Louis Freyberger, Engels accepted paternity of the child.

From the end of the 1840's onward, the Marx household lived in London and endured a long cycle of hardship which quickly dissipated the physical and emotional resources of Jenny Marx. The weight of the conflicting pressures involved in being Mrs. Marx was a direct cause of her steadily failing health, as were the deaths of the three children in the '50's. By July 1858 Marx was accurate in conceding to Engels that "My wife's nerves are quite ruined..."

In fact, her spirit had been destroyed by 1856 when she gave birth to a stillborn infant, her seventh pregnancy. Toward the end of that year she spoke of the "misery" of financial disasters, of having no money for Christmas festivities, as she completed copying out work toward *The Critique of Political Economy*. Despite several inheritances, the begging letters to Engels remained virtually non-stop; by 1860 at the latest, Jenny's once very handsome make-up had been turned to grey hair, bad teeth, and obesity. It was in that year that smallpox, contracted after transcribing the very lengthy and trivial *Herr Vogt* diatribe, left her deaf and pockmarked.

As secretary to Marx and under the steady strain of creditors, caused pre-eminently by the priority of maintaining appearances, Jenny's life was extremely difficult. Marx to Engels, 1862: "In order to preserve a certain facade, my wife had to take to the pawnbrokers everything that was not actually nailed down." The mid-'60's saw money spent on private lessons for the eldest of the three daughters and tuition at a "ladies' seminary" or finishing school, as Marx escaped the bill-collectors by spending his days at the British Museum. He admitted, in 1866, in a letter to his future son-in-law Paul LaFargue, that his wife's "life had been wrecked."

Dealing with nervous breakdowns and chronic chest ailments, Jenny was harried by ever-present household debt. One partial solution was to withhold a small part of her weekly allowance in order to deal with their arrears, the extent of which she tended to hide from Marx. In July, 1869 the Great Man exploded upon learning of this frugal effort; to Engels he wrote, "When I asked why, she replied that she was frightened to come out with the vast total (owed). Women plainly always need to be controlled!"

Speaking of Engels, we may turn from Marx the "family man" to a fairly chronological treatment of Marx in his immediate connections with contemporary politics. It may be noted here that Engels, his closest friend, colleague and provider, was not only a quite notorious "womanizer," but from 1838 on, a representative of the firm of Engels and Erman; in fact, throughout the 1850's and '60's he was a full-time capitalist in Manchester. Thus his *Condition of the Working Class in England* in 1844 was the fruit of a practical businessman, a man of precisely that class responsible for the terrible misery he so clearly chronicled.

By 1846 Marx and Engels had written *The German Ideology*,

which made a definitive break with the Young Hegelians and contains the full and mature ideas of the materialist concept of the progress of history. Along with this tome were practical activities in politics, also by now receiving their characteristic stamp. In terms of his Communist Correspondence Committee and its propaganda work Marx (also in 1846) stated: "There can be no talk at present of achieving communism; the bourgeoisie must first come to the helm." In June of the same year he sent instructions to supporters to act "jesuitically," to not have "any tiresome moral scruples" about acting for bourgeois hegemony.

The inexorable laws of capitalist development, necessarily involving the sacrifice of generations of "insufficiently developed" proletarians, would bring capital to its full plentitude—and the workers to the depths of enslavement. Thus in 1847, following a conference of professional economists in Brussels to which he was invited, Marx publicly noted the disastrous effect of free trade upon the working class, and embraced this development. In a subsequent newspaper article, he likewise found colonialism with its course of misery and death to be, on the whole, a good thing: like the development of capitalism itself, inevitable and progressive, working toward eventual revolution.

In 1847 the Communist League was formed in London, and at its second Congress later in the year Marx and Engels were given the task of drafting its manifesto. Despite a few ringing anti-capitalist phrases in its general opening sections, the concrete demands by way of conclusion are gradualist, collaborationist, and highly statist (e.g. for an inheritance tax, graduated income tax, centralization of credit and communications). Ignoring the incessant fight waged since the mid-18th century and culminating with the Luddites, and unprepared for the revolutionary upheavals that were to shake Europe in less than a year, the Communist Manifesto sees, again, only an "insufficiently developed" proletariat.

From this policy document arises one of the essential tactical mysteries of Marx, that of the concomitant rise of both capitalism and the proletariat. The development of capital is clearly portrayed as the accumulation of human misery, degradation and brutality, but along with it grows, by this process itself, a working class steadily more "centralized, united, disciplined, and organized."

How is it that from the extreme depths of physical and cultural oppression issues anything but a steadily more robotized, powerless, de-individualized proletariat? In fact, the history of revolts and militance of the 19th and 20th centuries shows that the majority do not come from those most herd-like and deprived, but from those least disciplined and with something to lose.

In April of 1848, Marx went to Germany with the Manifesto plus the utterly reformist "Demands of the Communist Party in Germany." The "Demands," also by Marx and Engels, were constituent of a bourgeois revolution, not a socialist one, appealing to many of the elements that directly fought the March outbreak of the revolution. Considering Marx's position as vice-president of the non-radical Democratic Association in Brussels during the previous year, and his support for a prerequisite bourgeois ascendancy, he quickly came into conflict with the revolutionary events of 1848 and much of the Communist League. Marx helped found a Democratic Society in Cologne, which ran candidates for the Frankfurt Parliament, and he vigorously opposed any League support for armed intervention in support of the revolutionaries. Using the opportunist rationale of not wanting to see the workers become "isolated," he went so far as to use his "discretionary powers," as a League official, to dissolve it in May as too radical, an embarrassment to his support of bourgeois elements.

With the League out of the way, Marx concentrated his 1848 activities in Germany on support for the Democratic Society and his dictatorial editorship of the *Neue Rheinische Zeitung*. In both capacities he pursued a "united front" policy, in which working people would be aligned with all other "democratic forces" against the remnants of feudalism. Of course, this arrangement would afford the workers no autonomy, no freedom of movement; it chose to see no revolutionary possibilities residing with them. As editor of the *NRZ*, Marx gave advice to Camphausen, businessman and head of the provisional government following the defeat of the proletarian upsurge. And further, astounding as it sounds, he supported the Democratic Society's newspaper despite the fact that it condemned the June, 1848 insurrection of the Paris proletariat. As politician and newspaper editor, Marx was increasingly criticized for his consistent refusal to deal radically with the specific situation or interests of the working class.

By the fall of 1848, the public activities of Marx began to take on a somewhat more activist, pro-worker coloration, as the risings of workers resumed in Germany. By December, however, disturbances were on the wane, and the volatile year in Germany appeared to be ending with no decisive revolutionary consequences. Now it was, and only now, that Marx in his paper declared that the working class would have to depend on itself, and not upon the bourgeoisie for revolution. But because it was rather clearly too late for this, the source of revolution would have to come, he divined, from a foreign external shock: namely, war between France and England, preceded by a renewed French proletarian uprising. Thus at the beginning of 1849, Marx saw in a Franco-British war the social revolution, just as in early 1848 he had located it in war between Prussia and Russia. This was not to be the last time, by the way, that Marx saw in the slaughter of national wars the spark of revolution; the workers-as-subject again fails to occur to Marx, that they could act—and did act—on their own initiative without first having to be sacrificed, by the generation, as factory slaves or cannon fodder. There were radicals who had seen the openings to revolution in 1848, and who were shocked by the deterministic conservatism of Marx. Louis Gottschalk, for example, attacked him for positing the choice for the working class as between bourgeois or feudal rule; "what of revolution?" he demanded. And so although Marx supported bourgeois candidates in the February (1849) elections, by April the Communist League (which he had abolished) had been refounded without him, effectively forcing him to leave the moderate Democratic Association. By May, with its week of street fighting in Dresden, revolts in the Ruhr, and extensive insurgency in Baden, events—as well as the reactions of the German radical community—continued to leave Marx far behind. Thus in that month, he closed down the *NRZ* with a defiant—and manifestly absurd—editorial claiming that the paper had been revolutionary and openly so throughout 1848–1849.

By 1850 Marx had joined other German refugees in London, upon the close of the insurrectionary upheavals on the continent of the previous two years. Under pressure from the left, as noted above, he now came out in favor of an independently organized German proletariat and highly centralized state for the (increasingly centralized) working class to seize and make its own. Despite the ill-will caused by his anything-but-radical activities in Germany, Marx was allowed to rejoin the Communist League and eventually resumed his dominance therein. In London he found support among the Chartists and other elements devoted to electoral reform and trade unionism, shunning the many radical German refugees whom he often branded as "agitators" and "assassins." This behavior gained him a majority of those present in London and enabled him to triumph over those in the League who had called him a "reactionary" for the minimalism of the Manifesto and for his disdain of a revolutionary practice in Germany.

But from the early '50's Marx had begun to spend most of his time in studies at the British Museum, where he could ponder the course of world revolution away from the noisome hubbub of his precarious household. From this time, he quickly jettisoned the relative radicality of his new-found militance and foresaw a general prosperity ahead, hence no prospects for revolution. The coincidence of economic crisis with proletarian revolt is, of course, mocked by the real history of our world. From the Luddites to the Commune, France in 1968 to the multitude of struggles opening on the last quarter of the 20th century, insurrection has been its own master; the great fluctuations of unemployment or inflation have often served, on the contrary, to deflect class struggles to a lower, survivalist plane rather than to fuel social revolution. The Great Depression of the 1930s brought a diminished vision, for example, characterized by German National Socialism and its cousin, the American New Deal, nothing approaching the destruction of capitalism. (The Spanish Revolution, bright light of the '30s, had nothing to do with the Depression gripping the industrialized nations.) Marx' overriding concern with externalities—principally economic crises, of course—was a trademark of his practical as well as theoretical approach; it obviously reflects his slight regard for the subjectivity of the majority of people, for their potential autonomy, imagination, and strength.

The distanciation from actual social struggles of his day is seemingly closely linked with the correct bourgeois life he led. In terms of his livelihood, one is surprised by the gap between his concrete activities and his reputation as revolutionary theorist. From 1852 into the 1860s, he was "one of the most highly valued" and "best paid" columnists of the *New York Daily Tribune*, according to its editor. In fact, one hundred and sixty-five of his articles were used as editorials by this not-quite-revolutionary metropolitan daily, which could account for the fact that Marx requested in 1855 that his subsequent pieces be printed anonymously. But if he wanted not to appear as the voice of a huge bourgeois paper, he wanted still more—as we have seen in his family role—to appear a gentleman. It was "to avoid a scandal" that he felt compelled to pay the printer's bill in 1859 for the reformist *Das Volk* newspaper in London. In 1862 he told Engels of his wish to engage in some kind of business: "Grey, dear friend, is all theory and only business is green. Unfortunately, I have come too late to this insight." Though he declined the offers, Marx received, in 1865 and 1867, two invitations which are noteworthy for the mere fact that they would have been extended to him at all: the first, via messenger from Bismarck, to "put his great talents to the service of the German people," the second, to write financial articles for the Prussian government's official journal. In 1866 he claimed to have made four hundred pounds by speculating in American funds, and his good advice to Engels on how to play the Stock Market is well authenticated. 1874 saw Marx and two partners wrangle in court over ownership of a patent to a new engraving device, intending to exploit the rights and reap large profits.

To these striking suggestions of ruling-class mentality must be added the behavior of Marx toward his children, the three daughters who grew to maturity under his thoroughly Victorian authority. In 1866 he insisted on economic guarantees for Paul LaFargue's future, critizing his lack of "diligence," and lecturing him in the most prudish terms regarding his intentions toward Laura, who was almost twenty-one. Reminding LaFargue that he and Laura were not yet engaged and, if they were to become so, that it would constitute a "long-term affair," he went on to express very puritanical strictures: "To my mind, true love expresses itself in the lover's restraint, modest bearing, even diffidence toward the adored one, and certainly not in unconstrained passion and manifestations of premature familiarity." In 1868 he opposed the taking of a job by Jenny, who was then twenty-two; later he forbade Eleanor from seeing Lissagaray, a Communard who happened to have defended single-handed the last barricade in Paris.

Turning back to politics, the economic crisis Marx avidly awaited in the '50's had come and gone in 1857 awakening no revolutionary activity. But by 1863 and the Polish insurrection of that year unrest was in the air, providing the background for the formation of the International Workingman's Association. Marx put aside his work on *Capital* and was most active in the affairs of the International from its London inception in September 1864. Odger, President of the Council of all London Trade Unions, and Cremer, Secretary of the Mason's Union, called the inaugural meeting, and Wheeler and Dell, two other British union officials, formally proposed an international organization. Marx was elected to the executive committee (soon to be called the General Council), and at its first business meeting was instrumental in establishing Odger and Cremer as President and Secretary of the International. Thus from the start, Marx's allies were union bureaucrats, and his policy approach was a completely reformist one with "plain speaking" as to radical aims disallowed. One of the first acts of the General Council was the sending of Marx's spirited, fraternal greetings to Abraham Lincoln, that "single-minded son of the working class."

Other early activities by Marx included the formation, as part of the International, of the Reform League dedicated to manhood suffrage. He boasted to Engels that this achievement "is our doing," and was equally enthusiastic when the National Reform League, sole surviving Chartist organization, applied for membership. This latter proved too much even for the faithful Engels, who for some time after refused to even serve as correspondent to the International for Manchester, where he was still a full-time capitalist. During this practice of embracing every shade of English gradualism, principally by promoting the membership of London trade unions, he penned his famous "the proletariat is revolutionary or it is nothing" line, in a letter to the German socialist Ferdinand Lassalle.

Lassalle and his General Union of German Workers (ADAV) harbored transparently serious illusions about the state; namely that Bismarck was capable of genuinely socialist policies as Chancellor of Prussia. Yet Marx in 1866 agreed to run for the presidency of the ADAV in the hopes of incorporating it into the International. At the same time, he wrote (to a cousin of Engels): "the adherence of the ADAV will only be of use at the beginning, against our opponents here. Later the whole institution of this Union, which rests on a false basis, must be destroyed."

Volumes could be written, and possibly have, on the manipulation of Marx within the International, the maneuverings of places, dates and lengths of meetings, for example, in the service of securing and centralizing his authority. To the case of the ADAV could be added, among a multitude of others, his cultivation of the wealthy bourgeois Lefort, so as to keep his wholly nonradical faction within the organization. By 1867 his dedicated machinations were felt to have reaped their reward; to Engels he wrote, "we (i.e. you and I) have this powerful machine in our hands."

Also in 1867 he availed himself publicly once more of one of his favorite notions, that a war between Prussia and Russia would prove both progressive and inevitable. Such a war would involve the German proletariat versus despotic Eastern barbarism and would thus be salutory for the prospects of European revolution. This perennial "war games" type of mentality somehow manages to equate victims, set in motion precisely as chattels of the state, with proletarian subjects acting for themselves; it would seem to parallel the substitution of trade union officials for workers, the hallmark of his preferred strategy as bureaucrat of the International. Marx naturally ridiculed anyone— such as his future son-in-law, LaFargue—for suggesting that the proper role of revolutionaries did not lie in such a crass game of weighing competing nationalisms. And in 1868 when the Belgian delegation to the International's Brussels Congress proposed the response of a general strike to war, Marx dismissed the idea as a "stupidity," owing to the "underdeveloped" status of the working class.

The weaknesses and contradictions of the adherents of Proudhon and Bakunin are irrelevant here, but we may observe 1869 as the high-water mark of the influence of Marx, due to the approaching decline of the Proudhonists and the infancy of Bakunin's impact in that year. With mid-1870 and the Napoleon III-engineered Franco-Prussian War, we see once more the pre-occupation with "progressive" vs. "non-progressive" military exploits of governments. Marx to Engels: "The French need a drubbing. If the Prussians are victorious then centralization of the working class...the superiority of the Germans over the French in the world arena would mean at the same time the superiority of our theory over Proudhon's and so on."

By July 1870 in an Address endorsed by the International's General Council, Marx added to this outlook a warning: "if the German working class allows the present war to lose its strictly defensive character and degenerate into a war against the French people, victory or defeat will prove alike disastrous." Thus the butchery of French workers is fine and good—but only up to a point. This height of cynical calculation appears almost too incredible—and after the Belgians and others were loudly denounced for imagining that the proletarian could be a factor for themselves in any case. How now could the "German working class" (Prussian army) decide how far to carry out the orders of the Prussian ruling class—and if they could, why not "instruct" them to simply ignore any and all of these class orders?

This kind of public statement by Marx, so devoid of revolutionary content, was naturally received with popularity by the bourgeois press. In fact, none other than the patron saint of British private property, John Stuart Mill, sent a message of congratulations to the International for its wise and moderate Address.

When the war Napoleon III had begun turned out as a Prussian victory, by the end of summer 1870, Marx protested, predictably, that Germany had dropped its approved "defensive" posture and was now an aggressor demanding annexation of the Alsace-Lorraine provinces. The defeat of France brought the fall of Louis Napoleon and his Second Empire, and a provisional Republican government was formed. Marx decided that the aims of the International were now two-fold: to secure the recognition of the new Republican regime in England, and to prevent any revolutionary outbreak by the French workers.

His policy advised that "any attempt to upset the new government in the present crisis, when the (Prussian) army is almost knocking at the doors of Paris, would be a desperate folly." This shabby, anti-revolutionary strategy was publicly promoted quite vigorously—until the Commune itself made a most rude and "unscientific" mockery of it in short order.

Well-known, of course, is Marx's negative reception to the rising of the Parisians; it is over-generous to say that he was merely pessimistic about the future of the Commune. Days after the successful insurrection began he failed to applaud its audacity, and satisfied himself with grumbling that "it had no chance of success." Though he finally recognized the fact of the Commune (and was thereby forced to revise his reformist ideas regarding proletarian use of existing state machinery), his lack of sympathy is amply reflected by the fact that throughout the Commune's two-month existence, the General Council of the International spoke not a single word about it.

It often escapes notice when an analysis or tribute is delivered well after the living struggle is, safely, living no longer. The masterful polemicizing about the triumphs of the Commune in his *Civil War in France* constitutes an obituary, in just the same way that *Class Struggles in France* did so at a similarly safe distance from the events he failed to support at the time of revolutionary Paris, 1848.

After a very brief period—again like his public attitude just after 1848–49 outbreaks in Europe—of stated optimism as to proletarian successes in general, Marx returned to his more usual colors. He denied the support of the International to the scattered summer 1871 uprisings in Italy, Russia, and Spain—countries mainly susceptible to the doctrines of anarchism, by the way. September witnessed the last meeting of the International before the Marx faction effectively disbanded it, rather than accept its domination by more radical elements such as the Bakuninists, in the following year. The bourgeois gradualism of Marx was much in evidence at the fall 1871 London Conference, as exemplified by such remarks as: "To get workers into parliament is equivalent to a victory over the governments, but one must choose the right man."

Between the demise of the International and his own death in 1881, Marx lived in a style that varied little from that of previous decades. Shunning the Communard refugees, by and large—as he had shunned the radical Germans in the '50's after their exile following 1848–49— Marx kept company with men like Maxim Kovalevsky, a non-socialist Russian aristocrat, the well-to-do Dr. Kugelmann, the businessman

Max Oppenheim, H.M. Hyndman, a very wealthy social democrat, and, of course, the now-retired capitalist, Engels.

With such a circle as his choice of friends, it is not surprising that he continued to see little radical capacity in the workers, just as he had always failed to see it. In 1874, he wrote, "The general situation of Europe is such that it moves to a general European war. We must go through this war before we can think of any decisive external effectiveness of the European working class." Looking, as ever, to externalities—and of course to the "immutable laws of history"—he contributes to the legacy of the millions of World War I dead, sacrificed by the capitulation of the Marxist parties to the support of war in 1914.

Refusing throughout his lifetime to see the possibilities of real class struggles, to understand the reality of the living negation of capitalism, Marx actively and concretely worked for the progress and fullness of capitalist development, which prescribed that generations would have to be sacrificed to it. I think that the above observations of his real life are important and typical ones, and suggest a consistency between that life and his body of ideas. The task of moving the exploration along to encompass the "distinctly theoretical" part of Marx, is expressly beyond the scope of this effort; possibly, however, the preceding will throw at least indirect light on the more "dis-embodied" Marx.

ORIGINS AND MEANING OF WWI

World War I, in Jan Patocka's words, "That tremendous and, in a sense, cosmic event"[1] was a watershed in the history of the West and the major influence on our century. Regarding its causes, nearly all the discussion has concerned the degree of responsibility of the various governments, in terms of the alliance system (ultimately, the Triple Entente of England, France and Russia and the Triple Alliance of Austria-Hungary, Germany and Italy) which, it is alleged, had to eventuate in worldwide war. The other major focus is the Marxist theory of imperialism, which contends that international rivalry caused by the need for markets and sources of raw material made inevitable a world war. Domestic causes have received remarkably little attention, and when the internal or social dynamics have been explored at all, several mistaken notions, large and small, have been introduced.

The genesis of the war is examined here in light of the social question and its dynamics; the thesis entertained is that a rapidly developing challenge to domination was destroyed by the arrival of war, the most significant stroke of counterrevolution in modern world history. If the real movement was somehow cancelled by August 1914, it is clear that the usual reference (in this case Debord's) to "the profound social upheaval which arose with the first world war"[2] is profoundly in error.

Some observers have noted, in passing, the prevalence of uncontrolled and unpredictable violence throughout Europe prior to the war, perhaps the most telling sign of the haunting dissatisfaction within an unanchored society. This could be seen in the major nations—and in many other regions as well. Halévy, for example, was surprised by the 1913 general strikes in South Africa and Dublin, which "so strangely and unexpectedly cut across the feud between English and Dutch overseas, between Protestant and Catholic in Ireland."[3] Berghahn saw that Turkey as well as Austria-Hungary "were threatened in their existence by both social and national revolutionary movements."[4] Sazonoz's *Reminiscences* refer to the sudden outbreaks of rioting in Constantinople, and to the Dashnaktzutium, Armenian radicals, of whom it was "difficult to discern" if they were more directed against Turkey or intent on fomenting a revolution at home.[5] And Pierre van Paasen's memoirs tell of a social peace disintegrating in prewar Holland: "A new spirit invaded the community. For one thing, the shipyard workers no longer drifted home at nights in small groups or singles. They came marching home...all of them singing, singing as if they wanted to burst their lungs, so that the windows rattled. What had come over these fellows?"[6]

Instead of analysis of this telling background, the coming of war is typically trivialized by a concentration on the assassination of the Austrian Archduke Franz Ferdinand, and the nature and duration of the ensuing carnage falsified as a surprise development. In fact, neither of these approaches to the meaning of the war hold up under a moment's scrutiny.

On the face of it, the Serbian militant who shot the Hapsburg Archduke did not so simply plunge Europe into hostilities; this can be seen first of all by the fact that six weeks passed between the June act and the August mobilizations. Zeman writes of this: "Indeed, in all the capitals of Europe, the reaction to the assassination of the heir to the Hapsburg throne was calm to the point of indifference. The people took little notice; the stock exchange registered hardly a tremor."[7]

As for the "surprise" as to the length and design of the war itself, it must be stressed that trench warfare—the hallmark of World War I—was anything but new. Employed 50 years before in the American Civil War, in the Crimea, and at Palevna (1877–78), as in the Russo-Japanese War of 1904–05, it is little wonder that military authorities predicted it. Ivan Bloch's six-volume *The Future of War* emphasized trench warfare and the totality of modern war; the work was discussed in ruling circles from the 1890s on. The adjustment of the record brings us closer to the thesis of war as a needed discharge of accumulated tensions, requiring a form and duration equal to the task of extinguishing radical possibilities.

L.T. Hobhouse viewed domestic problems in Europe as successively more clamorous, creating a crescendo of urgency. "Thus the catastrophe of 1914 was...the climax of a time of stress and strain."[8] Similarly, Stefan Zweig wrote of the outbreak of war: "I cannot explain it otherwise than by this surplus force, a tragic consequence of their internal dynamism that had accumulated...and now sought violent release."[9] The scale and conditions of the war had to be equal to the force straining against society, in order to replace this challenge with the horror and despair that spread from the battlefields to darken the mind of the 20th century West.

Beyond the initial value of war in promoting centralization and acceptance of authority, a far larger objective can be seen. In Wells' words, "greater happiness, and a continual enlargement of life, has been checked violently and perhaps arrested altogether."[10] Vibrant before the four years of death was the desire and expectation of significant change, not to be confused with the bourgeois ideology of positivism, ossified and insipid, which was being challenged in popular life.[11]

The monotonous, uniform present of industrial society, complete with Weberian forecast of increasing bureaucratization, was indeed becoming more and more miserably palpable. And leftist ideology seems just as increasingly threadbare as measured against this reality. War provided an escape from both daily life and the chance of its transcendence. By 1914, whatever emancipatory visions Marxism might once have represented were moribund; with the war, anarchism, which had seemed to Laurence Lafore "imposingly vigorous,"[12] was also demolished.

To examine the generalized internal crisis and the means by which it was successfully deflected and destroyed by World War I, the various countries—beginning, in rough order, with the less developed and ending with Germany and England—are surveyed here.

The act that eliminated the would-have-been Emperor of Austria-Hungary was by no means an atypical one: Russian Prime Minister Stolypin had been assassinated in 1911, as was Canalejas, Premier of Spain in 1912, and King George of Greece in 1913, to cite other prominent fatalities. In fact, there were several attempts upon the lives of Hapsburg royalty during the imminent prewar years, and even more than one against Franz Ferdinand on that particular notorious summer 1914 afternoon. All the more suggestive, then, that the Archduke paid his state visit on the anniversary of Kossovo, the national day of that restive vassal nation of the Hapsburgs. Similar in provocation would have been a visit by the British royalty to Dublin on St. Patrick's day in, say, 1916. And in passing, it is perhaps worth mentioning that the universally agreed upon figure for this and other Balkan dramas, the nationalist (or nationalist student, more exactly), is rather too readily typecast. Valiani noted the revival of anarchist affiliation and influence in Serbia and Bosnia,[13] and it is well established that Franz Ferdinand's assassins were hardly exclusively nationalist. War, of course, always requires a good excuse, especially when the state's real enemies are, more clearly than usual, its own citizenry; the Sarajevo outrage was tailor-made to the needs of the ailing regime.

The latifundist system of feudal rule on the land, allied with a quite usurious brand of capitalism, provided the background for a very potent social revolutionary dynamic that outweighed even the nationalist-separatist stresses of the exceedingly polyglot empire. In the ancient capital, a descending lassitude mirrored the crumbling rule; the leitmotif of countless works is Vienna's strange atmosphere of "something coming visibly to an end." Hofsthmannthal's Elektra cries, "Can one decay like a rotten corpse?"His striking play of the same name is the perfect artifact of imperial Vienna, in its vision of disaster. In fact, the drama is an extremely apt allegory of Europe at large, portraying the obsessive need for a bloodletting out of a terror of death.

As Norman Stone put it, "Official circles in Austria-Hungary calculated general conflict in Europe was their only alternative to civil war."[14] Thus the ultimatum served on Serbia, following the death by Serbians of Franz Ferdinand, was merely a pretext for war with Russia and that general conflict. War was declared on Serbia, with the corresponding involvement of Russia, despite the acceptance of the ultimatum; Serbia's capitulation, widely hailed as Austria's "brilliant diplomatic coup," therefore meant nothing. The immense significance of Austria's internal problems demanded war and a more complete reliance on its perennial school of civic virtues, the Hapsburg army.

Very critical to the success of this tactic was the organizational hegemony of the Marxian mass party over the working classes. The Austrian Social Democratic Party, most degenerate of the European left, was actually committed to the maintenance of the monarchy and its federative reorganization.[15]

When war came, it was billed as an unavoidable defense against the menacing eastern behemoth, Russia. The left, of course, cast its parliamentary votes in favor of war and immediately instituted war measures against work stoppages and other forms of insubordination. Although some Czechs threw down their arms upon being ordered against Russia, hostilities were initiated without serious resistance.[16] But, in the worlds of Arthur May, "Disaffection and discontent among the rank and file" took only months before the prosecution of the war was "seriously affected."[17]

Food riots were common by 1915 and had spread to the heart of Vienna by late 1916. Professor Josef Redlich's journal recorded that the population seemed pleased when Prime Minister Strugkh was shot to death by a renegade Socialist in October 1916. The Social Democratic Party was completely dedicated, meanwhile, to the "cooperation of all classes," and it organized scores of peace meetings—not of an antiwar variety, but to restrain the masses from breaches of the "domestic peace."[18]

With people wearied, bled dry by four years of apocalypse, rule was preserved following the collapse of the dynasty by the remaining servants of power. The Social Democrats continued their basic role—with the equally anti-revolutionary Christian Democrats—and were to govern Austria for 15 years, paralleling in many ways that postwar prelude to German National Socialism, the Weimar Republic. In Hungary, six months of Social Democratic rule was followed by the bureaucratic-totalitarian efforts of Bela Kun's Hungarian Soviet Republic (with Lukacs as Commissar of Culture); four months of this Leninist failure were enough to usher in the Horthy regime, what was to be a quarter-century of reaction.

War, in the case of Russia, did not prevent a revolution from occurring, but its mammoth ravages dictated the instant deformation of that revolution—the victory of the Bolshevik project. The class structure of Romanov society was too bankrupt to avoid demise; Z.A.B. Zeman wrote, for example, of the "amazing ease of the dynastic collapse in Russia."[19] But the unparalleled destruction and suffering of the millions of combatants (and non-combatants) in itself rendered a whole, breathing revolution impossible.

The Austro-Hungarian declaration of war on small, Slavic Serbia enabled a barely sufficient response to the Kremlin's consequent call to arms; Pan-Slavism, not Czarism, was the last pro-war chord that could be successfully struck by a doomed regime. Russia's war with Japan had been a clear attempt to direct internal ferment into calmer, patriotic channels; defeat set off the 1905 revolution. In 1914, only a victorious war could conceivably offer hope for the status quo. Barring war, "within a short time," as Germany's Prince von Bulow wrote, "revolution would have broken out in Russia, where it was ripe since the death of Alexander III in 1894."[20]

From 1909, various international incidents and crises, mainly in North Africa and the Balkans, arose with regularity to try to divert popular attention in Europe from the gathering social crisis. Throughout the West, authority was deeply on the defensive in this final period, and Russia is not an exception: since at least 1909 state weakness was a glaring constant. By then the memories of post-1905 repression were fading and "the temper of the factory workers was turning revolutionary again," according to Taylor.[21] And discontent was rising even faster due to the more reactionary policies of the regime following Stolypin's assassination in 1911. When the workers of the Lena gold fields were attacked by troops in April 1912, this act of savagery not only failed to cow the oppressed, but in fact it aroused workers all over Russia to a new wave of challenge.[22] In the two years before the war, the curve of social disorder steadily mounted, meaning that another year of peace would surely have seen new and even more serious upheavals.

Edmund Wilson observed that "by 1913 and 1914 there was a strike wave even bigger than that of 1905." By the spring and early summer of 1914, a movement, initiated especially by the Baku oil workers and women factory operatives of St. Petersburg, had brought "the proletariat again to the barricades."[23] As Arno Mayer succinctly put it, "during the first seven months of 1914, industrial unrest reached unparalleled intensity, much of it politically and socially motivated."[24] Thus the guns of August roared, the timing all but unavoidable.

The war to save oppressed and threatened Slavdom, launched with a momentary enthusiasm, was soon flagging. Meriel Buchanan's biography of her father, the British ambassador to Russia, bemoaned "how brief and frail was that spirit of devotion and self-sacrifice, how soon doubt and despair, impatience, lassitude, and discontent crept in."[25] Widely recounted was the lament of state ministers by mid-1915: "Poor Russia! Even her army, which in past ages filled the world with the thunder of its victories...turns out to consist only of cowards and deserters!"[26] Certainly by the widespread mass strikes of January and February 1916, the civil truce had been definitively broken.

The anarchist tide rose swiftly during the war for a time, despite the general draining effect of the gigantic bloodshed and the specific disillusionment caused by the pro-war position of Kropotkin. This latter accommodation to state power, widely seen of course as a betrayal of principle, was in fact shared by a majority of Russian anarchist ideologues, especially in Moscow.[27] The capitulation at the top led to the greater success of syndicalism among many anti-authoritarians, a more "practical," less "utopian" ideology. Another moment of the dimming of radical perspectives.

Kroptkin—like Rocker—located the reason for war in the competition for markets and the quest for colonies, ignoring, with the Marxists, the overarching domestic dynamic for an external, mechanistic etiology. And his untiring efforts to urge on the troops of the Entente to the greater killing of the Central Powers' counterparts evokes Marx and Engels, who could always be counted on to identify the more "progressive" state to support in a given war.

The collapse of the Romanov autocracy in March 1917 demonstrated that the spiritual exhaustion of the proletariat was not so advanced as to allow the greatly overdue dynasty any further borrowed time. Lenin, who had been surprised by every revolutionary outbreak in Russia,[28] could see in mid-1917 that the disintegration of the provisional government was soon to be a reality. His victory in that maimed dimension and the consequent Bolshevik counterrevolution is an all too familiar tale in its details.

Italy, turbulent through the 1890s and the first decade of the century, arrived at the prewar years in a volatile state. Propaganda in favor of conquest and expansion had failed to distract the submerged classes from the essential; at the elections of 1913 only three Nationalists were elected to the chamber.[29]

The months preceding the war were marked by rioting and strikes on a wide scale, culminating in the famous Red Week of early summer. During demonstrations by anarchists and republicans, violence broke out on the Adriatic coast; this week of June 1914 was to see its quick spread, into a general strike and countrywide riots. F.L. Carsten provides particulars: "In the Romagna and the Marches of Central Italy there were violent revolutionary outbreaks. Local republics were set up in many smaller towns, and the red flag was hoisted on the town hall of Bologna. Officers were disarmed; the military barracks were beseiged in many places."[30]

The populace displayed, in outlook and methods, an anarchic, autonomous temper that found its reflection in the anti-war position of the whole left. In this moment the syndicalist discovery of the myth of the nation seemed far away; that a national syndicalism was but a year off could hardly have been forecast with practical results. An overwhelming sentiment for neutrality cancelled Italy's alliance with Austria-Hungary and Germany, and rendered war far too dangerous a card to be played in hopes of defusing class war—for the time being.

By the spring of 1915, every major European nation had been at war for over half a year, with Italy being drawn steadily toward the abyss despite popular resistance. A friend of von Bulow states in May, "how the [Italian] Minister of the Interior had said to him that if there were a plebiscite there would be now war."[31] Zeman, likewise speaking of May 1915, observed that "Rome came to the verge of civil war."[32] Foreign elements engineered, with paid demonstrators, pro-interventionist riots against the neutralists—who received no police protection and suffered a vicious pro-war press. Rennell Rodd and others who thought they saw spontaneous enthusiasm for war there were largely deceived.

In mid-May the Turin workers declared a general strike, while the

Socialist Party debated its position regarding Italy's apparently imminent participation in the war. "All the factories were closed, all public services completely paralyzed. The strike was total among all categories of workers," according to Mario Montagna's memoirs, quoted by John Cammett. Cammett continues the narrative: "The entire working force of the city gathered before the Chamber of Labor, and then slowly marched—without the urging of speeches—toward the Prefecture to protest the war."[33] Fighting ensued but the strike came to an end on May 19, chiefly due to the isolation and demoralization brought on by the Party's refusal to support this self-authorized initiative. Meanwhile, the "revolutionary" syndicalists had become the first section of the Italian left to advocate war, arguing that reactionary Austria must not be allowed to defeat progressive France. On May 23, Italy entered the war.

Mussolini's radically rightward shift, in full swing at this time, is a particular symptom of the intense frustration caused by the left's inaction and betrayals. The young Gramsci, in fact, showed a passing sympathy for Mussolini's new pro-war position and his disgust with the passivity enforced on the proletariat.[34] When oppositional ideology and its arbiters assume such a renunciation of movement, the way is prepared for steadily more backward forms for thwarted class energies to assume. Forward avenues seem completely blocked and there was thus little alternative to the channel and dictates of war.

Giampero Carocci, among others, noted that after three and a half years of war, "the majority of workers and some of the peasants (particularly in the Po Valley, in Tuscany and in Umbria)" still "longed for revolution"[35]—but the pervasive postwar discontent was of an anxious, pessimistic kind.

The occupation of the factories, in the fall of 1920, bears the full imprint of a proletariat cheated and blocked by the left and battered by war. Despite the enormous scale of the takeovers, both the industrialists and the government simply let the neutered movement take its course, without state interference. In early September, the apparent conquests provoked some alarm, to be sure, but the ever more weary and confused workers stayed politely in the factories under control of the unions and the left;[36] "communist leaders refrained from every initiative," reported Angelo Tasca.[37] The restless and anxious occupiers saw neither the outlet to expand their action nor the energies by this point, to forge new ones. The seizure of virtually the entire industrial plant of Italy—not to mention the extensive land takeovers—simply died away, leaving a feeling of total defeat.[38] Mussolini's accession to power followed this fiasco by less than two years.

Recent historical analysis, especially that of A. James Gregor, has demonstrated the substantive continuity between Italy's most militant socialism—syndicalism—and fascism, with the war serving as essential mode of transition. The career of Mussolini, from activist and major theoretician of syndicalism to activist and architect of fascism, by way of World War I, is only one connection.[39] Syndicalism, then national syndicalism, provided the core social and economic content of ascendant fascism. The congruence begins with a common mass-mobilization, industrialization basis but does not end there; the essentials of nascent fascism were, in Gregor's words, "the product of syndicalist lucubrations, syndicalist sentiment, and syndicalist convictions."[40]

At the end of the century, French socialists and anarchists were swept into the mainstream of controversy over the legal treatment of Dreyfus, an army officer convicted of espionage. The arms of the republican family hence embraced new elements, whose integration had been open to question; in Dreyfusism we see an early appearance of the popular front, the recuperative answer to reaction, real or otherwise.

The depths were quickly plumbed. It is here that the Socialist Millerand, scandalizing the slow, became the first of his ideological brand to enter a government. A government, by the way, that had been recently disgraced by the infamous Panama finance scandal and which counted as its minister of war General Gallifet, butcher of the Commune. Minister of War Millerand would be the most chauvinist of prewar officials, later joined by his Socialist colleague, Albert Thomas, wartime minister of munitions.

It is not a surprise that so-called revisionism led to nationalism, nor that this course and its electoral methods would alienate the oppressed with its crass opportunism. In fact, there were many signs of a widespread disinterest in politics; Clemenceau's seventeen-point social reform program of 1906, for example, elicted no popular response.[41] An acute Cabinet instability began to emerge, due in part to the fact that the enragès of the far left made it increasingly harder for Marxists to cooperate with the center left. Oron Hale averred that the working class movement drifted away from parliamentarism toward radicalism in the five years before 1914.[42] And it was just before this period that Sorel, with customary acidity, warned: "A proletarian violence which escapes all valuation, all measurement, and all opportunism may jeopardize everything and rule socialistic diplomacy."[43]

But even in terms of orthodox political maneuvering, light is shed upon the threat to the existing order. An order, one might add, exhibiting such signs of decay as persistent financial scandals. The amazing murder of the editor of *Figaro* by the finance minister's wife brought these to new heights in March 1914.

The April elections, whose chief issue was the 1913 law prescribing three years' military service, returned "the most pacific chamber the country had ever known," in the words of Alfred Cobban.[44] The conscription law, by the complete failure of nationalist-rightist candidates, had been clearly repudiated.

Albrecht-Carré, Taylor, and others have spoken of this shift away from militarism at a time when France, according to von Bulow, "was the only European country in which in certain influential quarters, not in the people, it was justified to talk of 'war fever.'"[45] Prince Lichnowski, German ambassador to England, provided a still more complete picture in a diary entry of April 27: he described the French people's calm and "thoroughly pacific mood," while noting the difficulties which internal affairs presented to the governments."[46]

The April polling "proved," in Cobban's words, "that even in the existing state of international tension French opinion was profoundly pacific and non-aggressive."[47] President Poincaré, in June, was forced to appoint a left-wing regime under Viviani. Reversal of the conscription law was the first order of business; nevertheless, the radical and socialist deputies agreed not to press for this in exchange for vague promises regarding future passage of an income tax law, an obvious betrayal.

When the war crisis was played out in early August and Juarès, dean of the left, was assassinated by a chauvinist fanatic, it was Viviani who issued the left's call for nationalist unity; at this moment of spontaneous anti-war demonstrations, he announced that, "in the serious circumstances through which our country is passing, the government counts on the patriotism of the working class."

That the proletariat would have been the object of fear is evidenced by its growing militancy. Whereas in the 1890s there had been hundreds of small, local strikes, there were 1,073 in 1913, involving a quarter of a million workers. A good deal of alarm was generated by the scale and persistence of the strikes, seen by many as "symptoms of a profound unrest and social sickness," according to David Thomson.[48] Strikes of postal and telegraph workers in Paris called the loyalty of state employees into question, while agricultural workers' strikes often led to riots and the burning of farm owners' houses.

Radical tendencies on the terrain of work cannot, however, be attributed to prewar syndicalism with much accuracy. Syndicalist ideology proved an attraction for a time, due to revulsion with the dogma of socialist reformism, but there was—according to Stearns and others—no positive correlation between syndicalist leadership and strike violence, for example.[49] In fact, syndicalist leaders had to combat violence and spontaneous strikes just like any other brokers of organized labor. Syndicalist unions served the same integrative function as any others and manifested the same movement toward bureaucratization. It is hardly surprising that after 1910 there was growing talk of a "crisis of syndicalism."

During the first decade of the century, Gustave Hervé's doctrine of total military insurrection against the officer class became quite popular. Elie Halévy saw that "no sooner conceived, it spread like wildfire to many countries outside France."[50] He added that on the eve of war it was "still rampant in the rank and file of the French army."[51]

Hervé, editor of *La Guerre Sociale*, had called for revolution as the response to mobilization for war. But increasingly the socialist statesman, when war came he climaxed his anti-war career by begging to be allowed to serve in the army. Recalling Viviani's pro-war speech over the bier of Juarès, we find a fast evaporation of internationalist verbiage and observe how thin some of this rhetoric had been all along. The young males of the nation marched, leaving behind debasing contradictions of the left with a sense of relief.

By the end of 1916, however, desertions were occurring at a rate estimated at 30,000 a year. Spring 1917 saw wholesale desertion replaced by outright mutiny, causing open panic among the military high command. Whole divisions from the Champagne front were involved, for example, amid cheers for world revolution, for firing on the officers, and for a march on Paris.[52] But exhaustion and a sense of futility, built up of the war's mammoth violence and the long list of confusions and disillusionments that predated the war, were joined by the universal united front of unions and the left, to enforce the war and safeguard class society.

France was the *grand mutil*ée of the war: 1,400,000 dead, one of every 24 in the land. Out of all this, not even the postwar parodies of revolution would visit France.

Although the United States stands apart from Europe's traditions and conditions, it is also true that revolution, or its approach, is a world phenomenon as of the era under scrutiny. Taking a very few words' detour, many features paralleling prewar Europe are discernible in the American situation.

Henry May found that "During the prewar years, passion and violence seemed to many observers to be rising to the surface in all sorts of inexplicable ways."[53] And as in Europe, organized ideology could not find its vehicle in this upsurge. The tame Socialist Party was ebbing after having reached its peak in 1912, and the I.W.W., syndicalist alternative, failed to have much impact at any point.

The Federal Commission on Industrial Relations, sitting between 1910 and 1915, concluded that unionization was the answer to a violence, in Graham Adams' words, "which threatened the structure of society."[54] This recommendation was hailed by moderate and radical unionists alike,[55] and brings to mind the advice of a few that the I.W.W.'s industrial unionism was the specific brand needed to stabilize American capital relations. In fact, government-sponsored unions established the control apparatus of scientific management, under the War Industries Board, and survived long enough to administer the crucial blows to the three major post-war strikes, those in coal, steel, and Seattle, in 1919.

John Dewey had predicted that the war would introduce "the beginnings of a public control," and defended it thusly as a needed agency of socialization.[56] But America's entry was far from basically popular; Ellul concluded that U.S. participation "could be produced only by the enormous pressure of advertising and total propaganda on the human psyche."[57]

Zeman quotes a far from atypical, if anonymous, historian: "We still don't know, at any level that really matters, why Wilson took the fateful decision to bring the U.S. into the First World War."[58] John Higham provides an acceptable if understated reply: "Perhaps a vigorous assertion of American rights functioned...to submerge the drift and clash of purpose in domestic affairs."[59]

Before examining the two most developed countries, Germany and England, something of the depth of the prewar turmoil—and its pacification—can be seen in even the briefest glimpse at cultural changes.

Stravinsky, whose *Le Sacre du Printemps* virtually incarnated the promise of a new age, reminds one that the new music was noticeably supranational in its composition and appeal.[60] Between 1910 and 1914, more precisely, nationalism receded as a force in music, as it had in other fields. In painting, the movement toward pure abstraction emerged simultaneously and independently in several countries during the five years preceding the war.[61] Cubism, with its urgent re-examination of reality, was the most important element of the modern school and by far the most audacious to date—notwithstanding the frequent and entertaining accusation, in Roger Shattuck's words, that it was "an enormous hoax dreamed up by the hashish-smoking, pistol-carrying, half-starved inhabitants of Monmartre."[62]

Alfred Jarry's nihilistic anarchism, especially in his *Ubu* plays, constituted a one-man demolition squad, over a decade before Dada.[63] In Apollinaire, the new freedom and urgency in poetry, especially in French poetry, is obvious. Apollinaire, however, can also be viewed as an art-historical metaphor: having reached his height from 1912 to 1914, he volunteered in 1914 and was wounded in 1916. His passion and spontaneity were drained away, replaced by patriotism and a sense of artistic discipline; he died of his head wound in the last month of the war, November 1918. Apollinaire recalls vividly the condition of Jake in Hemingway's *The Sun Also Rises*, emasculated by the war.

Shortly before the war, a group of young players, eventually known as the "hypermodern" school, revivified chess in practice and principle, as exemplified most brazenly by Breyer's "After 1.P-K4, White's game is in the last throes."[64] This arcane case aims at underlining the point that throughout culture, in every area, an unmistakable daring, straining at limits was underway. "More freedom, more frankness, more spontaneity had been regained (in the decade before 1914) than in the previous hundred years," as Stefan Zweig looked back on it.[65]

The war drew a terrible dividing line across the advance of all this. The first battle cry of Dada in 1916 was already really the end of it, and the modernist movement of the 1920s acted out a drama conceived, dedicated and developed before the war.

The most anti-bourgeois moments of futurism, all of which were certainly pre-war, prefigured Dada in content and also stylistically (e.g., the use of incendiary manifestos). "In postwar Dada, the Futurist enthusiasm had been pacified, ironized and introverted," according to R.W. Flint.[66]

Shattuck mentions the "disintegrating social order" and a "sporty proletarian truculence" inspired by the avant-garde.[67] The lines of inspiration and energy were probably flowing, most importantly, the other way around but the connection itself is valid.

In H.G. Wells' *Joan and Peter* the younger working class generation is described as "bored by the everlasting dullness and humbug of it all."[68] If Paul Ricoeur could ask, over 50 years later, "if there is not, in the present-day unrest of culture, something which answers correlatively to the fundamental unrest in contemporary work,"[69] his question also fits the earlier world perfectly. For that previous unrest of work, the technological speedup of 1914–18 gave the answer; the "struggle against idiosyncrasy," toward completely standardized tools and tasks, received its final, critical impetus from the war.[70] "The time of full mechanization, 1918–1939," to use Siegfried Giedion's phrase,[71] was inaugurated.

Getting back to culture, a revolution of art forms gave clear testimony to the social crisis—not that the revolt against the rule of forms was always confined there.

German expressionism, a pinnacle of pre-war cultural revolt, aimed not only at shattering conventions but at the construction of a "utopian order, or disorder, believed to be freer and more life-enhancing than any to be found in the advanced industrial world just then approaching a new height of development," in the judgement of Hilton Kramer.[72]

The aspirations and innocence of these revolutionary artists were cruelly destroyed by the war. In its aftermath, the bitter expressionist protests of Georg Grosz and Otto Dix bespoke the shock and disillusionment, as with the surrealist nightmares of Dali. Literature is another example of the same result: Eliot, Joyce, Pound, Yeats and so many others—without exception, it appears, prophets of decay and death.

The authoritarian welfare state of Bismarck, several decades from its inception by the prewar years, enforced a state of affairs in Germany which was far from secure. The Eulenburg scandal, in two years of trials after 1907, aired intrigue, blackmail and rottenness in the Kaiser's immediate circle, causing state prestige to sink. Ballin, the Hamburg capitalist, spoke to the government in 1908 of "the growing domestic crisis," hoping that a tax decrease might help defuse it.[73] Already in March 1909 was the war alternative proposed, as Lyncker, chief of the military Cabinet, considered an "external conflict desirable" to move the nation out of "internal difficulties."[74]

Prince von Bulow recalled "a general disgruntlement," which he summarized in this way: "If in Bismarck's day people talked of 'disgust with the Empire,' it was now a case of 'disgust with the government'—a disgust which gained ground every day."[75] More specifically portentous was this high-placed opinion, also from his memoirs: "At the end of 1912 I heard from Dusseldorf that Kirdorf, one of the biggest Rheinish industrialists...had declared that if this goes on another three years Germany will have landed in war or revolution."[76]

In late 1913 and early 1914, the arrogant gestures of German officers against civilians in Alsace constituted the "Zabern Incidents," and aroused, in Carolyn Playne's words, "general indignation."[77] Indeed, a great outcry went up and the Reichstag voted, albeit somewhat impotently, a 293-54 no-confidence resolution. James Gerard saw this as an occasion of waning government power, and wrote that the German people seemed "to be almost ready to demilitarize themselves."[78]

To John Flynn, the Zabern hubbub merely contributed to the deepening of a domestic split which had already virtually paralyzed the country. As he viewed it, "There was a spirit—and a growing one—of resistance to arbitrary tendencies."[79] In this context the naval indiscipline aboard the S.S. Vaterland at Auxhaven in the spring of 1914 is similarly revealing. There the bold, spontaneous action of the 1,300 crewmen forced an immediate and unconditional acceptance of their demands, recalling the revolt in the Brazilian navy of late 1910.

Arthur Rosenberg described the political and social tension of Germany as "typical of a prerevolutionary period," concluding that without war in 1914, "the conflict between the Imperial government and the majority of the German nation would have continued to intensify to a point at which a revolutionary situation would have been created."[80] Chancellor Bethmann-Hollweg on the eve of war complained of the absence of nationalist fortitude in the land, lamenting this as a "decline of values," and a "spiritual degeneration." Complaining further of what he saw as the ruling classes' "solicitude for every current of public opinion," he defined his war policy to Riezler as a necessary "leap into the dark and the heaviest duty."[81]

At the same time, it is rather clear that this rising crisis, requiring the war to stem it, was not at all the doing of the left. Of the Social Democrats and their millions of adherents a hollowness was manifest. D.A. Smart wrote of the "widely felt stagnation in the party"[82] in 1913; Spengler, in the introduction to his *Decline of the West*, saw both the approaching world war and a "great crisis...in Socialism." Far from inconceivable, then, is the notion that the rulers feared a breakdown of their dependable official adversaries, not the party or unions themselves, especially given the signs of uncontrolled movement.

Industrial anger, in the shipyards, for example, was on the upswing and was most often directly combatted by the unions. The alienation of trade union membership, which was to characterize the latter part of the war, was strongly developing: local groups were breaking away from the central confederation in textiles, paint and metals.[83]

The Social Democratic Party, a function of the trade unions, was a loyal handmaiden of the state; its support of government tax bills made possible the military alternative, guaranteeing a harvest of proletarian cynicism. In 1914, Austin Harrison put it another way: "All kinds of men, German bankers, for example, often voted for the Socialists."[84] The workers' penchant for "sudden, unorganized" strikes, which has puzzled many commentators, underlined the contradiction and its threat.

During July, various Party leaders met with Bethmann-Hollweg, enabling him to reassure the Prussian Ministry of State on July 30 as to the left's abject loyalty: "There would be no talk of a general strike or of sabotage."[85] Utilizing the socialist tradition of defending war by advanced powers against less developed ones as progressive, 'opposition' and government were in agreement on anti-czarism as the effective public banner.

While making plans for preserving the Party machinery, Social Democracy voted unanimously for war credits on August 4, with an accompanying statement which stressed imperialism as inevitably generating war and explicitly refused any responsibility for the war. Robert Looker aptly termed this "a depth of political and moral bankruptcy…of such enormity that it went far beyond the crimes of particular leaders or parties."[86]

Rosa Luxemburg in early 1915 wrote that "the collapse itself is without precedent in the history of all times."[87] But it is interesting that she upheld the war (as legitimized by its enemy of autocratic Russia) for literally years until public pressure was overwhelmingly against it; similarly, she was neither in the lead of the rising of November 1918, which released her from prison, or of the Spartacist revolt, which she grudgingly backed. The Social Democrats—and the unions—were co-responsible with the army for managing the war effort in general. Their police role most importantly was the investiture of all the military authorities' security measures with a fading aura of 'socialism' toward the prevention of popular uprisings. When Luxemburg wrote in 1916 that "The world war has decimated the results of 40 years' work of European socialism,"[88] it would have been far more accurate to say that war revealed those results. And as if this role, in bringing on and protecting the process, were not enough, the Social Democrats, as the affective agency of state power surviving the war, drowned the abortive postwar rebellions in blood. Of course, the road to new horrors was wide open. As Lukacs recorded, "I witnessed the rise of fascism in Germany and I know very well that very many young people at that time adhered to fascism out of a sincere indignation at the capitalist system.''[89]

Returning for a moment to the actual arrival of war, there was indeed a sincere "indignation" reigning in 1914. Part of this was a nihilist dissatisfaction by many of ruling class backgrounds. Hannah Arendt detected, among those most permeated with the ideological outlook and standards of the bourgeoisie, a common absorption with "the desire to see the ruin of this whole world of fake security, fake culture, and fake life."[90] Ernst Junger expressed an exuberant hope that everything the elite knew, the whole culture and texture of life, might go down in "storms of steel."[91]

At the brink there was a certain relief, as well, caused by the decision itself. War gave a release to the exhausted nerves caused by the tension of weeks of waiting—followed, commonly, soon afterward by a confused despair.[92]

In October 1914, the diary of Rudolf Bindung, a young calvary officer, already contained virtually the whole lesson of the war: "An endless reproach to mankind...everything becomes senseless, a lunacy, a horrible bad joke of peoples and their history...It was the end of happy endings in life as in art."[93]

Never before, and nowhere more so than in England, had power—economic, political, administrative, military—achieved such a high degree of consolidation. Yet at this apogee its actual fragility was becoming palpable, in the tendency, in England and across Europe, toward unfettered and unpredictable mass opposition. That there existed a widespread challenge to the cohesion and integrity of nationalist states is unmistakable.

The crises since 1909 regarding North Africa and the Balkans, above all, have been mentioned; 'foreign affairs' progressed into a much closer parallel to its 'domestic' counterpart; with a much larger qualitative diversion finally needed to transcend the mounting social disharmony. The Agadir, Morocco, crisis of July and August 1911 exemplifies this development. During the seamen and dockers' strike, which was marked by unprecedented violence, especially in the ports of Liverpool and London, the arrival of the German gunboat *Panther* in Agadir became the occasion for growing official furor. When railway workers joined the strike, troops were called out and fighting ensued. The clash at home was settled on emergency terms, thanks to the Moroccan issue. Thereafter, domestic industrial warfare and foreign crisis both seemed to grow with equal intensity.

Another area of outbreak in England was a reaction to bourgeois suffocation, as seen in the strange physical fury of the votes for women cause. The mad fortitude exhibited by feminists in the period of 1910–1914—including pitched battles with police, and arson of cricket pavilions, racetrack grandstands, and resort hotels—certainly belied the utterly tame objective of female suffrage, an obvious reason for characterizing the movement as an outlet for suppressed energy. Reverend Joseph Bibby wrote of the suffragettes, "who set fire to our ancient churches and noble mansions, and who go about our art galleries with hammers up their sleeves to destroy valuable works of art." Having felt this explosion and the growing proletarian resolve, Bibby in 1915 welcomed the "chastening" effects of the war on these passions.[94]

The prewar Edwardian epoch was an age of violence wherein, according to Dangerfield, "fires long smoldering in the English spirit suddenly flared, so that by the end of 1913, Liberal England was reduced to ashes."[95] The memoirs of Emanuel Shinwell also testify to this quickening time: "The discontent of the masses spread, the expression of millions of ordinary people who had gained little or nothing from the Victorian age of industrial expansion and grandiose imperialism."[96]

The seeding time of 1914, in its ferment and fertility, seemed more than ripe for increasingly radical directions. R.C.K. Ensor felt that an undistracted concentration upon home issues may well have brought a revolution, especially, he thought, as reflected by the "prewar loss of balance about home rule."[97]

The social and parliamentary impasse over self-determination for Ireland—whether it should encompass the whole of the country or exclude Ulster in the north—boiled over in the summer of 1914. The south was ready to fight for a united Irish home rule, the loyalty of English troops was crumbling, and it looked, to R.J. Evans, for instance, "as if Britain was at last breaking up through her own weakness and dissension."[98]

Colin Cross wrote, apropos of the crisis over Ireland—and the industrial strife and suffrage violence as well—that "Had there been no European war in Summer 1914, Britain might well have lapsed into…anarchy." As Irish workers and peasants moved toward revolt, a divided England appeared "nearer to civil war than at any time since the 16th century," according to Cross.[99]

The whole English party system began to founder at the time of the Irish dilemma, especially given the split in the army. James Cameron summed up this moment with some eloquence: "From a hundred obscure places in Britain, from small-time barbers and ice-cream dealers and Diplomatic Secretaries the message went back to the European Foreign offices: the United Kingdom, if you could call it such, is riddled with dissension; indeed, there is the considerable likelihood of civil war."[100]

Harold Nicolson saw the background of the industrial upheavals of 1910–1914, with its unfolding "revolutionary spirit," as creating veritable panic among the upper classes; this "incessant labor unrest" plus the home rule clash brought the country, in his view, "to the brink of civil war."[101]

Plainly, class tensions were becoming unbearable, "too great to be contained in the existing social and world setting," in the words of Arthur Marwick.[102] In 1911 William Archer had conjectured that some "great catastrophe might be necessary for a new, viable world social order."[103] For England, as elsewhere, the whirlpool of contestation had grown critically turbulent over the four years leading up to mid-summer 1914. "The cry of civil war is on the lips of the most responsible and sober-minded of my people" George V warned participants of a Buckingham Palace conference on July 21, 1914.[104]

Indeed, it can be argued that to look more closely at the attitudes assembling the social crisis is to see nothing less than a nascent refusal against the whole miasma of modern organizational mediation.

A major social welfare enactment, for example, the National Insurance Act of 1911, served only to increase the discontent of the laboring classes.[105] And it was this act that accounted for growth in the trade unions, as the union bureaucracies provided functionaries needed for its administration. More distance from the workers, a greater closeness between unions and government. A 1912 bill proposing to greatly extend the franchise met with universal indifference.[106]

The Labor Party, voice of the unions and proponent of social legislation, likewise struck no chord with the populace; owing largely to the repulsion its bureaucratic nature evoked among the young especially, it engendered no enthusiasm at all.

But the voracious appetites at large could be clearly seen in the many major labor battles from 1910 on—and in their propensity for arson, looting, and violence, as well as the strong preponderance of unauthorized, anti-contract wildcat work stoppages. Halévy saw the unrest as "verging at times on anarchy," and determined that it was a "revolt not only against the authority of capital but against the discipline of trade unions"[107]—as if union discipline was not an essential element of capital's authority.

By 1912, syndicalism, and its close cousin, guild socialism, were attracting much attention. But popular excitement was actually a bit more elusive, not surprising since these projections, staffed by union officials and based on union structures, were all but indistinguishable from industrial unionism itself.

Unexceptionally, English unions, too, were strengthened by the war, but worker rebellions managed to continue, against high odds. The whole summer of 1916, for instance, featured much resistance throughout the provinces in England and along the Clyde to the north. By this time, and versus the disabling wartime array of forces, the struggles were not only against the state and the employers but especially in opposition to the union administrations. New mediation was called for and provided by the shop steward movement of union reform, a diversion essential to the containment of the workers. The Whitely Councils, a form of co-determination which increasingly emphasized the role of unions, was another wartime development aimed against proletarian autonomy. The parliamentary committees at work on a council formula recognized that the constant strife was the doing of the "undisciplined," not the unions. They "wanted to find a cure for the malaise that, before the war, had every year weighted more heavily on industry, and, in consequence, on all of English politics."[108]

A "Triple Alliance" among the miners', transport workers', and railwaymen's unions was formed during the spring and summer of 1914, leading not a few to the prediction that a general strike would have occurred in the fall, but for the war, as the culmination of the strike wave. This thesis totally confuses the official enemies of domination with its real ones.

In fact, the strikes were definitely not initiated by union leaders, architects of the Alliance, but in every case broke out locally and unofficially. The Alliance was not, according to G. A. Phillips, "a concession to the pressures of rank and file militancy; on the contrary, it was designed specifically to control and discipline such militancy." Union officials forged the new structure out of an immediate and overriding need to avert work actions, not facilitate them. Its constitution proclaimed that "every effort shall proceed among the three sections to create effective and complete control of the respective bodies."[109]

Concerning the actual arrival of war, even as the axe began to fall, "Nobody was 'for' the war, or cared at least to be expressly held to be so, and great numbers were urgently and articulately against it," in the judgment of Cameron.[110] Reginald Pound grasped the groundwork for the event: "Probably for the considerable part of the male population the war came, above all, as a relief from pointless labor, one of the major and possibly most dangerous discontents of 20th-century civilization.''[111]

World War I canonized the daily misery of the modern world, presenting its apotheosis of authority and technology most precisely in terms of work. Carl Zuckmayer's experience as a soldier summed up power's universal message that work is all: "the monstrous boredom, the exhaustion, the unheroic, mechanical day-to-day of war in which terror, fear, and death are inserted like the striking of a timeclock in an endless industrial process."[112]

In a world where the spectacle of opposition nowhere seriously asserted the abolition of wage-labor and its context, this frontal assault was as possible as it was necessary. The prewar revolution was smashed. It took 50 years for the recovery to begin.

TAYLORISM AND UNIONISM

Jenkins has observed that "The impression has begun to get about that the Industrial Revolution is not going to work out after all."[1] In light of the profound malaise of blue and white collar workers, the decline of output per worker since 1973, and increasing signs of a pervasive anti-union sentiment complementing anti-management restiveness, Jenkins' remark does not seem so shocking. The 1973 Health, Education and Welfare report, *Work in America*, remarked, in a similar vein, that "absenteeism, wildcat strikes, turnover, and industrial sabotage (have) become an increasingly significant part of the cost of doing business."[2]

The location of this quote from the HEW report in the section titled, "The Anachronism of Taylorism" is suggestive. Because of many mistaken notions about scientific management's historical role, much of industrial society is misunderstood. The genesis of Taylorism as "scientific management," and the developing relation of this system to trade unionism are especially crucial.

When Taylor began his efforts at the Midvale Steel Company in the 1880's, several members of the American Society of Mechanical Engineers were likewise interested in labor management. Industrial capitalism was running up against renewed resistance from the growing ranks of labor, still committed to a sense of work integrity and craftsmanship. Task management, or scientific management as it came to be called, began to take shape in the eighties as the way to break the worker's threatening resistance. The heart of this approach is the systematic reduction of work into discrete, routinized tasks, totally separated from any policy decisions about the job. Taylor realized that employees exert a vital influence because they possess crucial talents needed in any productive process. As he put it in his *Principles of Scientific Management*, "foremen and superintendents know, better than anyone else, that their own knowledge and personal skill falls far short of the combined knowledge and dexterity of all the workmen under them."[3] For capitalism to be firmly in control, it must monopolize information and techniques as surely as it controls the rest of the means of production. The worker must be permitted only to perform certain specific narrow tasks as planned by management.

Naturally, it made sense to publicly promote scientific management as geared directly to problems of profit and productivity, although its aim was control of production. In fact, at that time capital's problem was indeed not so much one of productivity. Giedion's comparison of American and German industry shows that Germany's greater reliance on worker skill was cheaper than the American tendency to mechanize.[4] Thus the introduction of Taylorism was primarily a social and even political response, rather than a matter of economics or "neutral" technology. The proponents of the new regimentation sought to invest it with an aura of impartiality, to evoke a theoretical legitimacy useful to capitalism as a whole.[5]

Despite these pseudo-scientific apologies for the Taylorist approach, the public rapidly developed a very negative view of it. As the Taylor Society admitted with suprising candor, scientific management was widely seen as "the degradation of workmen into obedient oxen under the direction of a small body of experts — into men debarred from creative participation in their work."[6] The public's accurate evaluation of scientific management practice finds its source in the contempt in which Taylor and his followers held workers. Referring to his experience at Bethlehem Steel, Taylor described the iron handler he encountered as stupid, phlegmatic, and ox-like.[7] Yet, despite attempts to downgrade their subjects, scientific management tracts are full of admonitions to proceed slowly, due to workers' resistance. It was regularly repeated that several years are needed to reorganize a plant on the scientific management basis.[8] The Taylor Society warned employers to expect strikes and sabotage, to proceed with cunning so as to infiltrate under false appearances, and to expect opposition at every step.[9] The struggle concerned progressive attempts to debase work.[10]

Although a survey of management and personnel journals[11] makes it clear that scientific management is the foundation of work organization everyday experiences bring the point home with painful clarity. Braverman notes that control assumed "unprecedented dimensions" with Taylor and it has engendered serious opposition. The works of Braverman, Marglin, and others since the mid-70's discuss the social/political control essence of Taylorism. What is less understood, however, is the nature of the struggle between workers and controllers, and the role of unionism in it.

The two standard works on the subject, McKelvey's *AFL Attitudes Toward Production* (1952) and Nadworny's *Scientific Management and the Unions* (1955) argue that organized labor switched from a hostile attitude toward Taylorism before WW I, to a warmly receptive one thereafter. This judgement is mistaken. The error stems from the perennial confusion of union attitude with rank and file attitudes. It would be much more accurate to say that workers seem to have opposed scientific management all along, while the unions seemed only briefly opposed, but have never really been against it.

Turning first to the union attitudes toward Taylorism in the pre-War period, we find anything but concerted opposition. In 1889, for example, when Taylor first presented his ideas to the American Society of Mechanical Engineers, John A. Penton, ex-president of the Brotherhood of Machine Molders, joined the discussion of Taylor's paper. This former union official, speaking "as a workman," was more lavish in his praise than any of the others. Urging that the paper be put into the hands of every employer and employee, Penton termed it "perhaps the most remarkable thing of its kind I ever heard in my life. I can sympathize with every word. His paper, I think, is a landmark in the field of political economy."[12]

In 1907, David Van Alstyne of the American Locomotive Company secured an agreement with the molders' and blacksmiths' union for the introduction of Taylorism in the company's U.S. and Canada shops. Though the molders and blacksmiths thus were prevented from fighting the degrading methods, the unorganized machinists in Pittsburgh walked out, "seething" with anger.[13]

Commons provided the cardinal reason for the unions' absence of hostility to Taylorism: ". . .the unions have generally come to the point of confining their attention to wages — that is, to distribution — leaving to employers the question of production."[14] If either McKelvey or Nadworny had examined collective bargaining agreements reached prior to World War I,[15] they would have most likely discovered the "management's rights" clause found in every U.S. union contract until the early 1980's. This clause vests the sole right to set work methods, job design, assignments, etc. with management; this is of fundamental importance in understanding why unionism could not oppose scientific management or any other kind of management system. If is easy to see why, when Taylorism became a public issue in 1911, AFL officials could not have found historical grounds for opposition.[16] Thus, when Nadworny mentions the arrangement made between Plimpton Press and the Typographical Union in 1914, whereby the union agreed to accept scientific management in return for closed shop recognition, or the arrangement between the New York garment industry and the International Ladies Garment Worker's Union in 1916, involving the same exchange, these are not aberrations.

In fact, well before the War the idea began spreading that unionization, with its standard "management's rights" clause contracts, was the best approach for fitting the Taylorist yoke on the workers. The efficacy of this "trojan horse" tactic of union mediation led Thompson to prescribe industrial unionism over the AFL's craft unionism as the best way the secure the Taylor system in industry. Describing "one plant where scientific management was fully developed and in complete operation, the management has itself authorized and aided the organization of its employees," Thompson went so far as to urge recognition of the Industrial Workers of the World, to secure "the necessary unanimity of action" in linking all the workers, not only the skilled ones, to Taylorism.[17]

The ostensibly radical I.W.W. might seem an unlikely candidate for the job of Taylorizing workers, but several Wobbly spokesmen actually saw in scientific management much of value toward stabilizing and rationalizing production "after the Revolution." And from the rest of the American Left, many other sympathetic voices could be heard. Enthusiasm for the system seemed to cut across ideological lines. Lenin's support of Taylorism is well-known, and John Spargo, an influential American Socialist, denounced everything about the Bolshevik Revolution save Lenin's adoption of scientific management.[18]

While the official union and radical spokesmen for the workers were finding no fault with scientific management, the workers were acting against it on their own. An attempt to introduce Taylorism at the huge Rock Island government arsenal in 1908 was defeated by the intense opposition it aroused. It is interesting that these "unorganized" workmen did not appeal to a union for help, but confronted the setting of piece rates and the division of tasks by themselves — and immediately demanded that the method be discontinued. Likewise, the beginnings of Taylorism at the Frankford arsenal were defeated by the hostility of the ("unorganized") employees there in 1910 and 1911. In October, 1914, the 3,000 garment workers of Sonnenborn and Company in Baltimore walked out spontaneously upon hearing that Taylorism was to be installed.[19]

The case of Taylorism at the U.S. arsenal at Watertown, Massachusetts in 1911 clearly demonstrates the need for not confusing unions with workers, "organized" or not. If this is as close as unions came in practice to opposing the new system, it is safe to say that they did not oppose it at all. When the idea of Taylorizing Watertown first arose in 1908, Taylor warned that the government managers must have the complete system. "Anything short of this leaves such a large part of the game in the hands of the workmen that it becomes largely a matter of whim or caprice on their part as to whether they will allow you to have any real results or not."[20]

It is clear that Taylor himself mistook the quiescence of the AFL unions, which represented various arsenal workers, for passivity on the part of the employees. He counseled a Watertown manager in 1910 "not to bother too much about what the AFL write (sic) concerning our system," and in March, 1911, just before the strike, he tried again to allay any management fears of worker resistance by pooh-poohing any AFL correspondence which might be received in the future.[21] He knew the unions would not seriously interfere; his elitism prevented a clear appraisal of worker attitudes.

When the time-study man, Merrick, openly timed foundry workers with a stop-watch, action was forthcoming immediately. Although union members, they did not call the union, but instead drew up a petition demanding the cessation of any further Taylorist intrusions. Being rebuffed, they walked out. Joseph Cooney, a molder in the foundry, testified early in 1912 to the Congressional committee examining Taylor's system, that there had been no contact between the workers and any union official and that the strike had been completely spontaneous.[22] Though an overwhelming majority of Watertown employees questioned by a consultant (hired by a group of workers) felt that the unions had no interest in agitating against scientific management,[23] the International Association of Machinists publicly proclaimed union opposition to the system shortly after the 1911 strike. Because this public opposition by the IAM in 1911 is practically the sole evidence supporting the thesis of pre-War union hostility in Taylorism,[24] it deserves a closer look.

In 1909, as McKelvey notes, the initial features of scientific management were installed at Watertown, without the slightest protest from the unions, including the IAM.[25] At about this time, the National League of Government Employees began to make inroads on the IAM, due to the dissatisfaction of the latter group's members. The rival organization had drawn away many members by the time of the 1911 strike,[26] and the IAM was thus forced to make a show of opposition if it wished to retain its hold among the workers. In similar fashion, the International Molder's Union had to give grudging support to a strike of Boston molders which had occurred without so much as informing the local union. The union leaders involved frequently made statements showing their actual support of Taylorism, and a careful reading of the 1911 AFL Convention record, also cited as evidence of anti-Taylorism by the unions, shows that Samuel Gompers avoided attacking directly the new work system in any substantial way.

The 1920s, with unionism's public embrace of scientific management and the falling away of union membership, was a victorious period for Taylorism. The age of the consumer began from the systematic destruction of much of the last autonomy of the producer. With the invaluable aid of unions, a healthy share of the content of work lives had been removed. Rorty saw the lack of militancy and initiative from workers in the early 1930s stemming directly from the technological processes to which they were enslaved.[27] The recent re-awakening of the struggle for a life of quality and meaning is informed with the knowledge that work itself is the major issue. It is unfortunate that the confusion about Taylorism and unionism continues, inasmuch as it bears heavily on an understanding of what trade unions really are.[28]

UNIONIZATION IN AMERICA

Throughout the Left there is a wrong impression of the labor struggles of the Depression, which obscures our understanding of the nature and origin of the increasingly anti-union 'revolt against work' of today.

Trade unions in the 1920s were generally in a weak and worsening position. While union membership constituted 19.4% of non-agricultural workers in 1920, only 10.2% were organized by 1930. The employee representation plans, or company unions, of "welfare capitalism" were being instituted as substitutes for unionism, in an effort at stabilized, peaceful industrial relations.

There were some, however, who even before the Crash realized that independent unions were essential for effective labor-management cooperation. In 1925, for example, Arthur Nash of the Golden Rule Clothing Company invited Sidney Hillman's Amalgamated Clothing Workers to organize his employees. Mr. Nash explained in this way: "I had a job that I could not do, and I just passed the buck to Mr. Hillman." Gerard P. Swope, president of General Electric, tried as early as 1926 to persuade the AFL to organize a nation-wide union of electrical workers on an industrial basis. Swope believed that having an industrial union might well mean "the difference between an organization with which we could work on a business-like basis and one that would be a source of endless difficulties." In 1928 George Mead wrote "Why I Unionized My Plant," describing in glowing terms his bringing the papermakers' union to his Wisconsin employees. Also in 1928, Secretary of Labor Davis asked that year's AFL convention to eliminate jurisdictional squabbling and get on with the kind of mass organizing that businesses desire. Another example of the pacifying, stabilizing possibilities of unionization followed the spontaneous strike movement of Southern textile workers in 1929. Commenting on AFL efforts to organize the union-less and uncontrolled mill workers, the *Chicago Tribune* in early 1930 expressed its support: "The effort of the Federation to organize the mill workers of the South deserves the endorsement of far-seeing businessmen throughout the country."

But with the onset of the Depression, the weakness of the AFL and its craft union approach became even more obvious. With the trend toward fewer skilled workers, the Federation's attempts to sell itself to industry as a frankly peace-keeping institution were increasingly out of touch with its capabilities. The Crash, moreover, did not awaken the craft union leaders to a new awareness of the changing industrial order. Noted businessman Edward Louis Sullivan classified the AFL as simply "reactionary."

In the early 1930s, some labor leaders became involved with a group of far-sighted businessmen who saw the need for mass unionization. John L. Lewis and Sidney Hillman, destined to play major roles in the formulation of the National Recovery Act of 1933 and the formation of the CIO, came to realize by 1932 that government and business might be enlisted in the cause of industrial unionism. Gerard Swope, the above-mentioned president of GE, unveiled his Swope Plan in 1931 with the help of employers like Chamber of Commerce president Henry I. Harriman. Self-government in industry, via extended trade associations which would operate outside anti-trust laws, was the basis of the plan. An essential facet was to be the unionization of the basic industries, with unions possessing the same kind of disciplinary power over the workers as the trade associations would exercise over individual firms.

In their enthusiasm for a controlled, rationalized corporate system, these labor and business leaders were as one. "Lewis and Hillman, in the end, differed little from Gerard Swope and Henry I. Harriman," in the words of Arthur Schlesinger, Jr. President Hoover labeled these plans "sheer fascism." By 1932, in fact, the government stood committed to labor's right to organize. Pre-dating the NRA by a year, the Norris-Laguardia Act not only outlawed the "yellow-dog" contract and certain kinds of injunctions but fully sanctioned the right to collective bargaining.

Section 7a of the NRA became the focus of attention after its enactment in June, 1933, however, and the reason seems two-fold. 7a's guarantee of labor's right to collective bargaining had the weight of a strong resurgence of labor unrest in 1933, as compared to the relative quiescence of 1932. Fully 812,000 workers struck in 1933, whereas only 243,000 had struck in 1932.

The second reason for the utilization of section 7a was that it was part of a whole stabilization program, which embodied the Swope Plan-type thinking on the need for a near-cartelization of business and the curtailment of much competition. Swope, not surprisingly, was one of the NRA's main architects—along with John L. Lewis.

With the NRA, the full integration of labor into the business system came a step closer to fruition. In the context of a continuing depression and increasing worker hostility, the need for industrial unionism became more and more apparent to government leaders. Donald Richberg, an author of both Norris-LaGuardia and NRA, decried craft unionism's failure to organize more than a small minority, and saw industrial unions as the key to industrial stability. As labor writer Benjamin Stolberg put it, in his *A Government in Search of a Labor Movement*, "The old-fashioned craft leader is through, for he is helpless to express the increasing restlessness of American labor." And Stolberg knew that President Roosevelt saw the need for unions, in order to safely contain that restlessness: "NRA was wholly an administrative measure...It shows that Mr. Roosevelt believes that what American industry needs desperately is the recognition and extension of the trade union movement."

Concerning FDR, there is ample evidence that Stolberg is correct and that Roosevelt consistently held to a basic belief in collective bargaining. As Assistant Secretary of the Navy, he sat on the Executive Board of the National Civic Federation, that early and important organization of heads of business and labor formed to promote amity through contracts and close communications. As Governor of New York, Roosevelt had been impressed by Swope's arguments and "had talked to John Sullivan of the State Federation of Labor in New York about the possibility of industrial unions being organized in plants like General Electric," according to Frances Perkins.

Perkins, FDR's Secretary of Labor, recounted the President's advice to a group of businessmen: "You don't need to be afraid about unions...You shouldn't be afraid to have them organize in your factory. They don't want to run the business. You will probably get a lot better production and a lot more peace and happiness if you have a good union organization and a good contract."

It was not surprising that Roosevelt's choice to head the NRA, General Hugh Johnson, "appreciates that industry cannot function without organized labor," in the judgement of Stolberg. Nor is the opinion of *Fortune*, that most prestigious of big business periodicals, surprising as regards the NRA as vehicle for unionization. In December, 1933, *Fortune* implied disapproval of the Ford Motor Company as being "ruled primarily by fear," while noting that firms unionized under NRA's 7a have the joint strength of both NRA and union officials to limit strikes. The phoney, staged strike became a safer bet at this time, owing to the NRA presence. In August 1933, for example, the ILGWU staged a strike of New York dressmakers, carefully arranged by union and NRA officials to last exactly 4 days and bring the unorganized dressmakers into the union and under an NRA code.

Where the AFL did not attempt stage-managed strikes, it worked to defeat authentic walk-outs. Louis Adamic concluded that "The Federation as a whole...sabotaged or suppressed all important rank-and-file or spontaneous movements in 1933 and 1934, especially those in steel and rubber. The one exception was the Bridges movement on the coast." It is far from clear, however, that even one exception occurred.

Under the leadership of Harry Bridges, the organizing of West Coast longshoremen had culminated in the famous San Francisco general strike of July, 1934. Charles Larrowe, the maritime labor historian, concludes that the only "benefit" obtained by the workers was their being brought under union contract: "The terms under which the prolonged, violent strike was settled were similar, to be sure, to some of the proposals for settlement made before the strike began. Looked at in this perspective it might seem that the strike served no purpose. But looked at in the larger context of collective bargaining, the strike was both unavoidable and necessary."

The settlement of the 1934 strike marked the beginning of a change in consciousness for San Francisco employers; though waterfront strife continued sporadically until 1937, the employers had begun to see that all that union officialdom really wanted was the closed shop, with the dues and power over the membership it entails. And for this, union discipline could then be put to the service of guaranteeing an absence of trouble from the longshoremen. Roosevelt, as indicated above, learned this lesson rather earlier; his Secretary of Labor, noting the lack of White House alarm over the SF general strike, commented on the power of union officials over union members: "Sensible labor leaders advised the men to get back to work, that this was not time for an unconsidered sympathetic strike, even if it was also in their own interest."

Fortune viewed Bridges as one of the "gifted, temperamental, power-wielding leaders of American maritime labor without whose compliance no decrees of the Maritime Commission are likely to keep the peace." The pro-Bridges article praised him and other labor leaders for introducing stability into shipping industry labor relations, adding that he was "no Communist."

San Francisco employers had come, by 1937, to fully appreciate the necessity of unionization as the key to a dependable work force. Irving Bernstein, in his authoritative history of Depression labor, tells us that in 1937 "the town's leading businessmen formed the Committee of Forty-Three hoping to persuade the unions to join in a program to stabilize labor relations. The labor people declined." The union chiefs declined, it should be added, because they feared membership reaction to institutionalized labor-management collusion of this kind. Bernstein continues: "But the Committee served a purpose—to commit San Francisco's employers to collective bargaining. And it was those with experience with Bridges and the ILWU, notably the two leading owners of steamship lines, Roger Lapham and Almon Roth, who led the way, forming the SF Employers Council which had as its purpose "the recognition and exercise of the right of the employers to bargain collectively."

Given the effective control over workers that only unions can manage, it was not at all out of place that San Francisco employers should have striven for collective bargaining, nor that the promotion and coordination of contracts quickly spread up and down the Pacific Coast.

Meanwhile 1934 and 1935 saw a deepening trend toward labor militancy and violence. The bloody Electric Auto-Lite strike in Toledo and the street warfare of the striking Minneapolis truck drivers were among the most spectacular of 1934, a year in which 40 strikers were killed. In less than eighteen months, between the summer of 1933 and the winter of 1934, troops were called out in sixteen states. The important point is that the AFL could not control this activism; though it might stall and sell out the workers, it could not provide the kind of organization that could enroll all of a firm's workers into a single, industry-wide union and bring peace under collective bargaining. Workers resisted the conservative craft form of organizations and the constant jurisdictional bickering that accompanied it and began to experiment with new organizational forms. For example, union locals in Hudson and Oldsmobile plants seceded from the AFL in August, 1934, to elect representatives from their own ranks and negotiate democratically. The *Wall Street Journal* discussed speculation as to the radicalism of the independents for several days, in articles such as "More on the Secession," and "Disaffection Spreads." Labor partisan Art Preis provides some revealing figures: "By 1935, the membership of the AFL federal auto locals had dwindled from 100,000 to 20,000. When the Wolman Board of the NRA took a poll in 1935 to determine 'proportional representation' in a number of plants in Michigan, of the 163,150 votes cast, 88.7% were for unaffiliated representatives;

8.6% for leaders of the AFL federal locals.''

If the NRA and its Section 7a was intended to fix labor "into a semi-public unionism whose organization was part of a government plan," in Stolberg's words, Washington in 1935 yet hoped to make good on the 1933 beginning. From the point of view of industrial peace, the impetus, as we have seen, was certainly stronger by 1935, when the Wagner bill was being considered. Supporters of the measure, like Lloyd Garrison and Harry Millis, put forth the "safety measure" theory, arguing the importance of assisting unionism and portraying the state as a friend of the worker, in order to combat worker radicalism. Leon Keyserling, legislative assistant to Senator Wagner, feared an uncontrolled labor movement, and saw a goal of government-sponsored labor relations which could reduce conflict and induce labor and business to work together in concert with government.

The pressing need for a government guarantee to unionism was readily appreciated and the Wagner bill breezed through the Senate in May by a 62–11 margin. Nonetheless, all of the standard accounts continue to assert business' steadfast opposition to the bill in spite of the evidence. The eminent business historian Thomas Cochran, for example, re-affirms the old thesis, only to admit that "the struggle in Congress appears very mild...All of this is hard to explain."

By this time, of course, leading elements of business and government saw collective bargaining as imperative for the steadying of the industrial order. Secretary Perkins is worth quoting at some length: *It may be surprising to some people to realize that men looked upon as the conservative branch of the Roosevelt administration were cooperative in bringing about a new, more modern and more reasonable attitude on the part of employers toward collective bargaining agreements. Averell Harriman of the Union Pacific Railroad, Carl Gray of the same railroad, Daniel Willard of the Baltimore and Ohio, Walter Teagle of the Standard Oil Company, Thomas Lamont of J. P. Morgan and Company, Myron Taylor, of U.S. Steel, Gerard Swope of General Electric, and Robert Armory, a textile manufacturer, were among those whom I asked for help from time to time in difficult situations, where the problem was to start collective bargaining negotiations. Roosevelt knew that these people had helped and was always very grateful to them.*

Nor was this "more reasonable attitude" merely a privately expressed one. Of many instances which could be cited, is the speech of Henry Heimann, head of the National Association of Credit Men (*Wall Street Journal*, August 21, 1934), which called for the abandonment of the company union idea and the control of labor in strong, national bodies.

By the time of the 1935 AFL Convention, the stage was set: workers in auto, rubber, radio, textiles, and steel were furious over the inaction, bad faith, and collusion with management that they saw in the AFL. The vast majority of General Motors workers, for example, regarded continued membership in an AFL auto local as proof of being a paid agent of GM, according to Wyndham Mortimer. Craft-style unionism stood in dire need of replacement by newer forms if unions were to contain the nation's workers.

John L. Lewis, the conservative and ruthless head of the United Mine Workers, was to lead the move toward industrial unionism. A Republican up to and during the 1932 presidential campaign, he ruled the often resistant miners by dictatorial methods. The servility and corruption of the union begat constant revolts from the ranks against Lewis. A miner interviewed by Studs Terkel testified to this state of affairs when he spoke of a UMW field representative being tarred and feathered "for tryin' to edge in with management," and declared that the "chairman of the local was thick with the superintendent of the mine." In October, 1933 *Fortune* related the miners' hatred of Lewis during the 1920s and the "Lewis Must Go" campaign of 1932. Generally quite pro-Lewis, "his repressive tactics in the union" were mentioned, and the article concluded with the judgement that the prospect of organizing 30,000,000 workers did not frighten Lewis—nor, by very strong implication, should it frighten business.

With Lewis' famous—and no doubt calculated—punch to the jaw of Bill Hutcheson, boss of the Carpenters Union and a major craft unionism spokesman, a split from the AFL was signalled. The blow, at the 1935 AFL convention, enabled Lewis to represent himself to the bitter and distrustful industrial workers as a new kind of leader. "By attacking Hutcheson, he was attacking the trade unionism these workers so bitterly hated...Hutcheson symbolized to millions of frustrated workers that craft-unionism policy that had defeated their spontaneous organizations," in the words of Saul Alinsky.

Within a month of the October convention, the Committee for Industrial Organization was formed by Lewis and a few others in the Federation who headed industrial-type unions. By early 1937, locals of those unions affiliated with the new CIO were expelled from all city and state AFL councils, making the break final and official.

The CIO began with a feudal structure in which all officers were appointed by Lewis, giving it an important advantage over its AFL predecessors. Whereas the AFL officials needed decades to emasculate the fairly autonomous city and state central councils and establish centralized national power, the CIO chiefs established complete control over collective bargaining and strike sanction almost from the outset. Leaders of both the AFL and CIO were "agreed on the necessity for circumscribing the increasing militancy in the basic industries...No one in the AFL or in the CIO was under any illusions that Lewis, Murray, Hillman, and Dubinsky were out to build a radically new kind of movement," as Sidney Lens put it.

The presence of Communists and other leftists within the CIO does not alter the picture, and not a few business leaders understood the anti-radical character of the new organization. For example, "when the CIO was organized and the left-led United Electrical Workers began to organize GE, Gerard Swope rejoiced," noted Ronald Radosh. Swope, the NRA architect, informed one of his GE vice-presidents that "if you can't get along with these fellows and settle matters, there's something wrong with you." The UEW was praised by Swope as "well-led, the discipline good." Radosh, in fact, concludes that "it was the more politically radical unions that led the integration of labor into the corporate structure."

Worker action continued to develop, however, in the relative absence of unions throughout 1935 and 1936. New forms of struggle and organization were adopted which deeply frightened business, government, and unions superiors alike. Employee-run independent unions sprang up, often employing radical tactics which challenged the traditional rights of management to define the nature of the job. The "skippy," for instance, was a very effective form of defiance that was spontaneously adopted by the man on the assembly line. Workers might quietly agree to skip every fifth fender or leave untightened every sixth bolt to protest intolerable job conditions. Rapidly the line would come to a halt in complete confusion, with enraged but helpless foremen at a loss to single out the participants.

The most threatening device and the one to become very widely utilized was, of course, the sitdown strike. Like the skippy, it more often than not was employed by the "unorganized"; in fact, the sitdown reflects worker suspicion of union structure and control. As Louis Adamic put it so well: "Most workers distrust—if not consciously, then unconsciously—union officials and strike leaders and committees, even when they have elected them themselves. The beauty of the sitdown or stay-in is that there are no leaders or officials to distrust. There can be no sell-out. Such standard procedure as strike sanction is hopelessly obsolete when workers drop their tools, stop their machines, and sit down beside them. The initiative, conduct, and control come directly from the men involved.'' The sitdown seems to have first become an established tactic in the rubber factories of Akron. Between 1933 and 1936 it became a tradition in Akron, developed largely because the union had failed to resist the speed-up.

The speed-up appears to have been the chief single cause of discontent throughout mass production. A 1934 study of the auto industry revealed that the grievance "mentioned most frequently...and uppermost in the minds of those who testified is the speed-up." Tactics like the sitdown were taken up when workers felt they had to challenge the employer's absolute right to control the work process, in the absence of union interest in questioning management prerogatives. The challenge to the speed-up came not only out of the sheer fatigue felt over the absolute rate of production, then, but also because the production worker was not free to set the pace of his work and to determine the manner in which it was to be performed. In the factories was joined the battle over who was to control the worker's life on the job. This was the real issue; as Mary Vorse put it, "the auto workers' discontent came in about equal parts from the speed-up and the absolute autocracy of the industry."

The struggle was waged not only by the auto workers, of course, but it was GM workers who waged one of the most important fights. And the role of the union as conservator for the existing relationships, rather than as challenger of them, may be clearly seen in the context of the great GM sitdown strike.

Actually the sitdown movement that was beginning to spread rapidly by late 1936 was anything but a part of CIO tactics. It "sprang spontaneously from an angered mass of workers. All American labor leaders would have been shocked, scared and instinctively opposed to the initiation or approval of this disorderly revolutionary upheaval," according to Saul Alinsky.

The 44-day GM sitdown began on December 28, 1936, when some 7,000 at Cleveland's Fisher Body plant struck. Two days later workers in Fisher Body No. 2 in Flint sat down and the spontaneous movement quickly spread throughout the GM system, bringing it to a standstill.

The former Harvard economist J. Raymond Walsh stated flatly that the CIO had certainly not called the strike: "The CIO high command...tried in vain to prevent the strike." As Wellington Roe wrote: "To the public, at least, Lewis was its originator. Actually Lewis had no more to do with the sitdown strike than some native of Patagonia." Although, as James Wechsler, Lewis' biographer, recorded, "he gave a superb imitation of a man who had worked everything out in advance."

Again, it was the lack of control over the assembly line that produced the sitdown among auto workers. Henry Kraus' book on the GM strike expressed it this way: "It was the speed-up that organized Flint, as it was the one element in the life of all the workers that found a common basis of resentment."

Though union officialdom feared the undisciplined sitdown movement, Lewis and the CIO realized that they must move fast if they hoped to keep up with and establish control over it. Hence Lewis declared on December 31, very early in the strike, that "the CIO stands squarely behind these sitdowns."

This tactic was essential at the time, though approval of sitdowns was revoked just as soon as the CIO could get away with it. Len De-Caux, editor of the CIO's United News Service, stated that "as a matter of fact, the first experience of the CIO with sitdowns was in discouraging them."

When the GM strike began, very few employees belonged to the CIO-affiliated United Auto Workers; in Flint only one in 400 belonged to the UAW. It was not, apparently, an easy matter for the CIO to achieve control over the strike. Kraus' account contains several instances of the difficulties encountered, including, "The strike committee had not yet completely established its authority and there were accordingly some resistance and friction at first with a certain tendency to anarchy of action." Wyndham Mortimer, another very pro-union source, admitted that "A very disturbing factor on the union side was that several members of our negotiating committee were convinced that no one in the leadership could be trusted, from John L. Lewis down."

Before centralized authority was effected, many radical possibilities remained open. Sidney Fine's authoritative *Sitdown* recognized the sitdowners' resistance to hierarchical procedures, commenting on the "fierce independence" displayed by the workers. The situation prompted Thomas Brooks to assay that "for a brief time, the CIO teetered on the brink of the revolutionary industrial unionism of the Wobblies." Alinsky states similarly that "the General Motors strike bordered on revolution."

The sitdowns in rubber, which had occurred, from Louis Adamic's observations, "without encouragement from any rank-and-file organizer," much less from any union, and which were almost invariably successful, reached a very important climax at GM. And inasmuch as the GM sitdowners were so vitally concerned with controlling the assembly line as the key issue, basic antagonism between workers and union was implied from the start. The CIO had to attach itself to the sitdown phenomenon and, at least initially, make a show of supporting the workers' actions, but there existed a vast chasm between the attitudes of that movement and the respect for management's rights of the CIO.

CIO leaders tried from the beginning to find a way to squelch the occupation of GM property. In a revealing passage, Secretary of Labor Perkins tells us: *The CIO came to the support of the automobile workers, although I know for a fact that John Lewis and Sidney Hillman and Lee Pressman, CIO counsel, made great efforts to get the men to leave the plant...But they would not publicly desert them.* CIO officials had no interest in taking up the issue of speed-up. Regulation of the speed of the line was listed as eighth of eight demands submitted by the UAW to GM on January 4. Predictably, the February 11 settlement dealt almost exclusively with union recognition and not at all with speed-up. The union had been granted sole-bargaining-agent status for six months in the 17 struck plants and looked forward to consolidating its position in the enforced absence of any rivals.

When Bud Simons, head of the strike committee in Fisher Body No. 1, was awakened and told the terms of the settlement, he said, "That won't do for the men to hear. That's not what we've been striking for." And when the union presented the settlement to the strikers, distrust mounted in relation to the unanswered questions as to speed of the line, authority on the shop floor, and working conditions.

The workers' forebodings were borne out by the negotiations which followed the evacuation of the plants. GM's policy was "above all, to preserve managerial discretion in the productive process, particularly over the speed of the line." The fundamental demand of the strike—to the strikers—had been "mutual determination" of the speed of production, but under the contract signed May 12 local management was ensured "full authority" in these matters. Alfred P. Sloan, Jr., GM president, became satisfied that the union was not out to challenge management's rights, and reported, "we have retained all the basic powers to manage."

In addition, the union became the effective agency for suppressing workers' direct action against speed-up or other grievances, pledging that "There shall be no suspensions or stoppages of work until every effort has been exhausted to adjust them through the regular grievance procedure, and in no case without the approval of the international officers of the union.''

Workers were plainly dissatisfied with the outcome of their sit-down, a fact usually ignored in the many accounts of the 'victorious CIO breakthrough' of the GM occupation. William Knudsen, GM vice-president, said that there were 170 sitdowns in GM plants between March and June, 1937, as workers who had become conscious of their great power did not automatically submit to union-management hegemony. Union officials scurried from place to place to quell these stoppages, which they considered a very serious threat to union authority. A *New York Times* article called "Unauthorized Sit-Downs fought by CIO Unions " described the drastic efforts used to end the sitdowns, including the dismissal of any union representative sympathetic to them. The same April 12, 1937 article ascribed the sitdowns to "dissatisfaction on the part of the workers with the union itself,'' and reported that "they are as willing in some cases to defy their own leaders as their bosses.''

Interestingly, the Communists were just as concerned with restoring proper order via traditional union structures as anyone else in the CIO. Even Eugene Lyons' hysterical *The Red Decade*, which found almost everything in the 1930s to be Party- controlled, did not try to say that the sitdown movement was Red-inspired or dominated.

A sitdown wave moved with amazing rapidity to all types of industry and business in the spring of 1937. *New Masses* of May 4 noted that "the strikes of the Woolworth and Grand girls gave a stunning surprise both to their employers and to the working-class movement.'' Evelyn Finn, a seamstress interviewed by Studs Terkel, told of the sitdown she was involved in: "The boss was goin' crazy. The union officials came down. They went crazy, too. It was a hilarious day.''

The ending of the movement could be effectively and lastingly engineered only from the inside. Before business and government could formulate a solution the union leaders themselves had put the lid on sitdowns. An industrial relations expert on the subject: "The sitdown is too easy a tactic for good discipline...because workers can secure grievance settlements by interrupting production through a sitdown, they may eventually think, what's the use of joining a union and paying dues if we can get what we want this way?''

The sitdowns were ended with the unions cooperating with management in the ouster of the workers, for of course the CIO had no intention of helping employees take power on the shop floor. As CIO official Mike Widman put it, "My union experience taught me that the direction of the working force is vested in management. The unions shall not abridge that right, so long as there is no discrimination or unfairness."

Walter Lippman, in the spring of 1937, warned recalcitrant businessmen "that the more they treat Mr. Lewis and the CIO as public enemies to be resisted at all costs, the more impossible they make it for Mr. Lewis to develop discipline and a sense of responsibility in the ranks..." By this time, however, many more employers were peacefully signed up with the CIO.

In March (1937), after three months of secret negotiations, US Steel's Myron Taylor signed a recognition agreement with Lewis, typifying the many industrialists impressed with CIO usefulness. The *New York World-Telegram* reported that "two financiers closely identified with Morgan interests said they had only praise and admiration for Mr. Lewis...apparently thoroughly in accord on the main theme that complete industrial organization was inevitable, they hinted that other industrial leaders may be just as receptive to unionization of their plants as is Myron C. Taylor, chief of Big Steel."

The critical CIO role in quelling or preventing sitdowns was certainly not lost on employers. In the steel industry, the CIO's Steel Workers' Organizing Committee found many willing customers, due to management's inability to control its employees unassisted. Charles Haines, producer of steel-making equipment and a member of one of the pioneering steel families of America, was representative of this management awareness. Stability was desired and hence the employers "were asking the SWOC to straighten out their labor difficulties," in May Vorse's words.

The bloody "Little Steel" strike was clearly an exception to the quickening trend of employer acceptance of unionism. Concerning the Little Steel strike, by the way, the CIO could have been successful, at least could have avoided the score of dead, had it not been so opposed to the use of the sitdown. Labor commentators Preis, Levinson, Lens, and others agree that the killing of pickets and demonstrators would have been obviated by the use of the sitdown tactic. And more than one writer has wondered if the whole "Memorial Day Massacre" march of unarmed strikers—and the likelihood of their being shot—was not planned by union leaders to produce union martyrs.

A contract with SWOC was a safeguard against work actions, and employers were appreciative. For example: "Major officials of the U.S. Steel Company have repeatedly and publicly attested the satisfactory character of their contractual relations with the unions," reported Robert Brooks. John L. Lewis was to the point when he said in 1937, "A CIO contract is adequate protection against sitdowns, lie-downs, or any other kind of strike."

Professor of labor relations Benjamin Selekman observed that "union leaders have sought to calm down the new members with their seemingly insatiable demands." Likewise, Carroll Dougherty judged that "The induction of large numbers of raw recruits untrained in unionism made guidance from the top necessary," adding, almost as an afterthought, "Yet there was danger that such guidance would develop into permanent dictatorship."

It didn't prove easy for the unions to impose discipline on the many new members. As we have seen, their "seemingly insatiable demands" were hardly uppermost in the minds of the union leaders; labor leaders must appear to support worker demands, if they are initially to interest them in union representation. "Only later does the union seek to instruct the individual member in his responsibilities, and such education is a slow process...Individual members must come to realize that they cannot take matters into their own hands," wrote John Dunlop.

Exclusive-bargaining-agent status, or the closed shop, is the primary institution by which the union enforces control of the workers. Golden and Ruttenberg, two SWOC officials, candidly argue in *The Dynamics of Industrial Democracy* that unions need power and responsibility to maintain discipline. With the closed shop, the union acquires, in effect, the power to fire unruly members; if a member is dropped from the union, he is dropped from his job. Golden and Ruttenberg, as so many other union spokesmen, point out that the union is likely to make noise until it gains the closed-shop arrangement, and that management rapidly comes to see the need for a strong (closed-shop) union, in the interest of a contained work force. The price of cooperation is thus the closed-shop, and it satisfies both the union and management.

By 1938, according to Brooks, only a "small minority" of employers opposed collective bargaining as guaranteed by the Wagner Act. It becomes easy to see why. Union leaders were "anxious to demonstrate to the management their responsibility, and their willingness to accept the burden of 'selling' the contract to the rank-and-file and keeping the dissidents in line," according to consultants Sayles and Straus. In many cases, unions simply replaced personnel departments.

As business came increasingly to the awareness of unions as indispensible to the maintenance of a relatively stable and docile labor supply, the ranks of labor exhibited more and more dissatisfaction with "their" new organizations. The 1945 *Trends in Collective Bargaining* study noted that "by around 1940" the labor leader had joined the business leader as an object of "widespread cynicism" to the American worker. Similarly, Daughterty reported that workers were chafing under the lack of structural democracy in the union. "There was evidence, by the end of 1940, that the rank-and-file were growing restive under such conditions."

Workers, after some initial enthusiasm and hopefulness regarding the CIO, were starting to feel the 'closed system' nature of compulsory unions. In discussing union-management cooperation in the steel industry, CIO officials Golden and Ruttenberg admitted, for example, that "to some workers" the cooperation only added up in practice to "a vicious speed-up."

Thus we return to the issue uppermost in the minds of industrial workers in the 1930's struggles. And Richard Lester seems to be quite correct in concluding that "the industrial government jointly established" possesses "disciplinary arrangements advantageous to management, rendering worker rebellions more and more difficult."

ORGANIZED LABOR VS. "THE REVOLT AGAINST WORK"

Serious commentators on the labor upheavals of the Depression years seem to agree that disturbances of all kinds, including the wave of sit-down strikes of 1936 and 1937, were caused by the "speed-up" above all.[1] Dissatisfaction among production workers with their new CIO unions set in early, however, mainly because the unions made no efforts to challenge management's right to establish whatever kind of work methods and working conditions they saw fit. The 1945 *Trends in Collective Bargaining* study noted that "by around 1940" the labor leader had joined the business leader as an object of "widespread cynicism" to the American employee.[2] Later in the 1940's C. Wright Mills, in his *The New Men of Power: America's Labor Leaders*, described the union's role thusly: "the integration of union with plant means that the union takes over much of the company's personnel work, becoming the discipline agent of the rank-and-file."[3]

In the mid-1950's, Daniel Bell realized that unionization had not given workers control over their job lives. Struck by the huge, spontaneous walk-out at River Rouge in July, 1949, over the speed of the Ford assembly line, he noted that "sometimes the constraints of work explode with geyser suddenness."[4] And as Bell's *Work and Its Discontents* (1956) bore witness that "the revolt against work is widespread and takes many forms,"[5] so had Walker and Guest's Harvard study, *The Man on the Assembly Line* (1953), testified to the resentment and resistance of the men on the line. Similarly, and from a writer with much working class experience himself, was Harvey Swados' "The Myth of the Happy Worker," published in *The Nation*, August, 1957.

Workers and the unions continued to be at odds over conditions of work during this period. In auto, for example, the 1955 contract between the United Auto Workers and General Motors did nothing to check the "speed-up" or facilitate the settlement of local shop grievances. Immediately after Walter Reuther made public the terms of the contract he'd just signed, over 70% of GM workers went on strike. An even larger percentage "wildcatted" after the signing of the 1958 agreement because the union had again refused to do anything about the work itself. For the same reason, the auto workers walked off their jobs again in 1961, closing every GM and a large number of Ford plants.[6]

Paul Jacobs' *The State of the Unions*, Paul Saltan's *The Disenchanted Unionist*, and B.J. Widick's *The Triumphs and Failures of Unionism in the United States* were some of the books written in the early 1960's by pro-union figures, usually former activists, who were disenchanted with what they had only lately and partially discovered to be the role of the unions. A black worker, James Boggs, clarified the process in a sentence: "Looking backwards, one will find that side by side with the fight to control production, has gone the struggle to control the union, and that the decline has taken place simultaneously on both fronts."[7] What displeased Boggs, however, was lauded by business. In the same year that his remarks were published, *Fortune*, American capital's most authoritative magazine, featured as a cover story in its May, 1963 issue Max Way's "Labor Unions Are Worth the Price."

But by the next year, the persistent dissatisfaction of workers was beginning to assume public prominence, and a June 1964 *Fortune* article reflected the growing pressure for union action: "Assembly-line monotony, a cause reminiscent of Charlie Chaplin's *Modern Times*, is being revived as a big issue in Detroit's 1964 negotiations,"[8] it reported.

In the middle-1960's another phenomenon was dramatically and violently making itself felt. The explosions in the black ghettoes appeared to most to have no connection with the almost underground fight over factory conditions. But many of the participants in the insurrections in Watts, Detroit and other cities were fully employed, according to arrest records.[9] The struggle for dignity in one's work certainly involved the black workers, whose oppression was, as in all other areas, greater than that of non-black workers. Jessie Reese, a Steelworkers' union organizer, described the distrust his fellow blacks felt toward him as an agent of the union: "To organize that black boy out there today you've got to prove yourself to him, because he don't believe nothing you say."[10] Authority was resented, not color. [11]

Turning to more direct forms of opposition to an uncontrolled and alien job world, we encounter the intriguing experience of Bill Watson, who spent 1968 in an auto plant near Detroit. Distinctly post-union in practice, he witnessed the systematic, planned efforts of the workers to substitute their own production plans and methods for those of management. He described it as "a regular phenomenon" brought out by the refusal of management and the UAW to listen to workers' suggestions as to modifications and improvements in the product. "The contradictions of planning and producing poor quality, beginning as the stuff of jokes, eventually became a source of anger...temporary deals unfolded between inspection and assembly and between assembly and trim, each with planned sabotage...the result was stacks upon stacks of motors awaiting repair...it was almost impossible to move...the entire six-cylinder assembly and inspection operation was moved away—where new workers were brought in to man it. In the most dramatic way, the necessity of taking the product out of the hands of laborers who insisted on planning the product became overwhelming."[12]

The extent and coordination of the workers' own organization in the plant described by Watson was very advanced indeed, causing him to wonder if it wasn't a glimpse of a new social form altogether, arising from the failure of unionism. Stanley Weir, writing at this time of similar if less highly developed phenomena, found that "in thousands of industrial establishments across the nation, workers have developed informal, underground unions," due to the deterioration or lack of improvement in the quality of their daily job lives."[13]

Until the 1970's—and very often still—the wages and benefits dimension of a work dispute, that part over which the union would become involved, received almost all the attention. In 1965 Thomas Brooks observed that the "apathy" of the union member stemmed from precisely this false emphasis: "...grievances on matters apart from wages are either ignored or lost in the limbo of union bureaucracy."[14] A few years later, Dr. David Whitter, industrial consultant to GM, admitted, "That isn't all they want; it's all they can get."[15]

As the 1960's drew to a close, some of the more perceptive business observers were about to discover this distinction and were soon forced by pressure from below to discuss it publicly. While the October, 1969 *Fortune* stressed the preferred emphasis on wages as the issue in Richard Armstrong's "Labor 1970: Angry, Aggressive, Acquisitive" (while admitting that the rank and file was in revolt "against its own leadership, and in important ways against society itself"), the July, 1970 issue carried Judson Gooding's "Blue-Collar Blues on the Assembly Line: Young auto workers find job disciplines harsh and uninspiring, and they vent their feeling through absenteeism, high turnover, shoddy work, and even sabotage. It's time for a new look at who's down on the line."

With the 1970's there has at last begun to dawn the realization that on the most fundamental issue, control of the work process, the unions and the workers are very much in opposition to each other. A St. Louis Teamster commented that traditional labor practice has as a rule involved "giving up items involving workers' control over the job in exchange for cash and fringe benefits."[16] Acknowledging the disciplinary function of the union, he elaborated on this time-honored bargaining: "Companies have been willing to give up large amounts of money to the union in return for the union's guarantee of no work stoppages." Daniel Bell wrote in 1973 that the trade union movement has never challenged the organization of work itself, and summed up the issue thusly: "The crucial point is that however much an improvement there may have been in wage rates, pension conditions, supervision, and the like, the conditions of work themselves—the control of pacing, the assignments, the design and layout of work—are still outside the control of the worker himself."[17]

Although the position of the unions is usually ignored, since 1970 there has appeared a veritable deluge of articles and books on the impossible to ignore rebellion against impossible work roles. From the covers of a few national magazines: Barbara Garson's "The Hell With Work," *Harper's*, June 1972; *Life* magazine's "Bored On the Job: Industry Contends with Apathy and Anger onthe Assembly Line," September 1, 1972; and "Who Wants to Work?" in the March 26, 1973 *Newsweek*. Other articles have brought out the important fact that the disaffection is definitely not confined to industrial workers. To cite just a few: Judson Gooding's "The Fraying White Collar" in *The Nation* of September 13, 1971, Marshall Kilduff's "Getting Back at a Boss: The New Underground Papers," in the December 27, 1971 *San Francisco Chronicle*, and Seashore and Barnowe's "Collar Color Doesn't Count," in the August, 1972 *Psychology Today*.

In 1971 *The Workers*, by Kenneth Lasson, was a representative book, focusing on the growing discontent via portraits of nine blue-collar workers. The *Job Revolution* by Judson Gooding appeared in 1972, a management-oriented discussion of liberalizing work management in order to contain employee pressure. The Report of the Special Task Force to the Secretary of Health, Education, and Welfare on the problem, titled *Work in America*, was published in 1973. Page 19 of the study admits the major facts: "...absenteeism, wildcat strikes, turnover, and industrial sabotage [have] become an increasingly significant part of the cost of doing business." The scores of people interviewed by Studs Terkel in his *Working: People Talk About What They Do All Day and How They Feel about What They Do* (1974), reveal a depth to the work revolt that is truly devastating. His book uncovers a nearly unanimous contempt for work and the fact that active resistance is fast replacing the quiet desperation silently suffered by most. From welders to editors to former executives, those questioned spoke up readily as to their feelings of humiliation and frustration.

If most of the literature of "the revolt against work" has left the unions out of their discussions, a brief look at some features of specific worker actions from 1970 through 1973 will help underline the comments made above concerning the necessarily anti-union nature of this revolt.

During March, 1970, a wildcat strike of postal employees, in defiance of union orders, public employee anti-strike law, and federal injunctions, spread across the country, disabling post offices in more than 200 cities and towns.[18] In New York, where the strike began, an effigy of Gus Johnson, president of the letter carriers' union local there, was hung at a tumultuous meeting on March 21 where the national union leaders were called "rats" and "creeps."[19] In many locations, the workers decided to not handle business mail, as part of their work action, and only the use of thousands of National Guardsmen ended the strike, major issues of which were the projected layoff of large numbers of workers and methods of work. In July, 1971, New York postal workers tried to renew their strike activity in the face of a contract proposal made by the new letter carrier president, Vincent Sombrotto. At the climax of a stormy meeting of 3,300 workers, Sombrotto and a lieutenant were chased from the hall down 33rd Street, narrowly escaping 200 enraged union members, who accused them of "selling out" the membership.[20]

Returning to the Spring of 1970, 100,000 Teamsters in 16 cities wildcatted between March and May to overturn a national contract signed March 23 by IBT President Fitzsimmons. The ensuing violence in the Middle West and West coast was extensive, and in Cleveland involved no less than a thirty-day blockade of main city thoroughfares and 67 million dollars in damages.[21]

On May 8, 1970, a large group of hard-hat construction workers assaulted peace demonstrators in Wall Street and invaded Pace College and City Hall itself to attack students and others suspected of not supporting the prosecution of the Vietnam war. The riot, in fact, was supported and directed by construction firm executives and union leaders,[22] in all likelihood to channel worker hostility away from themselves. Perhaps alone in its comprehension of the incident was public television (WNET, New York) and its "Great American Dream Machine" program aired May 13. A segment of that production uncovered the real job grievances that apparantly underlay the affair. Intelligent questioning revealed, in a very few minutes, that "commie punks" were not wholly the cause of their outburst, as an outpouring of gripes about unsafe working conditions, the strain of the work pace, the fact that they could be fired at any given moment, etc., was recorded. The head of the New York building trades union, Peter Brennan, and his union official colleagues were feted at the White House on May 26 for their patriotism—and for diverting the workers?—and Brennan was later appointed Secretary of Labor.

In July, 1970, on a Wednesday afternoon swing shift a black auto worker at a Detroit Chrysler plant pulled out an M-1 carbine and killed three supervisory personnel before he was subdued by UAW committeemen. It should be added that two others were shot dead in separate auto plant incidents within weeks of the Johnson shooting spree, and that in May, 1971, a jury found Johnson innocent because of insanity after visiting and being shocked by what they considered the maddening conditions at Johnson's place of work.[23]

The sixty-seven day strike at General Motors by the United Auto Workers in the Fall of 1970 is a classic example of the anti-employee nature of the conventional strike, perfectly illustrative of the ritualized manipulation of the individual which is repeated so often and which changes absolutely nothing about the nature of work.

A *Wall Street Journal* article of October 29, 1970 discussed the reasons why union and management agreed on the necessity of a strike. The UAW saw that a walk-out would serve as "an escape valve for the frustrations of workers bitter about what they consider intolerable working conditions," and a long strike would "wear down the expectations of members." The *Journal* went on to point out that, "among those who do understand the need for strikes to ease intra-union pressures are many company bargainers... They are aware that union leaders may need such strikes to get contracts ratified and get re-elected."[24] Or, as William Serrin succinctly put it: "A strike, by putting the workers on the street, rolls the steam out of them—it reduces their demands and thus brings agreement and ratification; it also solidifies the authority of the union hierarchy."[25]

Thus, the strike was called. The first order of the negotiating business was the dropping of all job condition demands, which were only raised in the first place as a public relations gesture to the membership. With this understood, the discussions and publicity centered around wages and early retirement benefits exclusively, and the charade played itself out to its pre-ordained end. "The company granted each demand [UAW president] Woodcock had made, demands he could have had in September."[26] Hardly surprising, then, that GM loaned the union $23 million per month during the strike.[27] As Serrin conceded, the company and the union are not even adversaries, much less enemies.[28]

In November, 1970, the fuel deliverers of New York City, exasperated by their union president's resistance to pleas for action, gave him a public beating. Also in New York, in the following March the Yellow Cab drivers ravaged a Teamsters' Union meeting hall in Manhattan in response to their union officials' refusal to yield the floor to rank and file speakers.

In January, 1971, the interns at San Francisco General Hospital struck, solely over hospital conditions and patient care. Eschewing any ties to organized labor, their negotiating practice was to vote publicly on each point at issue, with all interns present.

The General Motors strike of 1970 discussed above in no way dealt with the content of jobs.[29] Knowing that it would face no challenge from the UAW, especially, it was thought, so soon after a strike and its cathartic effects, GM began in 1971 a coordinated effort at speeding up the making of cars, under the name General Motors Assembly Division, or GMAD. The showplace plant for this re-organization was the Vega works at Lordstown, Ohio, where the work-force was 85% white and the average age 27. With cars moving down the line almost twice as fast as in pre-GMAD days, workers resorted to various forms of on the job resistance to the terrific pace. GM accused them of sabotage and had to shut down the line several times. Some estimates set the number of deliberately disabled cars as high as 500,000 for the period of December, 1971 to March, 1972, when a strike was finally called following a 97% affirmative vote of Lordstown's Local 1112. But a three-week strike failed to check the speed of the line, the union, as always, having no more desire than management to see workers effectively challenging the control of production. The membership lost all confidence in the union; Gary Bryner, the 29-year-old president of Local 1112 admitted: "They're angry with the union; when I go through the plant I get catcalls."[30]

In the GMAD plant at Norwood, Ohio, a strike like that at Lordstown broke out in April and lasted until September, 1971. The 174 days constituted the longest walkout in GM history.[31] The Norwood workers had voted 98% in favor of striking in the previous February, but the UAW had forced the two locals to go out separately, first Lordstown, and later Norwood, thus isolating them and protecting the GMAD program. Actually, the anti-worker efforts of the UAW go even further back, to September of 1971, when the Norwood Local 674 was put in receivership, or taken over, by the central leadership when members had tried to confront GMAD over the termination of their seniority rights.

In the summer of 1973, three wildcat strikes involving Chrysler facilities in Detroit took place in less than a month. Concerning the successful one-day wildcat at the Jefferson assembly plant, UAW vice president Doug Fraser said Chrysler had made a critical mistake in "appeasing the workers" and the Mack Avenue walkout was effectively suppressed when a crowd of "UAW local union officers and committeemen, armed with baseball bats and clubs, gathered outside of the plant gates to 'urge' the workers to return."[32]

October, 1973 brought the signing of a new three-year contract between Ford and the UAW. But with the signing appeared fresh evidence that workers intend to involve themselves in decisions concerning their work lives: "Despite the agreement, about 7,700 workers left their jobs at seven Ford plants when the strike deadline was reached, some because they were unhappy with the secrecy surrounding the new agreement."[33]

With these brief remarks on a very small number of actions by workers, let us try to arrive at some understanding of the overall temper of American wage-earners since the mid-1960's.

Sidney Lens found that the number of strikes during 1968, 1969, and 1971 was extremely high, and that only the years 1937, 1944–45 and 1952-53 showed comparable totals.[34] More interesting is the growing tendency of strikers to reject the labor contracts negotiated for them. In those contracts in which the Federal Mediation and Conciliation Service took a hand (the only ones for which there are statistics), contract rejections rose from 8.7% of the cases in 1964, to 10% in 1965, to 11% in 1966, to an amazing 14.2% in 1967, levelling off since then to about 12% annually.[35] And the ratio of work stoppages occurring during the period when a contract was in effect has changed, which is especially significant when it is remembered that most contracts specifically forbid strikes. Bureau of Labor Statistics figures reveal that while about one-third of all stoppages in 1968 occurred under existing agreements, "an alarming number,"[36] (almost two-fifths of them) in 1972 took place while contracts were in effect.[37] In 1973 Aronowitz provided a good summary: "The configuration of strikes since 1967 is unprecedented in the history of American workers. The number of strikes as a whole, as well as rank-and-file rejections of proposed union settlements with employers, and wildcat actions has exceeded that in any similar period in the modern era."[38] And as Sennett and Cobb, writing in 1971, made clear, the period has involved "the most turbulent rejection of organized union authority among young workers."[39]

The 1970 GM strike was mentioned as an example of the usefulness of a sham struggle in safely releasing pent-up employee resentment. The nation-wide telephone workers' strike of July, 1971 is another example, and the effects of the rising tide of anti-union hostility can also be seen in it. Rejecting a Bell System offer of a 30% wage increase over three years, the Communication Workers' union called a strike, publicly announcing that the only point at issue was that "we need 31 to 32 per cent,"[40] as union president Joseph Beirne put it. After a six-day walkout, the 1% was granted, as was a new Bell policy requiring all employees to join the union and remain in good standing as a condition of employment. But while the CWA was granted the standard "union-shop" status, a rather necessary step for the fulfillment of its role as a discipline agent of the work force, thousands of telephone workers refused to return to their jobs, in some cases staying out for weeks in defiance of CWA orders.

The calling of the 90-day wage-price freeze on August 15 was in large part a response to the climate of worker unruliness and independence, typified by the defiant phone workers. Aside from related economic considerations, the freeze and the ensuing controls were adopted because the unions needed government help in restraining the workers. Sham strikes clearly lose their effectiveness if employees refuse to play their assigned roles remaining, for example, on strike on their own.

George Meany, head of the AFL-CIO, had been calling for a wage-price freeze since 1969,[41] and in the weeks prior to August 15 had held a number of very private meetings with President Nixon.[42] Though he was compelled to publicly decry the freeze as "completely unfair to the worker" and "a bonanza to big business," he did not even call for an excess profits tax; he did come out strongly for a permanent wage-price control board and labor's place on it, however.

It seems clear that business leaders understood the need for government assistance. In September, a *Fortune* article proclaimed that "A system of wage-price review boards is the best hope for breaking the cost-push momentum that individual unions and employers have been powerless to resist."[43] As workers try to make partial compensation for their lack of autonomy on the job by demanding better wages and benefits, the only approved concessions, they create obvious economic pressure especially in an inflationary period. Arthur M. Louis, in November's *Fortune*, realized that the heat had been on labor officials for some time. Speaking of the "rebellious rank and file" of longshoremen, miners, and steelworkers, he said, "Long before President Nixon announced his wage-price freeze, many labor leaders were calling for stabilization, if only to get themselves off the hook."[44]

A *Fortune* editorial of January (1972) predicted that by the fall, a national "wave of wildcat strikes" might well occur and the labor members of the tripartite control board would resign.[45] In fact, Meany and Woodcock quit the Pay Board much earlier in the year than that, due precisely to the rank and file's refusal to support the plainly anti-labor wage policies of the board. Though Fitzsimmons of the Teamsters stayed on, and the controls continued, through a total of four "Phases" until early 1974, the credibility of the controls program was crippled, and its influence waned rapidly. Though the program was brought to a premature end, the Bureau of Labor Statistics gave its ceiling on wage increases much of the credit for the fact that the number of strikes in 1972 was the smallest in five years.[46]

During "Phase One" of the controls, the 90-day freeze, David Deitch wrote that "the new capitalism requires a strong, centralized trade union movement with which to bargain." He made explicit exactly what kind of "strength" would be needed: "The labor bureaucracy must ultimately silence the rank and file if it wants to join in the tripartite planning, in the same sense that the wildcat strike cannot be tolerated."[47]

In this area, too, members of the business community have shown an understanding of the critical role of the unions. In May 1970, within hours of the plane crash that claimed UAW chief Walter Reuther, there was publicly expressed corporate desire for a replacement who could continue to effectively contain the workers. "It's taken a strong man to keep the situation under control," Virgil Boyd, Chrysler vice-chairman, told the *New York Times*. "I hope that whoever his successor is can exert great internal discipline."[48] Likewise, *Fortune* bewailed the absence of a strong union in the coalfields, in a 1971 article subtitled, "The nation's fuel supply, as well as the industry's prosperity, depends on a union that has lost control of its members."[49]

Despite the overall failure of the wage control program, the government has been helping the unions in several other ways. Since 1970, for example, it has worked to reinforce the conventional strike—again, due to its important safety-valve function. In June 1970, the U.S. Supreme Court ruled that an employer could obtain an injunction to force employees back to work when a labor agreement contains a no-strike pledge and an arbitration clause. "The 1970 decision astonished many observers of the labor relations scene,"[50] directly reversing a 1962 decision of the Court, which ruled that such walkouts were merely labor disputes and not illegal. Also in 1970, during the four-month General Electric strike, Schenectady, New, York, officials "pleaded with non-union workers to refrain from crossing picket lines on the grounds that such action might endanger the peace."[51] A photo of the strike scene in *Fortune* was captioned, "Keeping workers out—workers who were trying to cross picket lines and get to their jobs—became the curious task of Schenectady policemen."[52]

A Supreme Court decision in 1972 indicated how far state power will go to protect the spectacle of union strikes. Four California Teamsters were ordered reinstated with five years' back pay as "a unanimous Supreme Court ruled (November 7, 1972) that it is unfair labor practice for an employer to fire a worker solely for taking part in a strike."[53] Government provides positive as well as negative support to approved walkouts, too. An 18-month study by the Wharton School of Finance and Commerce found that welfare benefits, unemployment compensation, and food stamps to strikers mean that "the American taxpayer has assumed a significant share of the cost of prolonged work stoppages."[54]

But in some areas, unions would rather not even risk offical strikes. The United Steelworkers of American—which allows only union officals to vote on contract ratifications, by the way—agreed with the major steel companies in March, 1973, that only negotiations and arbitration would be used to resolve differences. The Steelworkers' contract approved in April, 1974, declared that the no-strike policy would be in effect until at least 1980.[55] A few days before, in March, a federal court threw out a suit filed by rank and file steelworkers, ruling in sum that the union needn't be democratic in reaching its agreements with management.[56]

David Deitch, quoted above, said that the stability of the system required a centralized union structure. The process of centralization has been a fact and its acceleration has followed the increasing militancy of wage-earners since the middle-1960's. A June, 1971, article in the federal *Monthly Labor Review* discussed the big increase in union mergers over the preceding three years.[57] In a speech made on July 5, 1973, Longshoremen's president Harry Bridges called for the formation of "one big, national labor movement or federation."[58]

The significance of this centralization movement is that it places the individual even further from a position of possible influence over the union hierarchy—at a time when he is more and more likely to be obliged to join a union as a condition of employment. The situation is beginning to resemble in some ways the practice in National Socialist Germany, of requiring the membership of all workers in "one big, national labor movement or federation," the Labor Front. In the San Francisco Bay area, for example in 1969, "A rare—and probably unique—agreement that will require all the employees of a public agency to join a union or pay it the equivalent of union dues was reported in Oakland by the East Bay Regional Park District."[59] And in the same area this process was upheld in 1973: "A city can require its employees to pay the equivalent of initiation fees and dues to a union to keep their jobs, arbitrator Robert E. Burns has ruled in a precedent-setting case involving the city of Hayward."[60] This direction is certainly not limited to public employees, according to the Department of Labor. Their "What Happens When Everyone Organizes" article implied the inevitability of total unionization.

Though a discussion of the absence of democracy in unions is outside the scope of this essay, it is important to emphasize the lack of control possessed by the rank and file. In 1961 Joel Seidman commented on the subjection of the typical union membership: "It is hard to read union constitutions without being struck by the many provisions dealing with the obligations and the disciplining of members, as against the relatively small number of sections concerned with members' rights within the organization."[61] Two excellent offerings on the subject written in the 1970's are *Autocracy and Insurgency in Organized Labor* by Burton Hall[62] and "Apathy and Other Axioms: Expelling the Union Dissenter from History," by H. W. Benson.[63]

Relatively unthreatened by memberships, the unions have entered into ever-closer relations with government and business. A Times-Post Service story of April, 1969, disclosed a three-day meeting between AFL-CIO leadership and top Nixon administration officials, shrouded in secrecy at the exclusive Greenbriar spa. "Big labor and big government have quietly arranged an intriguing tryst this week in the mountains of West Virginia...for a private meeting involving at least half a dozen cabinet members."[64] Similarly, a surprising *New York Times* article appearing on the last day of 1972 is worth quoting for the institutionalizing of government-labor ties it augurs: "President Nixon has offered to put a labor union representative at a high level in every federal government department, a well-informed White House official has disclosed. The offer, said to be unparalleled in labor history, was made to union members on the National Productivity Commission, including George Meany, president of the AFL-CIO, and Frank E. Fitzsimmons, president of the IBT, at a White House meeting last week...labor sources said that they understood the proposal to include an offer to place union men at the assistant secretary level in all relevant government agencies...should the President's offer be taken up, it would mark a signal turning point in the traditional relations between labor and government."[65]

In Oregon, the activities of the Associated Oregon Industries, representing big business and the Oregon AFL-CIO, by the early '70's reflected a close working relationship between labor and management on practically everything. Joint lobbying efforts, against consumer and environmentalist proposals especially, and other forms of cooperation led to an exchange of even speakers at each other's conventions in the Fall of 1971. On September 2,the president of the AOI, Phil Bladine, addressed the AFL-CIO; on September 18, AFL-CIO president Ed Whalen spoke before the AOI.[66] In California, as in many other states, the pattern has been very much the same, with labor and business working together to attack conservationists in 1972 and defeat efforts to reform political campaign spending in 1974, for example.[67]

Also revealing is the "Strange Bedfellows From Labor, Business Own Dominican Resort" article on the front page of the May 15, *Wall Street Journal* by Jonathon Kwitney. Among the leading stockholders in the 15,000 acre Punta Cana, Dominican Republic resort and plantation are George Meany and Lane Kirkland, president and secretary-treasurer of the AFL-CIO, and Keith Terpe, Seafarers' Union official, as well as leading officers of Seatrain Lines, Inc., which employs members of Terpe's union.

Not seen for what they are, the striking cases of mounting business-labor-government collusion and cooperation have largely been overlooked. But those in a position to see that the worker is more and more actively intolerant of a daily work life beyond his control, also realize that even closer cooperation is necessary. In early 1971 *Personnel,* the magazine of the American Management Association, said that "it is perhaps time for a marriage of convenience between the two [unions and management]," [68] for the preservation of order. Pointing out, however, that many members "tend to mistrust the union."[69]

The reason for this "mistrust," as we have seen, is the historical refusal of unions to interfere with management's control of work. The AFL-CIO magazine, *The American Federationist,* admitted labor's lack of interest and involvement in an article in the January, 1974 issue entitled "Work is Here to Stay, Alas." And the traditional union position on the matter is why, in turn, C. Jackson Grayson, Dean of the School of Business Admistration at Southern Methodist University and former chairman of the Price Commission, called in early 1974 for union-management collaboration. The January 12 issue of *Business Week* contains his call for a symbolic dedication on July 4, 1976, "with the actual signing of a document—Declaration of Interdependence" between labor and business, "inseparably linked in the productivity quest."

Productivity—output per hour of work—has of course fallen due to worker dissatisfaction and unrest. A basic indication of the continuing revolt against work are the joint campaigns for higher productivity, such as the widely publicized US Steel-United Steelworkers efforts. A special issue on productivity in *Business Week* for September 9, 1972, highlighted the problem, pointing out also the opposition workers had for union-backed drives of this kind.[70] Closely related to low productivity, it seems, is the employee resistance to working overtime, even during economic recession. The refusal of thousands of Ford workers to work overtime prompted a Ford executive in April, 1974 to say, "We're mystified by the experience in light of the general economic situation."[71] Also during April, the Labor Department reported that "the productivity of American workers took its biggest drop on record as output slumped in all sectors of the economy during the first quarter."[72]

In 1935 the NRA issued the Henderson Report, which counseled that "unless something is done soon, they [the workers] intend to take things into their own hands."[73] Something was done: the hierarchical, national unions of the CIO finally appeared and stabilized relations. In the 1970's it may be that a limited form of worker participation in management decisions will be required to prevent employees from "taking things into their own hands." Irving Bluestone, head of the UAW's GM department, predicted in early 1972 that some form of participation would be necessary, under union-management control, of course.[74] As Arnold Tannenbaum of the Institute for Social Research in Michigan pointed out in the late 1960's, ceding some power to workers can be an excellent means of increasing their subjection, if it succeeds in giving them a sense of involvement.[75]

But it remains doubtful that token participation will in any way assuage the worker's alienation. More likely, it will underline it and make even clearer the true nature of the union-management relationship, which will still obtain. It may be more probable that traditional union institutions, such as the paid, professional stratum of officials and representatives, monopoly of membership guaranteed by management, and the labor contract itself will be increasingly re-examined[76] as workers continue to strive to take their work lives into their own hands.

NEW YORK, NEW YORK

"Amid All the Camaraderie is Much Looting this Time; Seeing the City Disappear." — *Wall Street Journal* headline, July 15, 1977

The *Journal* went on to quote a cop on what he saw, as the great Bastille Day break-out unfolded: "People are going wild in the borough of Brooklyn. They are looting stores by the carload." Another cop added later: "Stores were ripped open. Others have been leveled. After they looted, they burned."

At about 9:30 p.m. on July 13 the power went out in New York for 24 hours. During that period the complete impotence of the state in our most "advanced" urban space could hardly have been made more transparent.

As soon as the lights went out, cheers and shouts and loud music announced the liberation of huge sections of the city. The looting and burning commenced immediately, with whole families joining in the "carnival spirit." In the University Heights section of the Bronx, a Pontiac dealer lost the 50 new cars in his showroom. In many areas, tow trucks and other vehicles were used to tear away the metal gates from stores. Many multi-story furniture businesses were completely emptied by neighborhood residents.

Despite emergency alerts for the state troopers, FBI and National Guard, there was really nothing authority could do, and they knew it. A New York Times editorial of July 16 somewhat angrily waved aside the protests of those who wondered why there was almost no intervention on the side of property. "Are you kidding?" the Times snorted, pointing out that such provocation would only have meant that the entire city would still be engulfed in riots, adding that the National Guard is a "bunch of kids" who wouldn't have had a chance.

The plundering was completely multi-racial, with white, black and Hispanic businesses cleaned out and destroyed throughout major parts of Manhattan, Brooklyn, Queens and the Bronx. Not a single "racial incident" was reported during the uprising, while newspaper pictures and TV news bore witness to the variously-colored faces emerging from the merchants' windows and celebrating in the streets. Similarly, looting, vandalism, and attacks on police were not confined to the City proper; Mount Vernon, Yonkers and White Plains were among suburbs in which the same things happened, albeit on a smaller scale.

Rioting broke out in the Bronx House of Detention where prisoners started fires, seized dormitories, and almost escaped by ramming through a wall with a steel bed. Concerning the public, the Bronx District attorney fumed, "It's lawlessness. It's almost anarchy."

Officer Gary Parlefsky, of the 30th Precinct in Harlem, said that he and other cops came under fire from guns, bottles and rocks. "We were scared to death...but worse than that, a blue uniform didn't mean a thing. They couldn't understand why we were arresting them," he continued.

At a large store at 110th Street and Eighth Avenue, the doors were smashed open and dozens of people carried off appliances. A woman in her middle 50's walked into the store and said laughingly: "Shopping with no money required!"

Attesting to the atmosphere of a "collective celebration," as one worried columnist put it, a distribution center was spontaneously organized at a Brooklyn intersection, with piles of looted goods on display for the taking. This was shown briefly on an independent New York station, WPIX-TV, but not mentioned in the major newspapers.

The transformation of commodities into free merchandise was only aided by the coming of daylight, as the festivity and music continued. Mayor Beame, at a noon (July 15) press conference, spoke of the "night of terror," only to be mocked heartily by the continuing liberation underway throughout New York as he spoke.

Much, of course, was made of the huge contrast between the events of July, 1977 and the relatively placid, law-abiding New York blackout of November, 1965. One can only mention the obvious fact that the dominant values are now everywhere in shreds. The "social cohesion" of class society is evaporating; New York is no isolated example.

Of course, there has been a progressive decay in recent times of restraint, hierarchy, and the other enforced virtues; it hasn't happened all at once. Thus, in the 1960s, John Leggett (in his *Class, Race and Labor*) was surprised to learn upon examining the arrest records of those in the Detroit and Newark insurrections, that a great many of the participants were fully employed. This time, of the 176 people indicted as of August 8 in Brooklyn (1004 were arrested in the borough), 48 percent were regularly employed. (The same article in the August 9th *San Francisco Chronicle* where these figures appeared also pointed out that only "six grocery stores were looted while 39 furniture stores, 20 drug stores and 17 jewelry stores and clothing stores were looted.")

And there are other similarities to New York, naturally; *Life* magazine of August 4, 1967 spoke of the "carnival-like revel of looting" in Detroit, and Professor Edward Banfield commented that "Negroes and whites mingled in the streets (of Detroit) and looted amicably side by side..."

The main difference is probably one of scale and scope—that in New York virtually all areas, even suburbs, took the offensive and did so from the moment the lights went out. Over $1 billion was lost in the thousands of stores looted and burned, while the cops were paralyzed. During the last New York rioting, the "Martin Luther King" days of 1968, 32 cops were injured; in one day in July, 1977, 418 cops were injured.

The left—all of it—has spoken only of the high unemployment, the police brutality; has spoken of the people of New York only as objects, and pathetic ones at that! The gleaming achievements of the un-mediated/un-ideologized have all pigs scared shitless.

THE REFUSAL OF TECHNOLOGY

Of course everybody had to be given a personal code! How else could government do right by its citizens, keep track of the desires, tastes, preferences, purchases, commitments and above all location of a continent full of mobile, free individuals?

So don't dismiss the computer as a new type of fetters. Think of it rationally, as the most liberating device ever invented, the only tool capable of serving the multifarious needs of modern man.

Think of it, for a change, as him.

—*John Brunner*, The Shockwave Rider

Upon the utter destruction of wage-labor and the commodity, a new life will be situated and redefined, by the moment, in countless, unimagined forms. Launched by the abolition of every trace of authority and signified by the delights and surprises of an infinity of gift-creations, freely, spontaneously expressed by everyone.

Concepts like "economy," "exchange," "production" will have no meaning. (What is worth preserving from this lunatic order?) Perhaps mobile celebrations will replace our sense of cities, maybe even language will be obsolete.

But there are those who see revolutionary transformation in rather a different light; for them the Brunner quote is, tragically, not much of a burlesque.

Consider—if your stomach is strong—the following, from a 1980 ultra-leftist flyer, typical of the high-tech approach to the revolutionary question:

The development of computer technologies, now a threat to our job security, could be used to develop a network of global communications. In this way, our needs can be directly coordinated with the available labor-power and raw materials.

Leaving aside the pro-wage-labor concern for our job security, we find human activity (electronically) treated as so much "available labor power." Is this the language of desire? Could freedom, love and play flourish along such lines?

This computerized prescription is filled by taking "control of the global social reproduction network..." Capitalism, it need hardly be added, can be defined with some precision as the global social reproduction network.

Looking at the foundations of "advanced" technology—which our ultra-leftists, in their instrumentalism, always wish to ignore— even the most visionary of intentions would founder. High-tech as a vehicle, far from aiding a qualitative regeneration, denies the possibility of visionary development. The "great height now made possible" by computers and the like is, alas, only an expression of the perverse logic of historic class rule.

Technology has not developed neutrally, as if in the right hands it could benignly transform reality into something importantly different. The means and methods of social reproduction are necessarily in keeping with the stability of a social order. The factory system expressed the need for a disciplined proletariat; more modern modes progressively extend this "civilizing" process via specialized, usually centralized, technologies. The individual is everywhere reduced by the instruments of capitalism, as surely as by its wage-labor/commodity essence.

The purveyors of "alternative technology," it should be noted, promote a different illusion. This illusion lies in ideologizing fragments of possibly acceptable technology while ignoring that which will shape all of the future, class struggles.

Simple techniques for growing a huge amount of food in a few hours per year, for instance, are fraught with extremely significant implications; they present, in fact, some of the practical possibilities of living life exquisitely—as in a garden. But they can become real only if linked to the gigantic, necessary destruction of a world which impedes every utopian project.

Cioran asks, "If 'progress' is so great an evil, how is it that we do nothing to free ourselves from it without further delay?" In fact, this "freeing" is well underway, as seen in the massive "turn-off" felt toward its continuance.

General Dynamics vice-president Veliotis gave vent to a bitter ruling class frustration of the subject (summer 1980):

"I, for one, would be delighted if our vocational schools would bring us graduates who, if not trained, were simply trainable—could understand basic manufacturing processes, who could do shop math, could use standard tools and gauges."

More fundamental yet is a growing refusal to participate in education at all, given its direct linkage to "progress." The drop-out rate in

NYC high schools is now over 50%. The drop-out rate for all California high schools has risen from 12% in 1970 to 22% in 1980, occasioning predictions of "angry future workers and high juvenile crime rates."

The relationship between technology and education is also apt for the reason the latter provides, in its progression, such a useful, if obvious, analogy to the former. The fragmentation of knowledge into separate, artificially constructed fields constitutes the modern university—and social intelligence in general—in its ridiculous division of labor. This is the perfect analogy to technology itself; rather, it is more, inasmuch as both clearly work in tandem toward the ever-shrunken individual, dominated by a contrived, fractionalized scale of "information." The ignorance thus engendered and enforced reminds us of Khayati's allusion to the university: "Everything is said about our society except what it is."

Government thinker Willis Harman writes of the coming "information society," based on "revolutionizing everyday life with microcomputers." A horrible history surfaces with these words, as well as a forewarning of our future as cast by all similar techno-junkies, benevolent and otherwise.

Finally we return to the personal, which is of course the real terrain of the revolutionary axis. A character in Bellow's *Mr. Sammler's Planet* wonders:

And what is "common" about the "common life?" What if (we) were to do with "common life" what Einstein did with matter? Finding its energetics, uncovering its radiance.

The radiance and energetics will be there when we are all that "Einstein"; when every productivist, standardized separation—and every other mediation ("coordinated" or not)—is destroyed by us forever.

Everything in the past and present is waiting, waiting to detonate.

ANTI-WORK AND THE STRUGGLE FOR CONTROL

The debacle of the air controllers' strike and the growing difficulties unions are having in attracting new members (and holding new ones — decertification elections have increased for the last 10 years)[1] are two phenomena that could be used to depict American workers as quite tamed overall and adjusted to their lot. But such a picture of conservative stasis would be quite unfaithful to the reality of the work culture, which is now so *un*-tamed as to be evoking unprecedented attention and countermeasures.

Before tackling the subject of anti-work, a few words on the status of business might be in order. Bradshaw and Vogel's *Corporations and Their Critics* sees enterprise today as "faced by uncertainty and hostility on every hand." In fact, this fairly typical book finds that "latent mistrust has grown to the point at which lack of confidence in business's motives has become the overwhelming popular response to the role of the large corporation in the United States."[2] An early '81 survey of 24,000 prominent students, as determined by *Who's Who Among American High School Students,* showed a strong anti-business sentiment; less than 20 percent of the 24,000 agreed, for example, with the proposition that most companies charge fair prices.[3] Not surprising, then, are Peter Berger's conclusions about current attitudes. His "New Attack on the Legitimacy of Business" is summed up, in part, thusly: "When people genuinely believe in the 'rightness' of certain social arrangements, those arrangements are experienced as proper and worthy of support — that is, as legitimate. . . American business once enjoyed this kind of implicit social charter. It does not today."[4]

Within business, one begins to see the spread of work refusal. *Nation's Business* strikes what has become a familiar chord in its introduction to Dr. H.J. Freudenberger's "How to Survive Burn-Out": "For many business people, life has lost its meaning. Work has become mere drudgery, off-hours are spent in a miasma of dullness."[5] Similar is *Datamation's* "Burnout: Victims and Avoidances," because this disabling trauma "seems to be running rampant" among data processors.[6] Veninga and Spradley's *The Work Stress Condition: How to Cope with Job Burnout*[7] was condensed by the December 1981 *Reader's Digest.*

To continue in this bibliographic vein, it is worth noting that the sharp increase in scholarly articles such as Kahn's "Work, Stress, and Individual Well-Being," Abdel-Halim's "Effects of Role Stress - Job Design - Technology Interaction on Employee Work Satisfaction," and Behling and Holcombe's "Dealing with Employee Stress."[8] *Studies in Occupational Stress*, a series initiated in 1978 by Cooper and Kasl, dates the formal study of this facet of organized misery.

There is other related evidence of aversion to work, including this reaction in its literal sense, namely a growth of illnesses such as job-related allergies and at least a significant part of the advancing industrial accident rate since the early '60s. Comes to mind the machinist who becomes ill by contact with machine oil, the countless employees who seem to be accident-prone in the job setting. We are just beginning to see some awareness of this sort of phenomenon, the consequences of which may be very significant.

And, of course, there is absenteeism, probably the most common sign of antipathy to work and a topic that has called forth a huge amount of recent attention from the specialists of wage-labor. Any number of remedies are hawked; Frank Kuzmits' offering "No Fault: A New Strategy for Absenteeism,"[9] for example. Deitsch and Dilts' "Getting Absent Workers Back on the Job: The Case of General Motors," puts the annual cost to GM at $1 billion plus, and observes that "Absenteeism is of increasing concern to management and organized labor alike."[10]

There are other well-known elements of the anti-work syndrome. The inability of some firms to get a shift working on time is a serious problem; this is why Nucor Corp. offers a 4 percent pay hike for each ton of steel produced above a target figure, up to a 100 percent pay bonus for those who show up as scheduled and work the whole shift. The amount of drinking and drug-taking on the job is another form of protest, occasioning a great proliferation of employee alcoholism and drug abuse programs by every sort of company.[11] Tersine and Russell confront the "staggering" employee theft phenomenon, observing that it has become "more widespread and professional in recent years."[12] Turnover (considered as a function of the quit rate and not due to layoffs, of course), very high since the early 1970s, has inched up further.[13]

All of these aspects come together to produce the much publicized productivity, or output per hour worked, crisis. Blake and Moulton provide some useful points; they recognize, for example, that the "declining productivity rate and the erosion of quality in industry have caused grave concern in this country" and that "industry is pouring

more money than ever into training and development," while "the productivity rate continues to fall." Further, "attitudes among workers
themselves," including, most basically, an "erosion of obedience to
authority," are seen as at the root of the problem. Unlike many confused mainstream analyses of the situation — or the typical leftist denial
of it as either a media chimera or an invention of the always all-powerful
corporations — our two professors can at least realize that "Basic to
the decline in productivity is the breakdown of the authority-obedience
means of control"; this trend, moreover, "which is one manifestation
of a broader social disorder. . .will continue indefinitely without corrective action," they say.[14]

Librarian R.S. Byrne gives a useful testimonial to the subject in
her compendious "Sources on Productivity," which lists some of the
huge outpouring of articles, reports, books, newletters, etc., from a
variety of willing helpers of business, including those of the Work in
America Institute, the American Productivity Center, the American
Center for the Quality of Work Life, and the Project on Technology,
Work and Character, to name a few. As Byrne notes, "One can scarcely
pick up any publication without being barraged by articles on the topic
written from every possible perspective." The reason for the outpouring
is of course available to her: "U.S. productivity growth has declined
continuously in the past 15 years and the trend appears to be
worsening."[15]

The August 1981 *Personnel Administrator,* devoted entirely to the
topic, declares that "Today poor productivity is the United States'
number one industrial problem."[16] *Administrative Management*
reasons, in George Crosby's "Getting Back to Basics on Productivity," that no progress can occur "until all individuals begin viewing
productivity as their own personal responsibility."[17] "How Deadly Is
the Productivity Disease?" asks Stanley Henrici recently in the *Harvard Business Review.*[18] An endless stream, virtually an obsession.

Dissatisfaction with work and the consequences of this have even
drawn the Pope's attention. John Paul II, in his *Laborem Exercens*
(Through Work) encyclical of September 1981, examines the idea of
work and the tasks of modern management. On a more prosaic level,
one discovers that growing employee alienation has forced a search
for new forms of work organization.[19] The December 1981 *Nation's
Business* has located a new consensus in favor of "more worker involvement in decision-making."[20] James O'Toole's *Making America
Work*[21] emphasizes the changed work culture with its low motivation
and prescribes giving workers the freedom to design their own jobs,
set their own work schedules and decide their own salaries.

The productivity crisis has clearly led to the inauguration of worker participation, in a burgeoning number of co-determination arrangements since the mid-70s. The May 11, 1981 *Business Week* announced the arrival of a new day in U.S. management with its cover story and special report, "The New Industrial Relations." Proclaiming the "almost unnoticed" ascendancy of a "fundamentally different way of managing people," it claimed that the "authoritarian" approach of the "old, crude workplace ethos" is definitely passing, aided "immeasurably" by the growing collaboration of the trade unions. "With the adversarial approach outmoded, the trend is toward more worker involvement in decisions on the shop floor — and more job satisfaction, tied to productivity."[22]

Shortly after this analysis, *Business Week's* "A Try at Steel-Mill Harmony" recounted the labor-management efforts being made between the U.S. steel industry and the United Steelworkers "to create a cooperative labor climate where it matters most: between workers and bosses on the mill floor." The arrangements, which are essentially production teams made up of supervisors, local union officials, and workers, were provided for in 1980 contracts with the nine major steel companies, but not implemented until after early 1981 union elections because of the unpopularity of the idea among many steelworkers. "The participation-team concept...was devised as a means of improving steel's sluggish productivity growth rate,"[23] the obvious reason for a climate of disfavor in the mills.

In a series of *Fortune* articles appearing in June, July, and August 1981, the new system of industrial organization is discussed in some depth. "Shocked by faltering productivity," according to *Fortune*, American's corporate managers have moved almost overnight toward the worker involvement approach (after long ignoring the considerable Northern European experience), which "challenges a system of authority and accountability that has served most of history."[24] With a rising hopefulness, big capital's leading magazine announces that "Companies which have had time to weigh the consequences of participative management are finding that it informs the entire corporate culture." Employees "are no longer just workers; they become the lowest level of management,"[25] it says, echoing such recent books as Myers' *Every Employee a Manager.*[26]

The bottom line of such programs, which also go by the name "quality of work life," is never lost sight of. G.T. Strippoli, a plant manager of the TRW Corp., provides the guiding principle: "The workers know that if I feel there's no payback to the company in the solution they arrive at, there will be a definite no. I'm not here to give away the store or run a country club."[27]

In effect, in about 100 auto manufacturing and assembly plants, the co-management replaces the traditional, failed ways of pushing productivity. Auto, with virtually nothing to lose, has jumped for the effort to get workers to help run the factories. "As far as I'm concerned, it's the only way to operate the business — there isn't another way in today's world," says GM President F. James McDonald.[28] United Auto Workers committeemen and stewards are key co-leaders with management in the drive to "gain higher product quality and lower absenteeism."[29] Similar is the campaign for worker involvement in the AT&T empire, formalized in the 1980 contract with the Communication Workers of America.

The fight to bolster output per hour is as much the unions' as it is management's; anti-work feelings are equally responsible for the decline of the bodyguards of capital as they are for the productivity crisis proper. AFL-CIO Secretary-Treasurer T.R. Donahue has found in the general productivity impasse the message that the time has come for a "limited partnership — a marriage of convenience" with business.[30] *Fortune* sees in formal collaboration "interesting possibilities for reversing the decline" of organized labor.[31]

Business Week's "Quality of Work Life: Catching On" observes that shop-floor worker participation and the rest of the QWL movement is "taking root in everyday life."[32] Along the same lines, the October 1981 issue of *Productivity* notes that half of 500 firms surveyed now have such involvement programs.[33]

William Ouchi's 1981 contribution to the industrial relations literature, *Theory Z*, cites recent research, such as that of Harvard's James Medoff and M.I.T.'s Kathryn Abraham, to point out the productivity edge that unionized companies in the United States have over non-union ones.[34] And David Lewin's "Collective Bargaining and the Quality of Work Life" argues for a further union presence in the QWL movement, based on organized labor's past ability to recognize the constraints of work and support the ultimate authority of the workplace.[35]

It is clear that unions hold the high ground in a growing number of these programs, and there seems to be a trend toward co-management at ever higher levels. Douglas Fraser, UAW president, sits on the board of directors at Chrysler — a situation likely to spread to the rest of auto — and the Teamsters union appears close to putting its representative on the board at Pan-American Airways. Joint labor-management efforts to boost productivity in construction have produced about a dozen important local collaborative setups involving the building trades unions, like Columbus' MOST (Management and Organized Labor Striving Together), Denver's Union Jack, and PEP (Planning Economic Progress) in Beaumont, Texas. *Business Horizons* editorialized in 1981 about "the newly established Industrial Board with such luminaries as Larry Shaprin of DuPont and Lane Kirkland of the AFL-CIO" as a "mild portent" of the growing formal collaboration.[36] The board, a reincarnation of the Labor Management Board that expired in 1978, is chaired by Kirkland and the chairman of Exxon, Clifton C. Garvin Jr.

The defeat in 1979 of the Labor Law Reform Act, which would have greatly increased government support to unionization, was seen by many as almost catastrophic given labor's organizing failures. But the economic crisis, perhaps especially in light of generous union concessions to the auto, airlines, rubber, trucking and other industries, may provide the setting for a "revitalization" of the national order including a real institutionalization of labor's social potential to contain the mounting anti-work challenge.[37]

There is already much pointing to such a possibility, beyond even the huge worker participation-QWL movement with its vital union component. The 1978 Trilateral Commission on comparative industrial relations spoke in very glowing terms about the development of neo-corporatist institutions (with German "co-determination" by unions and management as its model).[38] *Business Week* of June 30, 1980, a special issue on "The Reindustrialization of America," proclaimed that "nothing short of a new social contract" between business, labor and government, and "sweeping changes in basic institutions" could stem the country's industrial decline.[39] Thus, when the AFL-CIO's Kirkland called in late 1981 for a tripartite National Reindustrialization Board, a concept first specifically advanced by investment banker Felix Rohatyn, the recent theoretical precedents are well in place. One of the main underlying arguments by Rohatyn and others is that labor will need the state to help enforce its productivity programs in its partnership with management.

Thus would spreading "worker involvement" be utilized, but shepherded by the most powerful of political arrangements. Wilber and Jameson's "Hedonism and Quietism" puts the matter in general yet historical terms: "Ways must be found to revitalize mediating institutions from the bottom up. A good example is Germany's efforts to bring workers into a direct role in decision-making."[40]

A change of this sort might appear to be too directly counter to the ideology of the Reagan government, but it would actually be quite in line with the goal of renewed social control minus spending outlays.

Washington, after all, has been trying to reduce its instrumentalities because this giant network of programs is past its ability to coherently manage, just as its cutbacks also reflect the practical failure of government social pacification programs.

Meanwhile, the refusal of work grows. One final example is the extremely high teen-age unemployment rate, which continues to climb among all groups and is the object of a growing awareness that a very big element is simply a rejection of work, especially low-skill work, by the young.[41] And legion are the reports that describe the habits of teen-agers who do work as characterized by habitual tardiness, a chronic absenteeism, disrespect for supervisors and customers, etc. Which recalls the larger picture drawn by Frederick Herzberg in his "New Perspectives on the Will to Work": "the problem is work motivation — all over the world. It's simply a matter of people not wanting to work."[42]

The gravity of the anti-work situation seems now to be approaching an unprecedented structural counter-revolution. Tripartism dates back to World War I, to Coolidge in peacetime, but the addition of a mass-participation schema is just beginning to emerge as a national hypothesis. Of course, this nascent reaction intersects with a political tide of non-participation (e.g., declining voter turnout, massive non-registration for the draft rolls, growing tax evasion). The larger culture of withdrawal, from the state as from work, will make this integration effort highly problematic, and may even produce a more effective exposure of capital's organization of life, given that organization's heightened dependence on its victims' active participation.

THE PROMISE OF THE '80s

For many, the 1970's were—and the 1980's bid fair to continue—a kind of "midnight of the century," an arrival at the point of complete demoralization and unrelieved sadness. What follows is one attempt to gauge the obviously unhappy landscape of capital's American rule and see whether there indeed exists no prospect for the ending of our captivity.

To begin with the obvious, the public misery could hardly be less of a secret; the evidence is legion. The March 1979 *Ladies Home Journal* featured "Get a Good Night's Sleep," in which epidemic insomnia is discussed. *Psychology Today* for April '79 is devoted to the spreading depression, asking rhetorically, "Is this the Age of Depression?" A month later, the UN's International Labor Organization reported that "mental illness affects more human lives than any other disabling condition," adding that the number of people suffering such disorders is "growing dramatically."

In terms of the young, the May 17, 1979 *Wall Street Journal* described authority's concern over the dimensions of teen-age alcohol abuse and cited the raising of the legal drinking age in an increasing number of states. Matthew Wald's "Alarm Over Teenage Drinking" echoed the point in the *New York Times* for August 16, 1979. *U.S. News and World Report* in the same week talked about drug use among the very young: "Increasingly, grade school pupils are being drawn into the ranks of narcotics users—often paying for their habits by taking part in crimes." Robert Press, in the August 17, 1979 *Christian Science Monitor* bemoaned the general ineffectiveness of parents' organizing efforts aimed at curtailing rising drug use. A two year study of Texas counties by Dr. Kenneth Nyberg, published in September 1979, indicates a universality to this problem, namely that kids' drinking and drug use among urban and rural areas is tending to occur at similarly high levels. Another noticeable aspect of the phenomenon was its reflection in the many dramas and "Afternoon Special" type television programs on young alcoholics, during the winter of 1979-80.

Of course, these references by no means exhaust the ways by which youth show the pain of living through this world. Nor do the young all make it. Scott Spencer's "Childhood's End," in May 1979

Harper's, tells us that the rate of childhood suicide is increasing radically. The scope of Spencer's concern is reflected in the subtitle: "A hopeless future inclines the young toward death." Nor should we neglect to include a staggering social fact dealing with the other end of the age spectrum, before turning our survey toward the adult majority. Senility, according to several doctors interviewed in *Newsweek* for November 5, 1979, is affecting millions, at far earlier ages and in a recent upsurge that qualifies it as epidemic.

The mountain of tranquilizers consumed in the U.S. each day is not a new situation, but by the late '70s the pressures against humans became more intense and identifiable. In general, this may be characterized by the *Harvard Medical School Health Letter* of October 1979: "...the concept of stress —a term that has become the banner designation for our human condition...." 1978 saw an unprecedented appearance of full-page ads in national magazines for such products as "STRESSTABS," a "High Potency Stress Formula Vitamin." In the first half of April 1979, the *Wall Street Journal* ran a four-part, front-page series on stress and its mounting, and seemingly inescapable toll on health and sanity. On May 1 ABC-TV's "World News Tonight" began a highly advertised four-part series of their own, called "STRESS: Is it killing you?" The November 1979 *American Journal of Nursing's* cover story was Smith and Selye's "The Trauma of Stress and How to Combat It."

Quite naturally, stress and wage-labor emerges as a pressing topic just at this time. The first volume in a series of *Studies in Occupational Stress* appeared in 1978, Cooper and Payne's *Work and Stress*. Articles on the subject, too, seem to fairly burst forth in the literature of industrial relations from 1978 and continue without let-up, through *New Developments in Occupational Stress*, published by UCLA's Center for Quality of Working Life in early 1980. That work is becoming viscerally unbearable is an idea reflected in the popular press, as well as in academic writings. Marcia Kramer's "Assembly-line hysteria—a fact, not fiction" recorded the incidence of stress-releasing mass psychogenic illness often occurring in monotonous work scenes, in the May 31, 1979 *Chicago Sun-Times*. Nadine Brozan's "Stress at Work: The Effects on Health," surveyed changing values and reactions toward work in the *New York Times* of June 14, 1979. Another topical piece was seen in the July 13 *San Francisco Chronicle*, in which Joan Chatfield -Taylor's "Job Burnout" described its timely subject as "a profound and lasting dread of work...mental and physical depletion ranging from fatigue to full-fledged nervous breakdown."

In late February 1979 United Auto Workers Vice President Pat

Greathouse told a Senate Subcommittee that occupational alcoholism alone may be draining the economy by $25 billion per year. He spoke of the widening use of drugs and alcohol, a growing menace to business and industry, which has motivated recovery programs being conducted jointly by union and management. "More Help for Emotionally Troubled Employees," *Business Week*, March 12, 1979, and an August 13, 1979 *Wall Street Journal* article by Roger Ricklef which described the boom in all-inclusive counselling services being set up for firms' employees, are but two stories on the new measures needed to try to cope with the massive, physically-registered alienation.

It is clear that we not only feel a higher level of everyday unhappiness, but that what many social psychologists observe as a very high degree of suppressed rage prevalent is surfacing in terms of conscious disaffection with the social system. *U.S. News and World Report*, February 26, 1979, registered alarm in its "'The Doubting American'—A Growing Breed." The article, like perhaps hundreds of others recently, noted the decline of "faith in leaders, institutions and the U.S. future," going on to state that "many Americans doubt the strength and even the validity of old values—and are skeptical about the quality of their lives...." A case in point was the public attitude concerning the spring 1979 disaster at the Three Mile Island nuclear plant; as the *Manchester Guardian* correctly assayed: "...in the country at large, people were overwhelmingly certain that the authorities were lying."

The May 1979 *Gallup Opinion Index* featured a poll measuring confidence in ten key institutions, and depicting a general decline from the already low degrees of trust these institutions attracted in 1973. Only one was the object of "a great deal of confidence" from more than 25% of the public, and the three most distrusted—organized labor, congress, and big business—could muster this rating from an average of only 12%. May 15 provided a specific example when the *Los Angeles Times* announced that the "Los Angeles Police Department has suffered a serious decline in public support..." according to their own *Times* poll. And May 21 unveiled a Gallup Poll which disclosed that "despite the best efforts of the Carter administration, energy experts and the oil companies," only 14% in the nation believed that a real gasoline shortage existed while 77% felt it to be artificial, contrived by the oil companies. The poll results had been finding their practical expression as well, as evidenced by the dismay voiced on March 11 by Energy Secretary Schlesinger: record levels of gas and oil consumption had been reached despite all the "energy crisis" appeals for restraint.

Coinciding with long lines at the gas pumps in 1979, *Time*'s June

18 issue included "Hoarding Days" in which the incidence of hoarding other goods—and the likelihood of its increase in the '80s —is caused principally by public distrust of government and its statements. "A Summer of Discontent" by Walter Annenberg decried the American unwillingness to sacrifice; the essay appeared in the June 16, 1979 issue of *TV Guide* and was a full-page reprint in the *New York Times* of June 14. Donald Winks' "Speaking out—with a forked tongue" was an editorial in the July 2 *Business Week*, which reminded that "rising mistrust of big government" is matched by strong public mistrust of business. On July 3 President Carter's popularity was assessed by an ABC News–Harris Poll; his job performance rating was 73% negative, lower than Nixon received as he left office in disgrace, the lowest for a president since modern polling began. There followed the exhaustively reported mid-July '79 crisis of the Carter regime, including the Camp David "domestic summit" from which talk of the mounting sense of "malaise" abroad in the land issued. His nationally televised July 15 speech included the following on the "crisis of confidence": "It is a crisis that strikes at the very heart and soul and spirit of our national will. We can see this crisis in the growing doubt about the meaning of our own lives and in the loss of a unity of purpose for our nation. The erosion of our confidence in the future is threatening to destroy the social and political fabric of America.'

Allegedly, the source for much of Carter's remarks in this vein was an April 23 memo from his pollster Patrick Caddell, dealing with a growing cynicism and pessimism with society. As 1979 drew to a close the general outlook was not seen to have changed, though the Iran situation provided a temporary deflection. Edward A. Wynn, writing in the October 4 *Wall Street Journal* ("Why Do We Expect Too Much?"), carped that "utopian" expectations lead to cynicism and disengagement. Calling for disciplinary efforts, he warned that a social order does not regenerate itself if the young generation is not socialized. A *New York Times*/CBS News Poll published November 12 found that two thirds in the U.S. feel that the nation is in worse shape than it was five years ago, while holding on to the belief that their personal futures look reasonably good. Significantly, the young are most optimistic about their personal future. A survey by *U.S. News & World Report* for the week of November 12 reported extremely similar findings.

From late '78 through mid-'79 the conclusions of a major study by the Survey Research Center of the University of Michigan attracted much public attention. Primarily seen as a study of job satisfaction, "a marked and significant decline" in specific satisfactions was registered between responses of the 1977 workers and those queried in 1969 and 1973. The June 4, 1979 *Business Week* discussed the results of this third nation al SRC survey as "a warning that worker discontent is rising," a typical summation.

Coincidentally, however, the next day's June 5 *Wall Street Journal* noted a further interpretation of the poll data of even wider significance. It was reported that the survey's director, Graham Stines, had recently drawn attention to the "life satisfaction" responses, indicating that the dissatisfaction in this area (e.g. overall health, happiness) was even greater than in terms of job discontent, and the workers tended to see less separation between work and non-work desires for satisfaction. The appearance of Robert Ogger's *A Little White Lie: Institutional Division of Labor and Life* also suggests that life—and society—is a totality which should provide all-around fulfillment. That an authentic life is absent is more consciously obvious, as individuals demand more from all spheres of living.

Concerning work, a few examples should suffice to indicate the general range of disaffection. Wright and Hamilton's "Education and Job Attitudes Among Blue Collar Workers," in the February 1979 *Sociology of Work and Occupations*, demonstrated that "education and job satisfaction are not significantly related." In other words, contrary to stereotypes, it is not only the more highly educated who are discontented. Neither, apparently, do the "seniors" fit the cliche image of docility, according to the 1979 publication by Action for Independent Maturity, entitled *How Do You Motivate the Older Worker?* Edward Harrison's "Discipline and the Professional Employee" from *The Personnel Administrator* for March '79 announced the increasing need of management to discipline professional workers. as opposed to the "rather rare" instances in the past. The March 26, 1979 *U.S. News & World Report* depicted labor's "Big Crusade of the '80s : More Rights for Workers," projecting the "mountain of complaints and litigation brought by workers against their bosses—court suits, grievances, arbitrations and charges brought to federal agencies." An April *Wall Street Journal* article on food service jobs, "Burger Blues," reported extremely high turnover and quoted a counter employee in Texas as to his loyalty to his bosses: "We have all learned how to successfully steal enough money...." Anxiety and resentment at AT&T, the nation's largest employer, was discussed in the May 28 and June 25 issues of *Business Week*. Similarly, *U.S. News & World Report* for July 30 and September 3, 1979 features articles which further elucidate the decline of the work ethic. In "Why 'Success' Isn't What It Used To Be" (July 30), it counsels that "employers will have to re-examine the traditional techniques for managing and motivating workers because people have a different way of looking at life.'' The September 3 "New Breed of Workers" was a cover story in which the cardinal adjectives were "restless" and "demanding."

Moving from the general to more specific cases on the "anti-work" front, consider the role of the lie-detector in industrial relations. *The Federationist* (AFL-CIO) discussed the fact of hundreds of thousands of psychological screenings and polygraph examinations using an increasing variety of devices, in its January '79 "The Intimidation of Job Tests." The piece cited the claim of Dr. Alan Strand, Industrial psychologist and president of Chicago's Personnel Security Corporation, that 100% of drug store employees steal with 80% stealing "significantly." Benson and Krois' "The Polygraph in Employment: Some Unresolved Issues," *Personnel Journal*, September '79, also examined this new development. Booming employee theft and falsified job applications have drastically increased lie detector usage, calling for some controls or standards, in their view. In the same month, the *Washington Post*'s John A. Jenkins discussed the controversial voice stress analyzers, wireless lie detectors used more and more by businesses "concerned about the honesty of their employees."

In Lawrence Stressin's "Employees Don't Take Anti-Theft Moves Lightly" (*New York Times*, March 4, 1979), resistance based largely on right-to-privacy grounds is seen, with the larger point that greater surveillance of workers has done little to stem "inventory drain." The April 16 *Forbes* cover story "The Game Where Everybody Loses But Nobody Gains," by Richard Phalon, finds big business bewailing the staggering figures involved: theft has surpassed the $40 billion a year mark, increasing at a compound rate of 15% annually. More rational than its title, the article goes on to credit the Department of Commerce with the observation that "Businessmen mistakenly assume that most inventory losses are caused by shoplifters when actually employees account for the major portion of inventory shrinkages." Commenting on the "horrendous" statistics involved, the piece notes also that "the security industry...is now grossing $23 billion a year." This last datum is clearly reflected in the full-page and even two-page ads by such firms as GTE ("Industrial Security") and INA Corporation ("Coping with White Collar Crime") appearing in business periodicals from mid-1979 on.

While the technical ingenuity of "computer criminals" is often mildly surprising to us, what is a real jolt to business is the great diversity of people robbing them. Associated Press writer Charles Chamberlain's "Spy TV Turns Up Surprises in Watching Industrial Plants" (June 24, 1979) *U.S. News & World Report* interview with Professor W.S. Albrecht, "expert on employee crime," was revealingly entitled "Surprising Profile of the White Collar Crook;" the "typical offender turns out to be someone just like the normal citizen...."

Another aspect of the anti-work trend is the most obvious one: the current and emerging ways by which the "labor force" breaks away from work as much as possible. Late January 1979 provided a most extreme case of rage in the person of Chicago snowplow driver Thomas Blair. After smashing some forty cars, killing one person, Blair was arrested screaming "I hate my job! I want to see my kids!" On a more widespread level are the findings of Caroline Bird's *The Two Pay-Check Marriage*, that men are losing their ambition and seek jobs which allow them more time with their families. Although inflation has forced a situation in which there are now more couples in which both parties work than those in which the woman stays home, Bird has observed "a definite decline in the work ethic, with men coming in late or telling the boss to go to hell if they don't like what is happening or even quitting." Another book in 1979 takes this theme further; *Breaktime: Living Without Work in a Nine to Five World*, by Bernard Lefkowitz, saw "average people" dropping out in protest "against a work culture whose values they no longer trust." *Breaktime* described the phenomenon as constituting a "quiet revolution taking place in the mainstream of American culture."

"Time Wasting at Work," in the March 5, 1979 *U.S. News & World Report* is representative of the recent outpouring of attention on "time theft." In mid-April, Robert Half of the placement service Philadelphia Inc. reported that the deliberate misuse and waste of on-the-job time was costing the economy $80 billion a year.

A further facet of work avoidance is the growth of part-time employment. Barney Olmsted's "Job Sharing: an emerging workstyle" (*International Labour Review*, May–June '79) explored the "innovative U.S. work pattern" of two people splitting one full-time job. In the same issue of the *ILR*, Olive Robinson found that the number and proportion of part-time workers in Europe has been rising for twenty years. "Big Market for Part-Time Help" by Lloyd Watson (*San Francisco Chronicle*, October 25, 1979) points up the same tendency in the U.S. What gives added significance to this trend can be grasped in studies like Miller and Terborg's "Job attitudes and Full-Time Employees" (*Journal of Applied Psychology*, Fall '79), which found that "Part-time employees were less satisfied with work, benefits, and the job in general."

The plight of the mass occupation of secretary is a reminder that antipathy to work has its more specific targets. "Help Wanted: a shortage of secretaries" (*Time*, September 3, 1979) took note of national aversion to the job, this severe under-supply despite a 6% unemployment rate and the most openings for secretarial positions of all the 300 Department of Labor classifications. The 20th Century Fox movie *Nine to Five*, which appeared in early 1980, reinforced the image of such corporate work as degrading and empty.

The four-day week, touted in the mid-'70s, produced no improvement in worker attitude or performance, beyond a sometimes-seen initial welcome. Talk of the three-day week, logically or illogically, has emerged from this failure. It is the scheduling of work time that has, most recently, occupied perhaps greater attention in management's hopes to quell the anti-work syndrome. "Flextime," or the choosing by employees of which hours in the day they will devote to wage-labor, has not, however, achieved results much dissimilar to working fewer days in the week. Similarly, it leads to an extension of its basic idea—in this case, to that of "flex-life"! "Live Now, Work Later" —though it may sound like a parody—was the quite serious article appearing in the *Financial Times of London*, early October '79. The idea of flex-time, already introduced in many firms, is simply extended to offer "the same kind of flexibility" to the entire work-life's scheduling. Worker disaffection is likewise behind this concept's appearance, introduced by no less a figure than Francis Blanchard, director general of the International Labour Organization.

Work, to which we will return at length further on, is of course only part of the arena of public disenchantment and withdrawal. The steady decline of voting, as discussed in books like E.C. Ladd's *Where Have All the Voters Gone?* (1978) and Arthur Hadley's *The Empty Polling Booth* (1979), is bringing popular support of government to lower and lower levels. Nor, by the way, does this phenomenon seem confined to the U.S.; the June and October 1979 elections in Italy and Japan, respectively, attracted the lowest turnouts since World War II.

And the participation of the young is the strongest portent for the future of the electoral diversion. Only 48% of the newly-enfranchised 18 to 20-year olds voted in 1972, 38% in 1976, and 20% in 1978. Fall '79 saw the inauguration of new efforts by national groups to reverse this downward spiral, including that of the National Association of Secondary School Principals. A United Press International story of October 23 reported that registration is "down throughout the country for all voters, but most notably for those 18 to 20," and described attempts to register high school seniors in the schools plus provide a new "voting education curriculum." *Time* (September 3) had also re-marked on the steady decline of young voters and the consequent registration drives in high schools, as typified by the new state laws deputizing school principals and teachers as registrars. Nonetheless, November '79 elections produced, in many places, such as San Francisco, the lowest turnouts in their histories. As T. W. Madron put it in the December '79 *Futurist*, the downward trend threatens "the entire American political system."

Without its re-creation by the citizenry, the modern political network indeed collapses. When Ralph Nader urges that voting be made mandatory, he is recognizing this essential need for participation. Bernard-Henri Levy, in his *Barbarism with a Human Face*, fleshes out this point a bit further: "There can be no successful dictatorship without the establishment of procedures through which people are invited or forced to speak."

The great socializer, education, is also beset by an advancing resistance, which exhibits both passive and active forms without precedent in their magnitude. Avoidance of school is seen, for instance, by a January '79 Oakland, California School District report, which discussed "the growing number of truants" and the various costs of such "unexcused absences." The May '79 Educational Press Association convention heard school officials term the 25% high school drop-out rate "a national disgrace." The Lalls' "School Phobia: It's Real and Growing," in which children experience panic and often severe physical symptoms in growing numbers (*Instructor*, September, 1979), is another example of passive resistance to school on an important level.

This withdrawal, no matter what form it takes, is obviously a major cause of the continually declining academic test scores. The pre-college Scholastic Aptitude Test, which measures high-schoolers' verbal and mathematical reasoning abilities, showed lowered scores for the tenth year in a row, it was announced on September 8. The average scores for the million high school seniors taking the SAT in 1979 are thus part of the downward current that began in 1969. The National Assessment of Educational Progress, a non-profit organization which monitors students' achievements in math and science, reported '79 declines comparable to those of the SAT scores. The July 3 *U.S. News & World Report*, in its "Science Skills Skidding in U.S. Schools," and "Problems!: Math skills are down again," in the September 24 *Time* registered these diminishing levels.

Carl Tupperman's *The Literary Hoax*, dealing with "the decline of reading, writing, and learning," suggests an even more widespread tendency of aversion from society's "knowledge." With Hunter and

Harman's "Adult Illiteracy in the United States: A Report to the Ford Foundation," this turning away becomes more obvious. Made public in September '79, the two-year study states that reading and writing problems are increasing, with as many as 64 million adult illiterates; "distrust of the institutions of the mainstream culture" is advanced as a key factor in this "American dilemma."

And within the educational system there are the most active forms of rebellion paralleling the quieter "crisis in our schools." A brief chronological sample will have to take the place of an easily voluminous catalog of student mayhem and teacher retreat.

Early in '79 two 11-year old schoolboys in Marianna, Florida, armed with a gun and a knife tried to take over their classroom but were forced out, police reported. On April 6, two Stafford (Connecticut) High School students were arrested for bombing a chemistry lab, which caused $100,000 damage. On April 24, four Isleton (California) Elementary School children laced a teacher's coffee with poison; aged 12 and 13. They were later convicted in juvenile court of attempted murder and conspiracy to commit murder. The May 21 *U.S. News & World Report* reported that "Now It's Suburbs Where School Violence Flares: From ice picks to explosives, a frightening array of weapons are contributing to disorder in the classroom—especially in areas once relatively untroubled." Also in May, the third arson incident within a month occurred in California's San Juan Unified School District, which brought the school year's arson losses to over $1 million. The school districts centering around Sacramento and San Jose are among other California areas—largely suburban—also registering extremely high arson and vandalism damages.

In June '79 a San Diego Teachers Association "violence inventory" was completed, showing increasing student violence; nearly one-fourth of San Diego teachers had been physically attacked by students during the '78–'79 school year. R.M. Kidder's "Where Have All the Teachers Gone?," in the July 19 *Christian Science Monitor* discussed the growing flight from the field, owing largely to resistant students. Education periodicals feature articles like Lee Cauter's "Discipline: You Can Do It!" and "Lessons in Anti-vandalism," both in the *Instructor*, September '79.

Meanwhile, even the most mass-circulation "entertainment" magazines are forced to devote space to the crisis. *People*, September 10, 1979 interviewed Willard McGuire, president of the National Education Association, in a piece entitled "Classroom Violence and Public Apathy: Why Teachers Are Quitting in Droves." McGuire talked about the "growing malady of 'teacher burnout,' a problem he believes "threatens to reach hurricane force if it isn't checked soon." McGuire's NEA had met earlier in the summer of '79 and had included one teacher, Emmit Williams, who understands rather well the meaning of "teacher burnout;" his home was burned by one of his students. Phyllis Burch, a teacher with 16 years experience in four states, essayed in the October 10 *San Francisco Examiner* that the foremost change in the schools since the mid-'60s has been "the mushrooming problems of violence, vandalism, and drugs in the classroom." Put more mildly, "A survey by the American Federation of Teachers indicates disruptive students are the main cause of stress experience by teachers" reported the November 20, 1979 *Wall Street Journal*. It is not a big surprise, then to find Neil Postman, author of *Teaching As a Subversive Activity* in 1969, to have written *Teaching as a Conserving Activity* in 1979—or to find his "Order in the Classroom!" in the September '79 *Atlantic*. Work, political participation, education all seem to be failing grandly as pillars of our society, especially perhaps in their roles as domestication of the young. It is not surprising that newer, less subtle devices must be projected to come to the rescue of a rotting social order.

Such a program was unveiled in Mid-February '79, with the Committee for the Study of National Service's report titled, "Youth and the Needs of the Nation." It declared that universal service for American youth is needed to curb "a cynicism and selfishness that can destroy society." "Too many...are drifting without purpose, and their apathy or self-centeredness is seldom cured by schooling," it added.

Actually, of course, this is a return to the draft, with the option of civilian duty in slums, parks and the like. Aside from its hoped-for results in terms of a national socializing force, it is also abundantly clear that the volunteer army, instituted in 1973, has been "a disaster verging on a scandal," according to Congressman Robin Beard in November '79.

The Economist, March 10, 1979, spoke of "severe problems of discipline" with the voluntary service, the immediate backdrop for talk of reviving conscription. AWOL (absent without leave), training, and attrition are major problem areas, with turnover very high in combat units and a third of all soldiers never finishing their first term of enlistment. Pentagon sources have increasingly been calling the overall status of the volunteer Army "hopeless"; allegedly, only a few elite units have any semblance of morale or dedication to national defense.

Beginning in May '79 a recruiting scandal spread, involving the enlisting of thousands of unqualified recruits; hundreds of Army recruiters have been relieved of duty for their illegal efforts at shoring up a growing shortage of volunteers. In mid-September the Army announced it would take enlistees with less than a tenth-grade education due to manpower deficiencies. Educational bonuses of up to $6000 were announced November 29, 1979 in a bid to attract qualified bodies in the face of the shortage.

A further perspective on G.I. attitudes was offered in the July '79 *American Journal of Sociology*, also a reminder of the point noted above on the blurring of work and non-work areas of life. Segal, Lynch, and Blair's contribution to the *AJS*, "The Changing American Soldier: Work-related Attitudes of U.S. Army Personnel in World War II and the 1970's," observed a comparable level of dissatisfaction between WWII AWOLs and typical soldiers in the all volunteer force. Within the '70s job satisfaction was seen to fall even more between February 1974 and the end-point of their data, August 1977. Aside from a suggested decline in military values between the 1940s and the '70s, it must also be recognized that there has been a "secular decline in job satisfaction in American society generally." Seth Cropsey's article in December '79 *Harper's* laments the severe shortage of volunteer troops, and makes a similar connection between the condition of the services and a larger trend in society: namely, that there exists a strong anti-military, anti-draft sentiment which shows no signs of changing.

A more vivid illustration of anti-military hostility could be seen from within the Navy. Blaine Harden, writing for the *Washington Post* in late June '79, chronicled the many fires aboard the carrier John F. Kennedy, believed to have been set by disgruntled sailors. In July, Naval officials announced that the period of April–July '79 contained twice as many suspicious fires aboard Atlantic Fleet ships as there had been during all of 1977 and 1978 on both Atlantic and Pacific vessels. At the beginning of November the *Los Angeles Times'* Robert Toth noted the almost $5 million fire damage to ships during 1979, postulating "deeper morale problems" involved.

Leaving the subject of national service and the desperately ailing military, the above cases of arson bring to mind that it is the nation's fastest growing crime, up "900% over a 16-year period," according to San Francisco Fire Chief Andrew Casper in September '79. August 31 had seen a $20 million apartment complex arson in Houston, the worst fire in the city's recent history. And less than a week later, an 18-year-old was arrested for starting a 5,000 acre fire in California's Los Padres National Forest.

Sabotage, too, seems to be providing spectacular and unprecedented examples of anti-society urges, and not only in the U.S. The *St.*

Catharine's Standard of December 9, 1978 carried, complete with photo, "Man Drives Truck Through Stores in Shopping Plaza." The story recounted the systematic destruction wreaked by a man who drove an armored truck through 35 stores in the Montreal area's Carrefour St. George, costing nearly $2 million. Crestview, Florida was the scene of a derailment on April 19, 1979 of two dozen cars on the Louisville and Nashville Railroad; sabotage was strongly suspected due to track damage caused by rifle bullets. On June 2, 1979 Los Angeles County Museum of Art officials said that eight paintings, including two by Picasso, had been slashed by someone using a metal object. A bulldozer smashed five cars in the parking lot of a Houston plastic firm June 13; the driver, finally halted by a collision with a railroad boxcar, had been recently fired from his job. Southern Pacific Railroad investigators announced on October 8, 1979 that saboteurs had derailed a 101-car freight train the day before near Santa Barbara; a barricade of lumber and concrete caused the crash, which closed the main rail line between Los Angeles and San Francisco.

If 1978 was a time when much national attention was given the fiscal survival chances of New York City as a public corporation, 1979 could perhaps be commemorated as the year in which its hope to survive as a coherent social entity became an open question. As the highest point of American urbanism, it deserves at least the following few, random readings from the front pages of the *New York Times*. March saw *NYT* stories covering the alarming jump in subway crime and the consequent decision to station police on every nighttime train. March 15 disclosed the "New York's illegal Garbage Dumping Gets Worse," as some roads in the Bronx and Brooklyn are "completely blocked" by mountains of unauthorized trash. "Graveyard Vandalism Continues," was another featured March topic. In May the *Times* front page for the 7th featured, "Vandals Ruin $80,000 Sculpture Outside A Madison Ave. Gallery." On the 10th Mayor Koch, in a "public safety" move eliciting mostly laughter from New Yorkers, was announced to have banned the drinking of alcohol in public places, such as street corners. The next day found a woman reportedly attacked by rats near NY's City Hall; officials closed off the area to battle the rodents. May 21, 1979 disclosed the high monetary and psychological cost of vandalism; it had already reached a dollar price-tag of 8 million by the end of 1978, to the Education and Parks Departments alone.

"Tens of Thousands of Derelicts Jam New York's Criminal Courts" appeared on the June 7 front page, within days of news stories on the description of drug abuse in City schools as "critical" by a congressional investigating committee. Narcotics Abuse Committee

Chairman Lester Wolff said the New York problem "reflects the state of affairs in all major metropolitan and suburban areas throughout the nation."

Turning to the subject of contemporary forms of violence in society at large, we encounter the "sniper." Lately it almost seems that every newscast includes a story on someone who has "flipped out" into a posture of lethal behavior, such as a man firing away from inside his barricaded apartment. A well-known case was that of Brenda Spencer, 16, who surrendered to police after shooting at an elementary school across the street from her San Diego home, killing its principal and custodian and wounding nine students; "I hate Mondays" she offered following the January 29, 1979 attack. In late April, a 64-year-old man opened fire on a group of seven police, wounding six of them and then killing two women and injuring more than 30 others who were present watching a San Antonio parade. A 30-year-old social worker shot and killed two FBI agents in their El Centro, California office on August 9, 1979 and then killed himself.

As un-reasoned as these suicidal acts may be, they are clearly a part of the syndrome of (often ill-defined) anger at authority, discussed throughout this essay. Marilyn Elias, in her June 1979 essay "Freelance Terrorists," lends a judgement that applies: "People seem willing to resort to drastic acts in an era marked by ebbing faith in such institutions as the family, the church, our economic system and the government."

Despite an everyday reality that enforces the calm of isolation and entropy, acts of collective as well as individual violence mount. Outbursts shatter the facade and contain mixed elements in their released rage; the '80s will, for a time, most likely bear this varied imprint as seen in a scan of some of 1979's group violence.

A Wichita rock concert "just broke into warfare," said a radio station director, when police shut off the power at the April 15 event. Hundreds of police firing shotguns and teargas required three hours to quell the riot, which saw squad cars destroyed by tire irons and four officers injured. San Francisco's "Dan White Riot" of May 21 caused over $1 million in damage to Civic Center buldings and looted stores and banks. A largely gay crowd of 5,000 also injured 60 police and burned 13 squad cars in an all-night explosion which laid siege to City Hall; begun as a protest against the extremely lenient legal treatment of a reactionary County Supervisor who had murdered a gay Supervisor and the mayor, the riot included many other elements and quickly transcended concern with legality or politicians. On the same night, a crowd of 1500 attacked firemen and police with rocks and bottles at the scene of a million-dollar factory fire in Redwood City, 25 miles south of the San Francisco outbreak. Also at the same time, end-of-semester vandalism at the University of Connecticut left smashed furniture and burning debris across the campus, in a rampage apparently caused by nothing so much as boredom.

Two days of rioting occurred in the famous Philadelphia suburb of Levittown—a name once synonymous with suburban conformity and tranquility—in late June, involving 3,000 people and 200 arrests. Truckers blockaded the area and joined teenagers and motorists in burning gas pumps and vehicles, throwing objects, including molotov cocktails at police and demanding more and cheaper fuel.

Four further examples from summer '79 demonstrate continuing non-individual violence in an array of forms. The Chicago White Sox annual teen half-price night, July 11, was billed as "Disco Demolition Night," but the anti-disco theme proved the excuse for 7,000 rioters to overrun and destroy the playing field. Red Lake Indian Reservation experienced two nights of arson and gunfire, including a three-hour firefight between Indians and federal police, on July 21 and 22. One man was shot to death during a July 27 rock concert in Cleveland which was marked by vandalism and rock and bottle throwing at police. An August UPI newswire from Slatington, Pennsylvania points out that even hamlets are not immune; it read: "The mayor of this tiny Lehigh County community Saturday declared a state of emergency and imposed a midnight–6a.m. curfew in an attempt to break up street corner crowds. Mayor David Altrichter said the groups were at times, 'urinating and defecating on Main Street!'" Curfew was also imposed on the central Connecticut city of Meriden on September 6, 1979 following a teen-age gang's rock-throwing attack on a police station. Mayor Walter Evilia said the assault came from "Hispanics, blacks and whites" living in and around a downtown housing project; "It's going to get like New York City soon," he told a reporter.

Dozens of melees could be cited involving people vs. police, but it is also true that a brutalized population is quite capable of brutalizing itself, as with gang violence or the tragic storming of a Cincinnati rock concert entrance on December 3, 1979 which resulted in 11 youths trampled to death. With both its liberatory and its backward aspects, however, we do appear to be embarking on the '80s in an increasing current of discomfort with passive spectatorship. Steven Jenkins, in his mid-April '79 *Newsday* piece "The Growing Spectre of Fan Violence in Sports," points to the mounting fragility of all types of sports spectacles, for example. Almost any large gathering seems vulnerable, as if physical closeness reminds us, bitterly, how far away real community is in this buy-and-sell existence.

Turning to specifics of the less graphic, everyday plane of the job, an unchecked tendency to stay away from it as much as possible is seen. *U.S. News and World Report* for July 3, 1978, in its "World Business" column, observed that in the United Kingdom, bonuses are offered for coming to work in an effort to check rising absenteeism; "Missing workers are an old problem, but it's getting worse." Allen and Higgins' "The Absenteeism Culture," in the January–February '79 *Personnel*, typifies a flood of interest in the subject by specialists. Similar was the March 14, 1979 *Wall Street Journal* article by James Robins, "Firms Try Newer Way to Slash Absenteeism As Carrot and Stick Fail: All Cures Seem Temporary." And the 1979–82 United Auto Workers contract increased the number of "paid personal holidays" to 26 from 12 provided under the previous covenant, bowing to auto workers' refusal to maintain attendance. Concerning the phenomenon in Canada, the November 13, 1979 *Wall Street Journal* noted Manpower, Incorporated's report of absenteeism's $8 billion per year price-tag there, plus the "growing tendency for workers to take a day off just because they don't feel like working"; their perspicacious psychologists opined that "frequent absentees may be trying to withdraw from life's tensions."

The frequency of people quitting their jobs is a related, and growing, matter. Characteristically, this is seen in the literature: Farrell Bloch's "Labor Turnover in U.S. Manufacturing Industries" *Journal of Human Resources*, Spring '79), H. Kent Baker's "The Turnover Trap" (*Supervisory Management*, June '79), and Robert Kushell's "How to Reduce Turnover" (*Personnel Journal*, August '79) for example. At the end of April '79 the Labor Department disclosed that job tenure of American workers decreased to an average of 3.6 years per job in 1978 from 3.9 years in 1973, with the tenure apparently shrinking at an accelerating rate. The October 10, 1979 *Wall Street Journal* announced an Administrative Management Society survey which observed that turnover among office employees averaged 20% in 1978, up from 14% in 1976.

In an early November '79 Princeton Features piece, "Revolution in the Workplace," Carper and Naisbett declared that a "growing demand for more satisfaction from life" has brought dissatisfaction with work to the point where "workers refuse to produce and even deliberately sabotage the products they make." This point may be highlighted by a few of the more sensational acts of employee sabotage, such as the November '79 damage to three of the world's largest electrical generators at Grand Coulee Dam in Washington state. In what investigators called "an inside job," 19 of the generator's coils had been broken with a crowbar, resulting in "millions of dollars" of damage. On February 15, 1979 a strike by mutuel clerks at New York's Aqueduct Race Track got out of control and all 550 mutuel betting machines were put out of action by sabotage. On May 7, 1979 it was discovered that lye had been poured into 62 uranium fuel elements at the Surrey nuclear plant in Richmond, Virginia; two employees were later arrested and convicted for the act. During September 21 and 22 of the same year, 4,000 Chrysler workers, anticipating a two-week shutdown of their factory, ripped the vinyl tops of the new cars, broke the windows, tore out dashboard wiring and started small fires throughout the plant.

Unlike the general charade/catharsis nature of strikes —though it may be noted that strikes appear to be more often taking illegal and violent forms—workers obviously are opposing work in a thousand ways, from purely visceral reactions against it to the most calculated attacks. This opposition registers itself most fundamentally in terms of productivity, or output-per-hour-worked.

The history of modern civilization is, in an important sense, a story of the steady growth of productivity. Unbroken for centuries, the foundation of industrial capitalism, rising productivity has now gone the way of the work ethic. And for the same reason: the falseness of trading away one's life in order to purchase things is a transparently barren death-trip.

1974 saw this reversal surfacing really for the first time, as that recession year's overall output-per-hour showed a gain of virtually zero. Since then, those who have attempted to manage the fate of the capital relationship have witnessed brief periods of small productivity gains being out-numbered by those of often substantial decreases. The Bureau of Labor Statistics announced a .3% productivity rise for private business in 1978, a tiny advance clearly reversed in 1979.

"Sharp Drop in Worker Productivity" read the May 30, 1979 Associated Press release, in which Labor Department analysis of first quarter figures showed "the steepest decline since 1974." A July 31 *Washington Post* story announced that "productivity of U.S. businesses fell more rapidly in the second quarter (of 1979) than it has since the government began keeping records in 1947." AP for November 29 proclaimed "Productivity in U.S. Still Declining," explaining that the third quarter drop was the first time since 1974 that three consecutive quarters had shown declines.

The overall trend has engendered countless articles, as society's defenders look desperately for solutions and the future of worker "efficiency" seems ever dimmer. February 5, 1979's *Time* featured "Perils of the Productivity Sag," while the March issue of *The Office* began to look at Northrup's plant design, "The continuing decline in productivity is considered a major problem in this country..." Campbell McConnell's "Why is U.S. Productivity Slowing Down?" discussed the "unsatisfactory gap between output and hours worked," in the April–May *Harvard Business Review*; the May-June *HBR* carried "Productivity—the Problem Behind the Headlines" by Burton Malhiel. *Industry Week* of May 14 spoke of "a new emphasis on office productivity," in its "Removing the Cages from the Corporate Zoo."

Meanwhile, unions and the left publicly exhibited their delusion, if not callousness, on the subject. Befitting their roles as champions of "honest toil" and the "good worker," the entire crisis is denied by them! The May '79 AFL-CIO *Federationist* and the June '79 *Monthly Review*, in "Bringing Productivity into Focus" and "Productivity Slowdown: A False Alarm," respectively, disputed the facts of diminishing work output and ignored the individual's primacy in productivity.

Returning to reality, Lawrence Baytos offered "Nine Strategies for Productivity" in the July '79 *Personnel Journal*, John Niler wrote of "Diagnosing and Treating the Symptoms of Low Productivity" in August's *Supervisory Management*, and the August 7 *Wall Street Journal* front-paged "White Collar Workers Start to Get attention in Productivity Studies: Employees Resist."

On June 4 and September 10, 1979 *Time* editorialized on the plight of America, in "The Weakness that Starts at Home" and "The Fascination of Decadence." Considering the mass circulation involved, we glimpse here the growing awareness of how critical the changing work posture is. The June essay deals with "a damaging slackness...in U.S. society at large" and locates a key part of the problem in "the state of American productivity, which after several years of declining growth has in recent months actually dipped below zero progress." September's opinion piece declared that "the work ethic is nearly as dead as the Weimar Republic," citing "the last business quarter's alarming 3.8% decline in productivity" as a symptom of decadence. It is a certainty that the '80s will see even more on capital's productivity dilemma, inasmuch as it cannot be "solved" without the destruction of that wage-labor/commodity relationship which is capitalism. *Business Week* of October 1, 1979, fretted over "Why It Won't Be Easy to Boost Productivity," and in mid-October Theodore Barry & Associates (management consultants) reported their findings that the average worker is productive during only 55% of working hours. James Fields, of the Barry firm, said this compares with 80 to 85%

spent productively working around the turn of the century; "the implications of that are staggering," declared Fields. The "team concept" of work improvement received a most negative judgement by Latane, Williams, and Harkins' "Social Loafing." The November '79 *Psychology Today* article concluded that output-per-hour actually declines in groups. And so on, into the new decade.

The proliferation of organizations like the American Productivity Center and Human Productivity Institute shows the demand by business for help. Similarly, Sylvia Porter's column, "Hot Careers for the 1980's" lists the top two fields as "management information systems" and "human resources" in which improving productivity is the "fundamental challenge" of each.

Corporate management has recently been forced toward a restructuring, as restive workers create more difficulties for their bosses. *Personnel Journal*, February '79. indicated this in Lawrence Wangler's "The Intensification of the Personnel Role: The personnel executive of the 1980's, with increased responsibilities and new challenges, will be viewed as a key decision-maker (and part-time magician)." This major expansion is also seen in "Personnel Widens its Franchise," which appeared in the February 26, 1979 *Business Week*; *Personnel Journal* for March reported a "new era" in federal industrial relations, due to revised laws and organization which put personnel administration on a par with financial management; publicized in Julius Draznin's "Labor Relations" column, this development was another spur to the private sector in the area. Donald Klingner's "Changing Role of Personnel Management in the 1980's" (*The Personnel Administrator*, September '79) pointed out that a fundamental change in the nature of the profession must follow the major shift of values underway at large. In mid-October Information Science, Inc. disclosed that a survey of 2,000 executives showed almost twice as many of them devoting from five to 20 hours a week to personnel matters as was the case five years ago; the respondents also indicated that pay for personnel execs has risen significantly.

Of personnel chiefs surveyed at a November '79 meeting of the American Society for Personnel Administration, 85% felt unions will have increased difficulty controlling their members during the '80s, according to the November 20 *Wall Street Journal*. It is this sense of union infirmity which is bringing on the great bolstering of personnel departments, and, more importantly, pushing increased union-management collaboration.

Whether or not unionism is seen as weakening, its vital, disciplinary role is unquestioned by America's corporate leadership. The appreciation of this role is exemplified by a May 21, 1979 *Fortune* article by Lee Smith, entitled "The UAW Has Its Own Management Problem." It focuses mainly on the auto companies' worries about the top Auto Workers' official who will be replaced by the end of 1983: "What the companies dread is a power vacuum created by a weak, inexperienced, and indecisive leadership." Noting "sullenness," a shift of values, and general distrust of institutions among the workers, a strong union is prescribed as the best defense against "chaos." Manufacturers "want to know whether or not the UAW leadership can deliver a manageable labor force," inasmuch as "a fundamental problem not just for the UAW but for most unions in this epoch has been the increasing disaffection of the rank and file, and with that, an erosion of discipline."

In the September/October '79 *Harvard Business Review*'s "Are Unions An Anachronism?" UAW and Communication Workers of America co-management programs with General Motors and AT&T, respectively, were adduced as joint efforts to effectively control the workplace that succeeded where neither party alone could have. The piece speaks of "the new discontents" creating the "post-industrial workplace problems" which have been growing "for over a decade," and concludes that authority must be shared in order to motivate "this kind of employee to produce."

Shared responsibility is the urgently needed cure for a "growing sense of social entitlement" which threatens to destroy wage-labor and society with it, according to James O'Toole's "Dystopia: The Irresponsible Society" in October '79's *Management Review*. Similar was R.M. Kanter's fear of an "authority vacuum" and his prescription, "to expand power, share it," in the *Harvard Business Review* for July/August '79 ("Power Failure in Management Circuits").

Management and unions have been advancing toward greater institutionalized collaboration, whereby joint management programs—labeled "worker participation," "job enrichment," "quality of work life" projects—aim at increased worker motivation. Business periodicals see the need for strong union partnerships in these developing setups, just as they have, for example, bemoaned the "anarchy" in the coalfields produced by a weak United Mine Workers Union, or applauded the United Steelworkers' partnerships with steel companies in pursuit of higher productivity.

Workers seem generally distrustful or cynical about such programs, like the major UAW-GM one at Tarrytown, New York, or the UAW-Harman International program in Bolivar, Tennessee which dates from 1973 and is discussed in an early 1980 University of Michigan study by Macy, Ledford, and Lawler. But unionists show a greater enthusiasm, as evidenced by Ponak and Fraser's finding of strong support for union-management cooperation in a study of middle-level union officials, entitled "Union Activists' Support for Joint Program" (*Industrial Relations*, Spring 1979).

The highest levels of power also see clearly the stakes involved, the need for new forms to contain the individual. In 1979 the Trilateral Commission published Roberts, Okamoto, and Lodge's *Collective Bargaining and Employee Participation in Western Europe, North America, and Japan*, a Task Force Report to the Commission. Its summary called for labor-management cooperation, lest "the marvels of modern technology and raised expectations lead to disaster." The reason for capital's embrace of the joint approach movement and workers' distrust (as shown by unchanged "performance" figures) is the same, of course. The September 4, 1979 *Wall Street Journal* quoted University of Michigan researchers that "the most common response that this country's labor unions make to the introduction of new technology is willing acceptance." This quote, from the "Labor Letter" of the *WSJ* certainly provides some of the reason for the opposition of interest felt by rulers and ruled in the unions.

The union-management committees and the other forms of "quality of work life" co-determination seem "on the brink of important growth in the U.S.," according to *Business Week*, September 17, 1979, which noted that representatives of 32 unions attended a Spring '79 American Productivity Center meeting aimed at such programs. The biggest top-level change, billed "a major breakthrough in U.S. labor history," was the UAW trade-off of $500 million in contract concessions for a seat on Chrysler's board of directors. Agreed to in October '79 and consecrated by the federal government in December, UAW president Douglas Fraser will obtain the directorship in May 1980, prompting such editorials as "Are Unions Knocking at Boardroom Doors?" (*Industry Week*, November 12, 1979). The move also sparked discussion of a possible shift toward the "social contract," in which unions and government agree upon and attempt to enforce various social programs at the national level; Fraser, for one, has declared himself quite interested in this direction for American unionism, following European examples.

Certainly there already exist labor-management bodies with broader social objectives than has generally been the case before. California's Council on Environmental and Economic Balance, or CEEB, was founded in 1973 and is composed of bankers, oil company executives, nuclear power industry representatives, land developers and the like, plus the heads of the state Building and Construction Trades Union Council, the Teamsters and the United Auto Workers. A great power in the state capitol, CEEB characteristically has done much toward lowering environmental laws and nuclear safeguard standards. Investigative reporting by David Kaplan in the Summer of '79 further uncovered that this "form of Fascism" intends a national organization with CEEB's set up across the country. Collaboration of this sort recalls the Golden, Colorado pro-nuclear rally on August 26, 1979 organized by Local 8031 of the United Steel Workers and paid for by Rockwell International, which operates the Rocky Flats nuclear weapons plant near Golden.

Institutionalized cooperation at the local level is incisively discussed by Urban Lehner, in his August 8, 1979 *Wall Street Journal* piece, "Committees of Labor and Management Enjoying Resurgence in Communities." The Evansville (Indiana) Area Labor-Management Committee, formed in 1975 and comprised of the local Alcoa, Whirlpool and Inland Container managements plus the local union chieftans, is portrayed as one of a growing number of joint bodies which try to solve communities' in-plant and at-large social problems. Plant vandalism was one of Evansville's biggest sore points; joint efforts at boosting productivity and general morale, and union-management planning for industrial expansion are other examples of such groups' functions. "In just the past year or so, new areawide committees have sprouted in Scranton, Pa., Portsmouth, Ohio, and St. Louis, and a longstanding committee in Pittsburgh has begun expanding its operations... 'They're really flourishing,' says John Stepp, an official of the Federal Mediation and Conciliation Service, which has helped set up a number of the committees."

Government help for unionism, in fact, has recently been increasing, especially in the form of helpful court decisions defending the power of unions over their members and extending their roles; this tendency is an invaluable aspect of the class collaboration directions indicated above.

Congress failed to pass the "Labor Reform" bill, or "commonsitus picketing" measure, in the late '70s prompting many to interpret this as a major shift away from appreciation of unions' benefits to the state and business. The bill, designed to greatly strengthen the leverage by which unions could corral new members and gain new jurisdictions, retains its importance in light of continued and growing worker restiveness against managment and unions. D. Quinn Mills' "Flawed Victory in Labor Law Reform" (*Harvard Business Review*, May–June '79), suggested that the victory was a pyrrhic one, that business really requires this "reform" to avoid soured "labor relations" in the '80s, as Labor must have help to unionize.

Denied for a time, this help becomes a must as will be discussed below. Meanwhile, there has been a steady increase in government assistance to unions on a more day-to-day level.

In early January '79 the U.S. Court of Appeals upheld the dismissal of an action brought by members of Electrical Workers (IBEW) Local 1547 in Alaska against the international union for its refusal to submit terms of a national contract to a membership ratification vote in 1977. The court decided that IBEW president Pillard was justified in interpreting the union's constitution in such a way as to negotiate and implement the agreement without ratification.

Early March '79 found a federal Appeals Court deciding against a membership suit in St. Louis, that the UAW could give union funds to whatever causes or organizations the "officers' discretion" dictated. At the same time a New York Court of Appeals sided with the Communication Workers of America executive board who fired shop steward Dave Newman merely for criticizing union policy; the judgement concluded that a steward's duty is to represent the policies of the "management of the union" and not the views of the members who elect them. The Supreme Court, in the summer '79 IBEW vs. Foust case, ruled that a union member could not recover damages over the failure of the union to fairly process his grievance. Although the right of fair grievance representation is guaranteed by law, and the individual was denied an opportunity to grieve his firing because the union would not represent his grievance within a time deadline, the Court decided that interference would antagonize the union, would "disrupt peaceful labor relations."

The state has also slowly but steadily expanded the purview of union authority. In March '79 the National Labor Relations Board reversed a 1971 decision and placed employees of condominiums and cooperatives within collective bargaining jurisdiction. This policy change was supported not only by unions but by New York's Realty Advisory Board, an employer bargaining association representing over 1,700 apartment buildings. On May 14, 1979, the Supreme Court declared the availability of food to employees during working hours and its price to be subject to union bargaining. Next day the *Wall Street Journal*'s "Labor Letter" said "Unions win expanded rights to picket and organize at shopping centers," noting that recent NLRB decisions have virtually overturned a 1976 Supreme Court denial of First Amendment protection to private shopping center access. And a continuing development is the setting up of collective bargaining systems for public employees; 1979 saw California, for instance, add local government workers to the list of those subject to "agency shop" set-ups requiring them to pay dues to a union, along with state employees, University of California workers, and others already served up to unions by state legislation.

The unions themselves are moving toward structures and policies aimed at more effective bureaucratic control of their members. Thus in early March '79 the merger of the 25,000-member United Shoeworkers of America with the 510,000 Amalgamated Clothing and Textile Workers Union was effectuated, and in June the Retail Clerks and Amalgamated Meat Cutters unions merged to form the 1.2 million-member United Food and Commercial Workers International Union, the largest in the AFL-CIO. *Business Week* of March 5, 1979 wrote of the impending Clerks and Meat Cutters consolidation, noting that the Retail Clerks president stated that his highly centralized union would bring most importantly, "structure" to the operations of the new body. Arnold Weber's May 14, 1979 *Wall Street Journal* article, "Mergers: Union Style" disclosed that 57 mergers involving 95 unions and employee associations took place between 1956 and 1978; of this 57, 21 took place since 1971, evidence of the quickening incidence of trade union amalgamation. "Labor stability" is thus promoted—which is logical on the part of Weber due to the diminished voice of the individual brought about by making union bosses more powerful and more distant. In the July 30, 1979 *Business Week's* "An AFL-CIO Without Meany" the Kirkland-era Federation is said to be committed to a policy of spurring more mergers: "One official predicts that the federation's 105 current unions will shrink to 70 by 1990." In late '79 AFL-CIO president Kirkland publicly invited the Teamsters and the UAW to re-affiliate with his umbrella body.

These few words on directions in unionism's structure bring to mind the European situation and its possible relevance to American developments. In England a strong parallel suggests itself from these comments by James Prior, Prime Minister Thatcher's minister responsible for union relations, interviewed in *Business Week*, April 16, 1979: "We have too many unions. And a lot of them are much too weak in administration, in ability to get a message across. The unions have lost a lot of control to the shop floor." The steady movement toward global unions, discussed for example in John Windmuller's 1980 work, *The Shape of Transnational Unionism*, has already been felt here. Paul Shaw had discussed it is his May '79 *Personnel Administrator* offering, "International Labor Relations' Impact on Domestic Labor Relations," in which he saw its number-one influence as pressure toward "much more industry-wide bargaining on a national basis."

Working people, policed by the unions and aware of their ever greater collusion with employers and the government, exhibit a rising anti-unionism. The flood of workers' charges against unions is being deflected by public rulings that are outrageous for their contempt of members' rights and their naked defense of unions' anti-worker activities. Some of the cases were cited above; another tactic is to simply not process worker complaints. NLRB members Pennello and Truesdale, for example, both spoke out in '79 against "peering over the shoulder" of the unions in the rising number of charges brought against them by their members.

"Trucking Turmoil," a front-page *Wall Street Journal* article of March 9, 1979, stressed the "undercurrent of discontent" among Teamsters. The NLRB's 43 annual report, released in mid-March, revealed that Board-conducted elections gave unions victories 46% of the time, for the second year in a row. The percentage of union victories has been declining: from 57% for 1968, to below 50% since 1975. Drupman and Rasin's "Decertification: Removing the Shroud," in the April '79 *Labor Law Journal*, found that "In the past ten years, there has been a dramatic increase in the number of employees seeking to decertify their collective bargaining representatives and become union-free." Further, these efforts are succeeding: "The rate at which unions are being decertified has increased continually over the last decade." Noting that a decertification petition may not be filed by an employer, it was delicately suggested that "today's employees do not consider unions to be a panacea for their concerns or desires."

Underlining this point further was "Approval of Labor Unions Sinks to Lowest Point on Record," featured in the June '79 Gallup Opinion Index. The Gallup measurement showed a decline of about 15% among both union and non-union families since June 1965. The downturn has been a steady one since '65, having reached in '79 the lowest point of public approval in Gallup's 43 years of polling. The August 27, 1979 *Fortune* carried A. H. Raskins's "Big Labor Strives to Break Out of Its Rut," with a subtitle which observed that Labor's ways "don't appeal to younger workers." An interesting specific of the article dealt with General Motors' 1979 decision to grant union workers preferential hiring rights for jobs at any of 12 non-union plants, all but one of which were in the South. UAW President Fraser conceded that only this GM policy gave the union its edge in representation elections at the plants.

Besides the charges filed (e.g. three times more NLRB grievance complaints than 10 years ago), and negative vote results, unions are also being hit by work actions as never before. Richard Sennett, in "The Boss's New Clothes," *New York Review of Books*, February 22, 1979, stated rather mildly that "During the last decade, the number of wildcat strikes has risen— strikes as much against the union bureaucracy, for example that of the United Mine Workers, as against the managerial bureaucracy." The Supreme Court decided in December '79 that unions are not liable for losses caused by their members' wildcats, a finding very consonant with Sennett's observation, recognizing that such acts are not an extension of union activity but antagonistic to it.

As with its denial of the productivity crisis, the left sees in this internal weakening of unionism another evidence of the hopeless nature of our era. Fortunately close to extinction, ground away as a separate force like so many other illusions, the left now more than ever shows its congruence with the world we must shatter. Like the basic rule of authority, it seeks to demoralize, confuse and divide that which proceeds past ideology, the painful-enough progress of the autonomous social movement. Insignificant in itself, we may use its typical viewpoints to chart, then, the difference between lived truth and those in general who fear it.

The image of ever-more security-conscious consumers, happily supporting the rules of the economy, is one maintenance of that economy—though this lie is so rapidly eroded by reality. In fact, as being uninsured vies with the filing of personal bankruptcy as the greater commonplace, and "wrathful jurors' demands" push damage suit settlements against wealth "sky-high," respect for the commodity is obviously ebbing. Almost weekly, the assessments of the "subterranean economy" of "illegal" and/or unreported income seem to include more millions of people and billions of dollars; former Treasury Secretary William Simon said in November '79 that the refusal to pay taxes had reached the level of notorious Italy, and reflected Americans' "thumbing their noses at the system." Meanwhile, '79 saw epidemics of bank robberies with records set in the major cities, looting to the point of requiring the National Guard after every hurricane or sizable tornado, and unprecedented, soaring shoplifting.

And the "rightist trend" seen in the "Ku Klux Klan rise" scenario is also at strong variance with the fact that people increasingly feel "in it together," all sorely mauled by increasingly visible sources. Taylor, Sheatsley, and Greenley's "Attitudes Toward Racial Integration," in *Scientific American* for June '78; the February '79 National Conference of Christians and Jews' massive survey; and the August '78 and '79 Gallup Polls, among other data, showed "dramatic" drops in race bias, a "markedly" growing toleration for persons of other races and creeds.

The myth of impending economic doom, finally, is a favorite diversion among those who wish to keep the struggle to live contained on the already-won plane of survival. The March '79 Supreme Court decision upholding unemployment benefits for strikers and extending them to students typify the guarantees in effect, and, in light of the collapsing capital relationship, lend more plausibility to the thesis that post-survivalist struggles occur with the stakes of total revolution much more accessible. In 1970 Herman Kahn predicted a frenzy of social travel developing in the new decade. Ten years later, Stephen Papson's *Futurist* article, "Tourism: Biggest Industry in the Twenty-First Century?" sees its arrival "with the growth of affluence," as emblematic of the need "to get away from all routine, not just one's work."

But "getting away" isn't that easy and the frustration corrodes. A way of death is dying but it may survive us. Arming ourselves with an accurate sense of our inter-subjectivity in its complex fight with this alien place is necessary to help us strike hard and well.

THE '80s SO FAR

From new levels of boredom and the digital/TV screen mentality of the high technology onslaught, to mounting physical pollution and economic decay, only the incidentals of alienation have changed at all in the past four years. A climate of (often mis-directed) violence is also greatly in evidence; as so many elements of modern life cheapen living, the tragic relevance of "life is cheap," once thought applicable mainly elsewhere, emerges around us. In the mid-'80s the potential promise lies solely in the conclusion that this world is even closer to collapse.

Society's negation has moved forward; and in the decomposition of the old world it is increasingly accurate to speak, with Sanguinetti, of that "false consciousness which still reigns, but no longer governs." As the century runs down, so does, faster and faster, its store of effective illusion.

There is no guarantee how much humanness will survive to replace repressive emptiness with an unfettered life spirit. For an agonizing toll is being registered on all our sensibilities. As the refrain of John Cougar's best-selling record of 1982, "Jack and Diane", put it, "Oh yeah, life goes on/Long after the thrill of living is gone."

The supermarket tabloids also reflect the rampant sense of generalized pain and loss, with their weekly parade of features on depression, fear of pain, stress and the like; and similarly, a flow of advertising for Stressgard, Stress Formula vitamins, etc. A September 21, 1981 *Time* essay, "The Burnout of Almost Everyone" reads: "Today the smell of psychological wiring on fire is everywhere...Burnout is preeminently the disease of the thwarted; it is a frustration so profound that it exhausts body and morale." In the mid-'80s this condition seems to be even more widespread, if possible; for example, Procaccini and Kiefaber's popular 1983 work, *Parent Burnout*, and *Time*'s June 6, 1983 cover story, "Stress", introduced by a contorted, screaming face.

A prior psychological and social stability is giving way to an assault upon the young by the realities of dominated life. Marie Winn's *Children Without Childhood* (1983) describes a fundamental shift away from the condition of children as innocents protected from the world, from a conception of childhood that was the norm until just a very few years ago. Intimate awareness of drugs and violence at very early ages, for example, is a brutalizing consequence of the awareness of the falseness of such institutions as the nuclear family, religion and government.

Not only is the traditional family continuing to fall apart, but love itself seems to be worn down more quickly by the strains and deprivation of the twilight of capitalism. The 1980 census figures reveal a marked trend toward the one-person household, to the accompaniment of articles such as "The Reasons Men and Women are Raging at Each Other All of A Sudden" (*Cosmopolitan*, November, 1982).

Naturally, many of the young seem profoundly horrified by what they are expected to live under. "Suicide Among Preschoolers On the Rise" was the topic of a May 15, 1983 UPI feature, while the *U.S. News and World Report*'s June 20, 1983 "Behind a Surge in Suicides of Young People " discussed the suicide trend among youth. *Newsweek* for August 15, 1983 reported that the 15- to 24-year-old age group is the only segment of the population whose death rate has increased in recent years, and that among 15- to 19-year olds, suicide is now the second leading cause of death, after traffic accidents—many of which, in fact, are suspected suicides.

Anorexia nervosa (self-induced starvation) and bulimia (a pattern of gorging followed by vomiting) are rapidly spreading phenomena among women. First registered in the popular media in the mid-'70s, the growth of these afflictions has been discussed in such articles as "The Binge-Purge Syndrome" (*Newsweek*, November 2, 1981) and "Anorexia: the 'Starvation Disease' Epidemic" (*U. S. News and World Report*, August 30, 1982). The October 1983 *Ms.* asks, "Is the Binge-Purge Cycle Catching?" while noting that "At least half the women on campus today suffer from some kind of eating disorder."

A sudden surge in heroin use among various social classes, from blue-collar workers to Kennedy offspring, drew much media attention during the second half of 1983.

Continued growth in the dimensions of alcohol abuse has brought a big turnabout from the '70s, namely, the tendency of states to raise the legal drinking age. A *Redbook* (June 1982) survey "revealed the startling news that problem drinking is increasing dramatically among women who are under the age of 35." The *Wall Street Journal* of February 8, 1983 addressed the connection between brawling, falling grades, and drinking in "Colleges Try to Combat Rampant Alcohol Use, But With Little Effect." The first federally funded study on the subject in fifty years, *Alcohol and Public Policy: Beyond the Shadow of*

Prohibition, attracted attention in summer 1983 with its recommendation of a national campaign to slash alcohol consumption.

At the same time, the report of the National Commission on Excellence in Education, issued in May, had been causing more of a stir by its devastating indictment of the American education system; the 18-month study warned of "a rising tide of mediocrity that threatens our very future as a nation and a people," as kids have perhaps never been so turned off by school.

Gambling has been multiplying so rapidly as to be measured in fractions of the national economy and to cause some social critics to refer to it as a curse that reflects basic changes in public attitudes toward work and money. "Gambling Rage: Out of Control" (*U. S. News and World Report*, May 30, 1983) depicts a growing popular "urge to buck the odds and take a chance—on anything."

Another development receiving scrutiny in the early and mid-'80s is massive avoidance of taxes. "The Tax-Evasion Virus" (*Psychology Today*, March 1982) employed a medical metaphor to opine that "In the epidemiology of cheating, there is...contagion—and no vaccine in sight." Featured in *Business Week* for April 5, 1982 was "The Underground Economy's Hidden Force," a lengthy discussion of the "startling growth" of the refusal to report income for the purpose of avoiding taxes, which posits distrust of government as its central element. *Time*'s March 28, 1983 cover story, "Cheating by the Millions," also focused on the growing, open acceptance even of blatant tax evasion. *Time* noted that tax revenue lost to fraud tripled from 1973 to 1981 and project that '83 losses (possibly $300 billion) may entail a ten-fold jump over those of 1973.

In the military, reports of sabotage and the near-universal use of drugs continue to appear routinely, along with articles indicating the unreliability of enlisted persons as mindless instruments of destruction. The total fiasco of the April 1980 mission to rescue the American embassy hostages in Iran reflected, to many, the combat unreadiness of armed services personnel as a whole. During the following two years, political commentators of every stripe were astonished by the wholesale non-compliance which met a pre-draft registration law, as about one million 19- and 20-year-olds ignored the federal requirement to sign up. (In the spring of 1982 an annual reserve duty call-up in the Ukraine had to be cancelled when too few reported.)

If the "New Nationalism" component of the still-born New Right movement of the early '80s seemed to exist mainly as a media creation, like the Moral Majority, the alleged rise of the Ku Klux Klan also proved non-existent. In 1925, 40,000 had marched in a Washington,

D.C. rally; at their next Washington show of strength, on November 27, 1982, fewer than 40 appeared. And the thousands of counter-demonstrators on hand, breaking the confines of leftist ritual provided for them, used the occasion to riot, looting shops and injuring ten police.

The election of Reagan produced no social or ideological results for the Right; its efforts in favor of school prayer and creationism, and against abortion and conservation, clearly failed. A Louis Harris poll of January 1983 expressed Americans' desire for tougher anti-pollution laws, counter to the Reagan administration's hopes to use the depth of recession for a severe weakening of environmental statutes. Meanwhile, articles like "Behind the Public's Negative Attitude Toward Business" (*U.S. News & World Report,* July 12, 1982) and "A Red Light for Scofflaws" (*Time* Essay, January 24, 1983), which editorialized about the "extreme infectiousness" of the current spirit of generally ignoring laws of all kinds, are published frequently.

In a February 1983 Louis Harris poll on alienation, a record 62% registered a bitter estrangement from the idea of the supposed legitimacy of the rich and powerful, and leadership in general. "Clearly, alienation has cut deeper into the adult population of America than ever before," concluded Harris. Robert Wuthnow, "Moral Crisis in American Capitalism" (*Harvard Business Review*, March–April 1983), analyzed an unprecedented "fundamental uncertainty about the institutions of capitalism." And as the percentage of voters declines still further, young people are demonstrating an utter disinterest in politics. "Civics Gap: Alarming Challenge" (*U.S. News & World Report*, April 25, 1983) featured former Commissioner of Education Ernest L. Boyer, who spoke of an "upsurge of apathy and decline in public understanding" of government among students.

In the world of work, or should one say anti-work, the '80s continue to evidence a deepening disaffection. The reports and studies fuel countless stories on high turnover, the chronic "productivity crisis," growing "time theft," and the sharp increase (since 1974) of people interested only in part-time work, as well as on-the-job stress, unemployment insurance "abuse," etc.—the aspects of work refusal are virtually countless and unabating. *Dun's Business Month* for October 1982 dealt with the $40 billion a year "High Cost of Employee Theft," describing it as a "major cause of business failures," while in June 1983, followed with "How to Foil Employee Crime: Inside Thefts Can Destroy a Business—And Often Do." The continued strong growth in the use of lie detectors by employers is one obvious corollary to this facet of the vanishing work ethic.

Another prominent part of the syndrome, in terms of mid-'80s emphases, is referred to in *Business Horizons*' "Employee Substance Abuse: Epidemic of the Eighties" (July/August 1983), and by *Newsweek*'s "Taking Drugs on the Job" cover story (August 22, 1983), which outlined its "enormous" dimensions and cost to the economy.

The movement toward worker participation as a stabilizing principle gains ground against the backdrop of anti-work phenomena. The recession of 1981–83 was used by managers as a pressure to seek the best terms for the new rules; it did not prevent their institution, contrary to most predictions. Authority relations, in this area as elsewhere, will have to be increasingly participationist or they will collapse all the sooner.

In mid-September 1982, the first nationally sponsored conference on labor-management cooperation was held, with some 900 union, company, and government officials taking part. The Labor Department announced it would promote and encourage shop floor collaboration, a new U.S. policy aimed of course at undercutting worker indiscipline.

Chrysler Corporation Chairman Lee Iacocca, in a December 1982 speech to the Commercial Club of Boston, spoke of the crucial need to "get everyone on the same team—labor, management, and the government." He repeated this idea on June 30, 1983 to enthusiastic union representatives as the first businessman to address Michigan's AFL-CIO convention in its 25-year history. Similarly, the "Let's Work Together" series of spots by the radio and TV networks' Broadcasting Industry Committee to Improve American Productivity were widely aired, and Ford's two-page ad entitled "A Breakthrough in Labor Relations Has Helped Create the Highest Quality Vehicles in America" appeared prominently in 1983.

Since the '70s the new organizational model, at all levels, has been steadily moving forward. The spring 1982 *Journal of Contemporary Business* focused on "Theory X, Y, Z, or ?: Reshaping the American Workplace." John Simmons and William J. Mares' "Reforming Work" (*New York Times*, October 25, 1982) reported a "dramatically increased employee participation in management and ownership," aimed at reducing alienation and reversing the productivity decline, and amounting to "a quiet revolution...taking place on shop floors and in offices across America." The shift to tripartite negotiations in auto, steel and construction were examples of a tendency toward collaboration that must be expanded, according to "Ideology Revisited: America Looks Ahead" by David A. Heenan (*Sloan Management Review*, Winter 1982). Its stress on implementing a "one nation indivisible" solution reflects the powerful dis-integrative energies at large and points in the direction of a fascist choice of alternatives.

Among the many other influential references in fairly recent publications are Donald N. Scobel's "Business and Labor—from Adversaries to Allies" in the November–December 1982 *Harvard Business Review*, and D. Quinn Mills' March 1983 *Monthly Labor Review* offering, "Reforming the U.S. System of Collective Bargaining," which concludes that a new, official collaborative set-up is essential to avoid a high degree of "economic and social unrest" which would be counter to the interest "of the Nation as a whole."

Meanwhile, by the middle of 1983, the newsweeklies and monthly magazines had devoted much space to Harvard's Robert Reich, a Democratic Party advisor, whose "The Next American Frontier" advocates tripartite planning as an alternative to Reagan's neo-free market failures and beyond. The August 28, 1983 *New York Times Magazine* discussed an emerging national policy emphasis in this area, centering on the Industrial Policy Study Group made up of bankers, union officials, politicians, and high-tech corporation heads, and meeting at the AFL-CIO national headquarters. This corporatist tendency (see Frank Hearn, "The Corporatist Mood in the United States," *Telos* No. 56, useful for its bibliographic notes) is not confined to the U.S.; on August 1, 1983 a new USSR "Law on Work Collectives," featuring worker participation, was enacted under the direction of Andropov, who came to power in late 1982 expressly to combat a severe Soviet work refusal.

Of course before the '80s there were digital watches, pocket calculators, and *Star Wars*. But easily the biggest social impact of the early to middle years of the decade, occurring with the developing changes in work organization, has been that of the high-tech explosion with its promise of video games and computers for every business, dwelling and school.

1982 was the full inauguration of this blitz, as observed by such articles as "Computers for the Masses: The Revolution Is Just Beginning" early in the year (*U.S. News & World Report*, January 3, 1982), and *Time*'s January 3, 1983 cover story, "A New World Dawns," which proclaimed the computer Man of the Year for 1982.

The outlines are well-known to everyone, even though the meaning of this latest technological wave has been publicly discussed almost not at all. Suddenly we are in the Information Age, its benign—and inevitable—consequences to be merely accepted as facts of life. A two-page IBM ad announced the "new era" under the heading, "Information: There's Growing Agreement that It's the Name of the Age We

Live in." A TRW, Inc. ad of 1983 began, "There was a time when there was time. Once we could spend time with a new piece of information," proceeding to boast of the speed with which its computer systems can deal with "trillions of bits of information." But the processing of data—"information"—has nothing to do with understanding, and what comes to mind here is the social affliction just around the corner suggested in Tom Mooney's 1982 novel, *Easy Travel to Other Planets*, that of "information sickness."

It is also becoming ever more obvious that technology renders each succeeding generation more technology-dependent, further separated from nature, more fully colonized by the inauthentic and empty. The notion of people as appendages of machines, evoked in terms of 19th century industrialism, is even more relevant today. Apple Computer offered its product to the late 1983 consumer with the counsel, "Think of It as a Maserati for Your Mind," in a debasement of individuality and creation echoed by the claims that typing an instruction on a computer results in art or that word processors enable one to write. We become weaker, reduced, infantilized.

Meanwhile this barren future's dawning is heralded, especially for the young who may be expected to have been prepared for this contrived world, by the ugliness and boredom of today's. "Computer Camps for Kids," reveals a July 19, 1982 *Newsweek* article, followed by a look at education in that magazine's December 27, 1982 issue, entitled "The Great Computer Frenzy." The Apple Company announced in July 1983 its plan to provide free computers for every public school in California that asked for one, as colleges began to require that students purchase computers as part of registration. Howard Rheingold's "Video Games Go to School" (*Psychology Today*, September 1983) discussed the "profound transformation" of education represented by the introduction of classroom computers.

Benjamin Compain's "The New Literacy" (*Science Digest*, March 1983) matter-of-factly states that the ability to manipulate a computer will soon be the criterion of literacy. One can perhaps already see some of the products along this line of high-tech culture, such as the vacuous *USA Today*, "the Nation's Newspaper via Satellite," which arrived in 1983. The irony in the contrast between the claims of fulfillment and empowerment as promised by further "progress" and its real sterility and impoverishment is stunning. And occasionally it is almost funny, as in the case of CBS-TV's July 7, 1983 presentation, "1984 Revisited." The program zeroed in on the rise of the computer state and the consequent loss of privacy, etc. and was sponsored by Exxon Office Systems, whose frequent commercials featured a view of endless video display terminals lined up in a huge, faceless office, which could have graced the cover of any distopian novel.

Amitai Etzioni's *An Immodest Agenda: Rebuilding America Before the 21st Century* (1982) takes aim at an individualism that in the view of this sociologist, has disastrously advanced since the '60s to the point of threatening American society itself. The search for self-fulfillment, which involves a "retreat from work" and an "inability to defer gratification," affects 80% of the population and, according to Etzioni, is crippling virtually all the institutions that mediate between the individual and the state. While this "Immodest Agenda" is essentially a warning and a wish by one hoping to preserve and even renew the present order, others can see in high-tech the tools of uniformity and "objective" restraints necessary to do precisely that.

Computer entrepreneur Steven Wozniak staged an "Us Festival" in Southern California over the 1982 Labor Day weekend, intended to help transcend the threatening forces of the "me generation" by introducing the 400,000 music fans to a giant computer pavillion and such high-tech wonders as fifty-foot video screens. Steven Levy's "Bliss, Microchips and Rock & Roll" (*Rolling Stone*, October 14, 1982) called this effort "the marriage of rock and computer technology." The efficacy of this spectacle may be doubted, however, especially considering the fate of the second Us Festival, also held in San Bernadino county, during Memorial Day weekend, 1983. Several injuries occurred, and part of the crowd tore down fences, threw bottles at sheriff's deputies and rammed their cars into police cruisers.

Certainly the project of computerizing work in the neo-Taylorist direction of quantifying and tightly regulating employee output, is a major part of technology's combat with troublesome and capricious humanity. John Andrew's "Terminal Tedium" (*Wall Street Journal*, May 6, 1983) is typical of many articles describing the strong antipathy to computer-systematized work. Workers in a Blue Shield office in Massachusetts, for example, denounced the electronic set-up as simply an unbearable sweatshop and told Andrew they wouldn't be there long. In the May 15, 1983 *New York Times*, Richard McGahey ("High Tech, Low Hopes") wrote of the oppressive, low-paid work, such as computer assembly, that underlies the clean, dazzling facade of the new developments and warned of "increased class tensions."

With industrial robotics one detects high technology's wishful thinking that capital could reproduce itself while dispensing with an undependable proletariat. The growing number of "telecommuters", or those performing piece-work at home before computer screens, expresses some of this urge and is also part of a more general, isolating impulse at large. From the jump in one-person households to increased emphasis on "home entertainment center" equipment, portable music headgear and the like, we seem to be shrinking away from our social selves. High technology accelerates a sense of false self-sufficiency; an early 1983 ad for the Oregon Museum of Science and Industry cited new breakthroughs in home computers, including the not wholly unserious prediction that "Soon your refrigerator will talk to you even if no-one else will."

And yet despite the great barrage of enticements of all kinds (not forgetting economic pressures) in the schools, the media and elsewhere, much popular resistance to the computer age exists. Since Harold Hellman's 1976 work, *Technophobia*, more recent works have sounded the same theme, for example, *Blaming Technology* (1981) by Samuel C. Florman and *Science Anxiety* (1981) by Jeffrey V. Mallow. More recently, lots of articles have shown that girls still avoid mathematics, as well as video games, and detail a probably sharply growing distrust of technology among various groups throughout society. September's *Science '83* asked, "Are Kids Afraid to Become Scientists?", and wondered why more than half of U.S. high school students drop out of science and math by the 10th grade.

Behind all the ways work and technology can be reformulated and repackaged stands their basic domination and the resultant weariness and frustration felt so universally today. A world is faltering. It is defined by absurdities and so draining that our participation must be demanded if it is to continue to exist. The "issue" of "quality of life" is spurious. If as Fourier said, "Civilization becomes more odious as it nears its end," we at least can see not only the odium but more prospects for its end.

PRESENT-DAY BANALITIES

When contestation publicly re-emerged in the '60s, after virtually a half- century of dormancy, its militancy often betrayed a very underdeveloped sense of vision. Since World War I and subsequent depression and wars, hot and cold, this explicit renewal of the negative found itself on a new terrain and the spirit of revolt only scratched the surface before being diffused by a variety of factors.

From the end of that decade a significant deepening in the erosion of the dominant values and orientation has taken place, escaping the notice of those who forget that political struggles are predicated on more inchoate (even spontaneous!) social developments. Hence, a few words are in order regarding that which should be taken for granted as the minimum intelligence for any understanding of the '80s. To those whose comprehension of the "Reagan Era" is limited to lamenting the demise of the '60s, an apology for disturbing their slumber.

By way of introduction, two sets of contrasts. In November 1965 a power failure darkened New York City but the law-abiding restraint of its citizens was evident and widely praised by authority; internalized repression seemed to be wholly intact. When a similar blackout occurred there in 1977, however, "the party began from the minute the lights went out," as one participant described it. Massive and inter-racial looting commenced, even to the point of the setting up of distribution centers of free goods, and the only reported violence was suffered by those few police foolhardy enough to try to restore "order."

When John F. Kennedy was shot in 1963 the immediate reaction of many was shock and tears. Upon Reagan's shooting in 1981, when it wasn't yet known whether he would survive, the laughter of children became the topic of scores of journalists' commentaries.

Even anecdotally, then, the superficiality of the notion of a real ascendancy of Reaganism is immediately suggested. The efforts to introduce prayer and a biblical anti-evolution doctrine into the schools and to do away with abortion and environmental protection are, of course, in their failure, one measure of that, as is the November 1985 Roper poll which found that only 4 percent respect "Moral Majority" Falwell.

When the tendency is toward a deeper and deeper disillusionment with the American Dream, a picture of America that was invented in Hollywood half a century ago cannot be successfully promoted and will only emphasize the extent of disaffection by its effort. The slightly more

234

modern angle of the Right's propaganda is the re-invention and elevation of the acquisitive, middle-class careerist, the Yuppie, whose cultural dominance has been loudly trumpeted. But already the articles detailing the "dissatisfaction, anxiety, and physical problems" ("Life of a Yuppie Takes a Psychic Toll," *U.S. News & World Report*, April 29, 1985) of the upwardly-mobile are deflating this tiresome success image.

Likewise, the once-touted return of martial spirit under Reagan has largely been exposed. Most important in this context was the vast non-compliance of young men in the early '80s to the instituting of pre-draft registration requirements. The failure of the military to attract enlistees is seen in the enormous recruiting campaigns currently needed and in articles like "Honeymoon Over for Volunteer Armed Forces?" (*U.S. News & World Report*, June 10, 1985). Another conservative source, columnist George Will, also spoke (August 19, 1985) of this vulnerability by an important conclusion: "The more complex the military organization and the more sophisticated the technology, the more the success of the system depends on morale."

A crucial parallel involves the world of work, where the use of polygraph or "lie-detector" tests by employers has now passed the one million per year mark. A 1984 survey of merchants by American Hardware Mutual Insurance found that "80 percent of store owners think their employees are more likely to steal than ten years ago." Ward Howell International, a national employment agency, disclosed that false resumes and misrepresentation of job qualifications in general, based on their 1985 study, is very widespread and on the rise. Meanwhile, fast food chains are reportedly recruiting older workers at retirement homes because they can't find enough teenagers to fill shifts—despite the fact that 17.7 percent of U.S. teens are out of work. Along with these data are reports that drug use in the workplace has never been more prevalent, and a November 1985 announcement by the Labor Department of the largest single year increase in work-related injuries and illnesses since such figures began to be reported in 1973; the 11.7 percent jump resumes an earlier trend and can be reasonably linked to refusal of work as a major factor.

The vitality of the revolt against work syndrome is seen in the steadily growing popularity of participative management systems, which recognize that the "workers themselves must be the real source of discipline," as a July- August 1985 *Harvard Business Review* offering put it. The industrial relations literature is full of evidence that capital requires the voluntary participation of employees for its stability, if not survival. The unions, of course, provide the most important agency for this cooperation; the "landmark" 1984 contract between the United Auto Workers and General Motors- Toyota, for example, increased "access to plant decision-making" (*Christian Science Monitor*, June 27, 1985), and was also the first time a UAW dues increase was negotiated with the boss rather than voted by union delegates, which infuriated auto workers.

From a social control perspective, the judgement that the management of information will be more efficient than what prevails in a non-computerized economy establishes the foundation of the Information Society. But the Scientific Management movement of the '80s, a neo-Taylorist monitoring of typists, phone operators and all the rest by computers, is providing no easy road to a satisfactory productivity. The overwhelming response is one of anger, as humans resist fitting into the new, rationalized future and Silicon Valley, its new mecca, offers less a picture of gleaming success than one of pollution and lay-offs. The possibility that the impoverishment of daily life might even render work relatively satisfying, due to the vacuum of substance elsewhere, is rendered unlikely by technology's progressive degradation of work. There is no area of authenticity, no place to hide, and no one can miss this commonplace. The bumpersticker, "The worst day fishing is better than the best day working," remains true, as does the also popular "Different day, same bullshit."

Anguished commentaries about declining civic virtue are not confined to such data as the declining percentage of registered voters who do so, or to miscreants on the job, but also draw their content from a most irresponsible consumer culture. One favorite in this vein deals with increasing shoplifting, including the stories of the complete non-involvement of shoppers presented with very visible incidences of stealing. The near- universal placement of electronic alarms on store exits testifies to the extent of the phenomenon, as high tech vies with eroding allegiance to the work-and-pay rules. The present record level of the prison population, the growing state lottery mania, and the unchecked growth of the "underground economy" all testify to the shift in values. Concerning the latter subject, figures from the Internal Revenue Service show that tax cheating now costs the government over $100 billion as compared to less than $20 billion at the end of the '60s.

A deeper, visceral disaffection can be detected among the young, in terms of remarkable behavior patterns. *Psychology Today*'s January 1985 cover story asked, "Why Are Middle-Class Children Setting Their Worlds on Fire?" The alienation registered by widespread child arson is also evident in two November 1985 Gallup polls which showed that 12 percent of teenage girls suffer symptoms of anorexia nervosa (self-starvation) or bulimia (binge-and- purge syndrome), a much higher figure than had been previously estimated. In June 1985 national Center for Disease Control statistics were released that demonstrated a jump of 50 percent in the suicide rate of young men aged 15 to 24 from 1970 to 1980.

A September 1984 Gallup poll had found that only 23 percent of U.S. teenagers do not drink, the lowest figure recorded by the Gallup

Organization, and *Family Circle* and the Parents' Resource Institute for Drug Education reported in September 1985 that their four year study indicated a spread of drinking and drug abuse into the grammar schools.

During the same week of September 1985 Bishop James Malone, president of the National Conference of Catholic Bishops, declared that new emphasis on the teaching of sexual morality is "urgently needed," and U.S. Education Secretary William Bennett urged conservative activists to join him in a fight to restore a "coherent moral vision" to America's public schools.

Reality offers little or nothing to support the idea that even during the high noon of Reaganism has there been any renewal of faith in the promise of American life; quite the contrary, the increased enrollment in college business courses not withstanding. The idealist illusions of the '60s are mainly dead, and the failed counter-revolution of the Right is equally irrelevant. If the future is unclear, it at least seems obvious that a corrosive skepticism has dissolved much of the old foundation for repression and lies.

One could reply that this negation has only left us even more miserable; look at the growing levels of emotional disability, as reported not only by the National Institute of Mental Health but by a glance at the covers of the supermarket tabloids, with their continuing attention to depression, loneliness and stress or the great numbers of TV commercials devoted to pain relievers, alcohol treatment centers and the like. There is even a refusal of literacy taking place, with about 30 million illiterate adult Americans, and some have discussed this in terms of an intentional aversion to the whole of modern life. Horkheimer's later pessimism could be cited to echo current references to entropy and despair, "the feeling," as he put it, "that nothing further can be expected, at least nothing that depends on oneself."

And yet the psychologists seem to agree that we all have much rage inside, and there is, arguably, less than ever for authority to rely on for our continued suppression. A senescent order seems to have no cards left to play, beyond more technology; nothing in its ideological pocket, nothing up its sleeve. As Debord wrote in the late '70s, "it no longer promises anything. It no longer says: 'What appears is good, what is good appears.' It simply says 'It is so.' "

MEDIA, IRONY AND "BOB"

It is not my purpose here to lament the fact that culture has been liquidating itself for some time now. Artists no longer want to tell us anything—they have nothing left to say. With postmodernism the idea of style itself enters a stage of bankruptcy; its incoherent banality turns postmodernism into the fast-food chain of expression and reflects the exposed condition of representation in general.

In its enervated, late capitalist decline, art is increasingly no more than a specialized colony of the media. The vapid acquiescence of, say, a Warhol has made it easier for corporations like Mobil and Xerox to understand that all art, at base, serves authority. Thus their sponsorship of culture for the masses exists not only to improve their negative public images but also to promote the artistic for its own qualities. Philip Morris, to cite a most instrumental use of art, employs oversized graphics at the world's largest cigarette factory to create a culturally valorized workplace, in order to motivate and pacify workers. Media-style art uses symbols to drown out the employees' alienation and argue the existence of a shared cultural unity between owners, managers, and workers. This intention brings to mind perhaps the deepest function that Muzak attempts; one of its foremost psychologists and advisors, James Keenan, explained that "Muzak promotes the sharing of meaning because it massifies symbolism in which not a few but all can participate." Reaching 80 million people a day, Muzak is one of the grosser tactics in power's struggle against the global devaluation of symbols.

The Surrealists, among other avant-gardes, set themselves the goal of aestheticizing life. Today this goal is being realized at a time when avant- gardism is nearing extinction; the ubiquity of art as manipulation is achieving this aestheticization, and is no more than advertising and styles of consumerism. The fact that the world's best photography is expressed as TV commercials is a perfect illustration of the technologized, commodified culture striving to reach everyone.

This would-be conquest by media easily puts all the goods of culture in its service, as it must when there are so many signs that the whole spectacle of simulated life is running out of gas.

If the spiritless melange in painting known as postmodernism implies, by its recycling of elements from earlier eras, that development is at an end, so the tired current of "instant nostalgia" indicates a similar condition for massified art, media and the spectacle in general. The successful representation of life now relies, for its last resource or energy, on the re- use of ever more recent cultural memories. Occasionally the mass media themselves even make this recycling explicit, as in a TV commercial for lemonade: "Look what's happened to way back when/ Now everything old is new again."

It is among responses to this manipulated life, of course, that the deepest interest must lie, our weighing of the movement and meaning of responses. Irony, for example, was possibly always disconnective or defusing, in its tendency to substitute an easy joke for a too direct response to a loaded conversation or other critical situation. But if it was always in that sense "a form of appeasement," in Bill Berkson's phrase, for this undermining of dialogue, irony is now automatic and establishes complicity in a deeper sense. So much is "camp", and whatever subversive potential that once might have resided there is long dead. An ironic or sarcastic response to the world is nearly always present today; it is a cliche, a convention rather than a sign of independence.

Skepticism—or at least its image—is built into the parade of images and roles, though the reasons why it is needed cannot be comforting to those who do not wish to give up the synthetic. If "nihilism" is as close to everyone's grasp as rock music or the seven hours of television consumed on average per day, one can see, equally, that such "nihilism" is not enough and that the spectacle's strength is being strained. The further alienation must be represented and sold to us—consider "Miami Vice," for example, (and that it features cops is mostly irrelevant) with its ultra-hipness and angst—the more careful we must be to avoid its cultural-political recuperation and the more depth is required to do just that.

The rock videos of MTV at times seem to threaten the very integrity of the subjective; their frequent surrealism projects more powerful images than the Surrealists achieved, with more power to colonize imagination. David Letterman mocks the TV industry and his own format while enriching media; who would really be surprised to see explicitly "radical" angles presented there?

Meanwhile, the Church of the Subgenius is virtually a cultural industry in itself and its digs at religion, work, etc. pack no more punch than Letterman. In fact, culture needs such farce to pep up its dying appeal. Not surprisingly, "Rev." Ivan Stang, Subgenius founder, writes regularly for *High Performance: A Quarterly Magazine for the New Arts Audience* to help meet the art-head demand for new antics by his Church. The radical edge of the very popular Subgenius ensemble is not far from that of "Saturday Night Live", or that of *Artforum*, in which ready references to Adorno and Baudrillard can be found immediately following dozens of pages of gallery ads.

But if media, following art, and culture in general, tend to swallow up the critical and blunt the negative, that negative is not to be lost sight of. Despite the best efforts of hip, cynical substitutes reality certainly remains problematic, eluding media's grasp.

To cite just one area of apparent non-colonization, the refusal of work continues and deepens. *Time* for April 28, 1986 bemoaned "A Maddening Labor Mismatch," in which growing worker shortages co-exist with continued unemployment. The rejection of jobs by the young stands out most of all, especially considering the higher teenage and young-adult jobless rates. The May 20, 1986 *Fortune* cover story announced a shocking failure, that of the zero impact computers have had on output-per-hour in the office: "U.S. business has spent hundreds of billions of dollars on them, but white-collar productivity is no higher than it was in the late Sixties." And blue-collar productivity has presented an equally dismaying picture to authority; Wickham Skinner's "Productivity Paradox" (*Harvard Business Review*, July/August 1986) revealed that "American manufacturers' near-heroic efforts" have simply not gotten more work out of industrial workers.

Irony and images of estrangement, neutered as they are by the limits of culture, do not contain our disaffection. That disaffection undermines, as it must, the very basis of the ironic and artistic points of view.

NOTES

Beginning of Time, End of Time

1. Oswald Spengler, *The Decline of the West*, v. 1 (New York, 1926), p. 131.
2. Elias Canetti, *Crowds and Power* (New York, 1962), p. 397.
3. Guy Debord, *Society of the Spectacle* (Detroit, 1977), thesis 125.
4. Max Horkheimer and Theodor W. Adorno, *Dialektik der Aufklarung* (Amsterdam, 1947), p. 274.
5. Cioran, not to mention a host of anthropologists, makes this confusion; it is one reason he could say, "There is no going back to a pre-linguistic paradise, to a supremacy over time based upon some primordial stupidity." E.M. Cioran, *The Fall Into Time* (Chicago, 1970), p. 29. Another reason is the failure to imagine this "going back" as necessarily a social transformation on the order of the most basic "revolution."
6. Spengler, op. cit., p. 390.
7. Herbert Marcuse, *One-Dimensional Man* (Boston, 1964), p. 326.
8. Lucien Levy-Bruhl, *Primitive Mentality* (New York, 1923), p. 93. Paul Radin's *Primitive Man As Philosopher* (New York, 1927) is, it should be noted, a necessary corrective to Levy-Bruhl's view of early thought as non-individuated and dominated by "mystic" and "occult" patterns. Radin demonstrated that individuality, self-expression and tolerance mark early humanity.
9. H. and H.A. Frankfort, *The Intellectual Adventure of Ancient Man* (Chicago, 1946), p. 23.
10. Marie-Louise von Franz, *Time: Rhythm and Repose* (London, 1978), p. 5.
11. Jacquetta Hawks, *Man on Earth* (London, 1954), p. 13.
12. John G. Gunnell, *Political Philosophy and Time* (Middletown, Conn., 1968), p. 13; Mircea Eliade, *Cosmos and History* (New York, 1959), p. 86.
13. Cited by Thomas J. Cottle and Stephen L. Klineberg, *The Present of Things Future* (New York, 1974), p. 166.
14. Ibid., p. 168.
15. The hunter-gatherer mode occupied more than 99% of the span of human life.
16. Eric Alden Smith and Bruce Winterhalder, *Hunter Gatherer Foraging Strategies*, (Chicago, 1981), p. 4.
17. See, for example, Marshall Sahlins, *Stone Age Economics* (Chicago, 1972).
18. G.J. Whitrow, *Along the Fourth Dimension* (London, 1972), p. 119.
19. Mircea Eliade, *Myth and Reality* (New York, 1963), p. 51; E.R. Dodds, *The Ancient Concept of Progress* (Oxford, 1973), p. 3; W.K.C. Guthrie, *In the Beginning* (Ithaca, 1957), p. 69.
20. Norman O. Brown, *Love's Body* (New York, 1966), p. 148.
21. Walter Benjamin, *Illuminations* (New York, 1978), p. 328.
22. Mircea Eliade, *Shamanism* (Princeton, 1964), pp. 508, 486.
23. Loren Eisely, *The Invisible Pyramid* (New York, 1970), p. 113.
24. Claude Levy-Strauss, *Structural Anthropology* (New York, 1976), p. 28.
25. Grinnell, op cit., p. 17.
26. Grahame Clark and Stuart Piggott, *Prehistoric Societies* (New York, 1965), p. 43.
27. Erich Kahler, *Man the Measure* (New York, 1943), p. 39.
28. Leslie Paul, *Nature Into History* (London, 1957), p. 179.
29. Kahler, op. cit., p. 40.
30. Roderick Seidenberg, *Posthistoric Man* (Chapel Hill, 1950), p. 21.
31. Arnold Gehlen, *Man in the Age of Technology* (New York, 1980), p. 13.
32. Cited by Kahler, op. cit., p. 44.
33. Cited by Adolph E. Jensen, *Myth and Cult Among Primitive Peoples* (Chicago, 1963), p. 31.

242

34. Emile Durkheim, *Elementary Forms of Religious Life* (New York, 1965), p. 22.
35. Eliade, *Myth and Reality,* op. cit., pp. 95-96.
36. Elman Service, *The Hunters* (Englewood Cliffs, N.J., 1966), pp. 80-81. Recent work seems to bear out this picture; for example, John Nance, *The Gentle Tasaday: A Stone Age People in the Philippine Rain Forest* (New York, 1975).
37. Perhaps especially Sigmund Freud, *Civilization and its Discontents* (London, 1949).
38. E.M. Cioran, *The New Gods* (New York, 1974), p. 10.
39. Horkheimer and Adorno, op. cit., p. 14.
40. Morton Fried, "Evolution of Social Stratification," from Stanley Diamond, ed., *Culture in History* (New York, 1960), p. 715.
41. Gale E. Christianson, *The Wild Abyss* (New York, 1978), p. 20.
42. Lawrence Wright, *Clockwork Man* (New York, 1968), p. 12.
43. G.J. Whitrow, *The Natural Philosophy of Time* (Oxford, 1980), p. 56.
44. Henry Elmer Barnes, *The History of Western Civilization* (New York, 1935), p. 25.
45. Richard Glasser, *Time in French Life and Thought* (Manchester, 1972), p. 6.
46. Martin P. Nilsson, *Primitive Time-Reckoning* (London, 1920), p. 1.
47. William Irwin Thompson, *The Time Falling Bodies Take to Light: Mythology, Sexuality and the Origins of Culture* (New York, 1981), p. 211. Walter Benjamin's well-known "There is never a document of civilization which is not at the same time a document of barbarism," could be said to apply first and foremost to the calendar.
48. Mircea Eliade, *The Forge and the Crucible* (New York, 1971), p. 177.
49. There seems to be a striking parallel here to Marcuse's profound valorization of memory (even including a mutual endorsement of the cyclical view of time). See Martin Jay, "Anamnestic Totalization: Reflections on Marcuse's Theory of Remembrance," *Theory & Society* Vol. 11 (1982): No. 1.
50. J.B. Bury, *The Idea of Progress* (New York, 1932), pp. 8-9.
51. Christianson, op. cit., p. 86.
52. Nicolas Berdyaev, *The Meaning of History* (London, 1936), p. 1.
53. Wright, op. cit., p. 39.
54. Glasser, op. cit., p. 54.
55. Lewis Mumford, *Interpretations and Forecasts, 1922-1972* (New York, 1972), p. 271.
56. Lewis Mumford, *Technics and Civilization* (New York, 1934), p. 16.
57. Glasser, op. cit., p. 56.
58. Norman Cohn, *The Pursuit of the Millenium* (Fairlawn, N.J., 1957), p. 186.
59. The celebration of the Feast of Fools, which reached its height in Europe at this time, was a mocking of religious authority. It involved a grotesquely costumed figure representing the higher clergy, led into church seated backwards on an ass with garments inside out, and dancing or reversing the order of the liturgy.

   Also, it is not inconceivable that the Black Plague, which decimated Europe from 1348-1350, was in a sense a massive, visceral reaction to the attack of modern time.
60. Jacob Bronowski, *The Ascent of Man* (Boston, 1974), p. 78.
61. Yi-Fu Tuan, *Space and Place* (Minneapolis, 1977), p. 123.
62. Fernand Braudel, *Capitalism and Material Life, 1400-1800* (London, 1967), p. 60.
63. Ernst Kantorowiscz, *The King's Two Bodies* (Princeton, 1957), p. 274. Gustav Bilfinger, in the 1890s, also understood the change from the medieval to the modern age as a change in the nature of time.
64. Jacques LeGoff, *Time, Work and Culture in the Middle Ages* (Chicago, 1980), p. 51.
65. S. Lilley, *Men, Machines and History* (London, 1948), p. 44.
66. Mumford, *Technics and Civilization*, op. cit., p. 14.
67. Marx to Engels, January 28, 1863, *The Letters of Karl Marx* (Englewood Cliffs, N.J., 1979), p. 168.
68. Charles Newman, introduction to Cioran's *Fall into Time,* op. cit., p. 10.
69. Arnold Gehlen, *Man in the Age of Technology* (New York, 1980), p. 94.
70. Horkheimer and Adorno, op. cit., p. 7.

71. Sebastian de Grazia, *Of Time, Work, and Leisure* (New York, 1962), pp. 310-311.
72. John Milton, *Paradise Lost* (Oxford, 1968), X, 1054-5.
73. Octavio Paz, *Alternating Currents* (New York, 1973), p. 146.
74. E.P. Thompson, "Time, Work-Discipline, and Industrial Capitalism," *Past and Present* #38 (December 1967).
75. For example, John Zerzan, "Industrialism and Domestication," *Fifth Estate*, April, 1976.
76. Time re-began for the new Republic on September 22, 1792. Year One of the new calendar disclosed that the number of no-work holidays had been cut in half, a radically unpopular idea!
77. Benjamin, *op. cit.*, p. 264.
78. Georges Poulet, *Studies in Human Time* (New York, 1956), p. 273.
79. Robert Louis Stevenson, *Virginibus Puerisque and Other Papers* (New York, 1893), pp. 254-5.
80. Benjamin, *op. cit.*, p. 253.
81. Stuart Ewen, *Captains of Consciousness: Advertising and the Roots of the Consumer Culture* (New York, 1976), p. 198.
82. John Zerzan, "Origins and Meaning of World War I," *TELOS* 49 (Fall 1981), pp. 97-116.
83. Raymond Klibansky, "The Philosophic Character of History," in Raymond Klibansky and H.J. Paton, editors, *Philosophy and History: The Ernst Cassirer Festschrift* (New York, 1963), p. 330.
84. John Berger, *Permanent Red* (London, 1960), p. 112.
85. "History is a nightmare from which I am trying to awaken." James Joyce, *Ulysses* (New York, 1961), p. 34.
86. Donald M. Lowe, *History of Bourgeois Perception* (Chicago, 1982), p. 117.
87. Theodor W. Adorno, *The Jargon of Authenticity* (Evanston, Ill., 1973), p. 88.
88. For example, Huxley's *After Many a Summer Dies the Swan* (New York, 1939) and *Time Must Have a Stop* (New York, 1944).
89. N.J. Berrill, *Man's Emerging Mind* (New York, 1955), pp. 163-4.
90. Ludwig Wittgenstein, *Notebooks, 1914-1916* (Chicago, 1979), p. 74e.
91. Joost A. M. Meerloo, *The Two Faces of Man* (New York, 1954), p. 23.
92. Raoul Vaneigem, *The Revolution of Everyday Life* (London, 1975), p. 220.
93. *Ibid.*, p. 228.
94. Consider Jacques Ellul, *The Technological System* (New York, 1980) as to whether it is time or technology that "comes first." All of the basic, society-dominating traits he attributes to technology are, more basically, those of time. Perhaps a tell-tale sign that he is still one remove away from the most fundamental level is the spatial character of his conclusion that "technology is the only place where form and being are identical." p. 231.
95. Service, *op. cit.*, p. 67.
96. Richard Schlegel, *Time and the Physical World* (E. Lansing, 1961), p. 16.
97. Samuel Beckett, *Waiting for Godot* (New York, 1954), p. 32.
98. George W. Morgan, *The Human Predicament: Dissolution and Wholeness* (Providence, 1968), p. 41.
99. Loren Eisely, *The Invisible Pyramid, op. cit.*, p. 102.
100. Robert Lowell, *Notebook, 1967-68* (New York, 1969), p. 60.
101. Herbert Marcuse, *Eros and Civilization* (New York, 1955), p. 213.
102. Norman O. Brown, *Life Against Death* (Middletown, Conn., 1959), pp. 95, 103, for example.
103. Christopher Lasch, *The Culture of Narcissism* (New York, 1978), p. 53.
104. Burt Alpert, *Getting Godel's Goat: A Stoned Jogging Journal Through Hofstadter* (San Francisco, 1982), p.1.
105. Aldous Huxley, *After Many a Summer Dies the Swan, op. cit.*, p. 117.

244

106. Theodor W. Adorno, *Negative Dialectics* (New York, 1973), p. 370.

107. Benjamin, *op. cit.*, p. 263.

108. Cited by Spengler, *op. cit.*, p. 103.

109. For example, Julian Jaynes, *The Origin of Consciousness in the Breakdown of the Bicameral Mind* (Boston, 1977), p. 280.

110. William Morris, *News from Nowhere* (London, 1915), p. 278.

Language: Origin and Meaning

1. Claude Levi-Strauss, *The Savage Mind* (Chicago, 1966), p. 245.

2. Theodor W. Adorno, *Minima Moralia* (London, 1974), p. 72.

3. Friedrich Nietzsche, *The Will to Power* (New York, 1967), p. 428.

4. Paul A. Gaeng, *Introduction to the Principles of Language* (New York, 1971, p. 1.

5. Rosalind Coward and John Ellis, *Language and Materialism: Developments in Semiology and the Theory of the Subject* (London, 1977), p. 1.

6. Hans-George Gadamer, *Truth and Method* (New York, 1982), p. 340. Also, Susanne K. Langer, *Philosophy in a New Key* (Cambridge, 1980), p. 103: "Language is, without a doubt, the most momentous and at the same time mysterious product of the human mind."

7. A.S. Diamond, *The History and Origin of Language* (New York, 1959), p. 6. The physicist-philosopher David Bohm has proposed a new model of language called the "rheomode," aimed at reversing this development by re- establishing the primacy of the verb. His aim is to reduce the subject-object split, so pronounced in the West since Descartes and increasingly an area of contestation by other such "holistic" scientists as well, such as Fritjof Capra and David Dossey.

8. Benjamin Lee Whorf, "Science and Linguistics," S.I. Hayakawa, ed., *Language in Action* (New York, 1941), pp. 311-313.

9. H.E.L. Mellersh, *The Story of Early Man* (New York, 1960), pp. 106- 107.

10. Arnold J. Toynbee, *A Study of Early Man* (New York, 1947), p. 198.

11. Ernst Cassirer, *An Essay on Man* (New Haven, 1944), p. 135.

12. It may be worth referring here to the hermaneutic motto that "Man *is* language," expressive of the drift toward a "linguistic" phenomenology with Heidegger and Ricoeur. In *Being and Time* Heidegger specifically maintains that perception becomes what it is only with respect to the fundamental context of language, and Ricoeur finds that all experience is already mediated via a world of symbols. See Don Ihde, *Existential Technics* (Albany, 1983), p. 145.

13. George Steiner, *After Babel: Aspects of Language and Translation* (New York, 1975), p. 229.

14. "...words, symbolic and wholly unlike their objects." George Santayana, *Dominations and Powers* (New York, 1951), p. 143.

15. E.M. Cioran, *The Fall Into Time* (Chicago, 1970), p. 12.

16. Roland Barthes, "Literature and Signification," *Cultural Essays* (Evanston, 1972), p. 278.

17. Max Horkheimer, "The End of Reason," Andrew Arato and Eike Gebhardt, eds., *The Essential Frankfort School Reader* (New York, 1978), p. 47.

18. Cassirer, *op. cit.*, p. 25.

19. Mayra Bloom, "Don't Teach Your Baby to Read" (letter to editor), *Co- Evolution Quarterly* (Winter 1981), p. 102.

20. The fairly extensive literature on the supposed ability of animals to learn language is not relevant here; the efficacy of training primates or others only demonstrates that it is possible to domesticate them. The nature and origin of language as domestication is not thereby addressed.

21. Noam Ziv and Jagdish N. Hattiangad, "Essence vs. Evolution in Language," *Word:*

Journal of the International Linguistics Association (August 1982), p. 86.

22. "The beginning of communication by symbolic languages in mankind cannot be dated, even approximately." Vanne Goodall, *The Quest for Man* (New York, 1975), p. 203.

23. Bernard Campbell, *Mankind Emerging* (Boston, 1976), p. 193.

24. "Speech was given to man to disguise his thoughts." Appropriately, this quote is attributed to Tallyrand, diplomat and statesman (1754-1838).

25. Peter Caws, "The Structure of Discovery," *Science* No. 166 (1969), p. 1380.

26. Olivia Vlahos, *Human Beginnings* (New York, 1966), p. 140.

27. Emile Durkheim, *Division of Labor in Society* (Glencoe, 1960), p. 50.

28. Julian Jaynes, *The Origins of Consciousness in the Breakdown of the Bicameral Mind* (Boston, 1976), p. 130.

29. Jaynes sees language emerging no sooner than the Upper Paleolithic age (c. 40,000 B.C.), when stone tool technology experienced an accelerated development. But even among those whose conception of language puts its emergence at a vastly earlier epoch, the late Stone Age is understood as pivotal; e.g. "whatever the state of language before the Upper Paleolithic, it must have undergone spectacular changes afterwards." John E. Pfeiffer, *The Creative Explosion* (New York, 1982), p. 71.

30. Frederick Engels, *The Part Played by Labor in the Transition from Ape to Man* (Peking, 1975), pp. 4-6.

31. This is not to deny there is some division based on sexual differentiation. But ascribing too great a role to the sexual division of labor would also be a mistake, one which seems to be routinely made. Consider the apparently contradictory two sentences by which a leading anthropologist sums up the matter: "The division of labor by sex is virtually universal. Men hunt and gather; women primarily gather and hunt small game; both sexes fish and gather shellfish." Richard B. Lee, "Is there a Foraging Mode of Production?" *California Journal of Anthropology*, (Spring 1981), p. 15.

32. Sigmund Freud, *The Standard Edition of the Complete Psychological Works of Sigmund Freud* (London, 1953-1974), Vol. 15, p. 167.

33. Jacques Lacan, *The Function of Language in Psychoanalysis* (Baltimore, 1968).

34. Mircea Eliade, *Shamanism* (Princeton, 1964), p. 99.

35. John Zerzan, "Beginning of Time, End of Time", *Fifth Estate*, (Summer 1983).

36. Russell Fraser, *The Language of Adam* (New York, 1977), p. 1.

37. Walter Benjamin, "On Language as Such and on the Language of Man," *Reflections* (New York, 1978), p. 328.

38. Norman O. Brown, *Love's Body* (New York, 1966), p. 257.

39. "...a name is the vastest generative idea that was ever conceived." Langer, *op. cit.*, p. 142.

40. Mikel Dufrenne, *Language & Philosophy 7* (Bloomington, 1963), p. 101.

41. Oswald Spengler, *The Decline of the West* Vol. I. (New York, 1929), p. 123. "Animals do not realize that we name them. Or else they do realize it, and that may be why they fear us." Elias Canetti, *The Human Province* (New York, 1978), p. 14.

42. Quoted by Pierre Clastres, *Society Against the State* (New York, 1977), p. 166.

43. R.B. Lee, *op. cit.*, p. 14.

44. Quoted by David R. Harris, "Alternative Pathways Toward Agriculture," Charles A. Reed, ed., *Origins of Agriculture* (The Hague, 1977), pp. 180- 181.

45. Max Horkheimer and Theodor W. Adorno, *Dialectic of Nature* (New York, 1972), p. 32.

46. Mario Pei, *The Story of Language* (Philadelphia, 1965), p. 199.

47. Roland Barthes, *Writing Degree Zero* (New York, 1968), p. 10.

48. Cassirer, *op. cit.*, p. 87.

49. Max Muller, "The Philosophy of Mythology," addendum to *Introduction to the Science of Religion* (London, 1873), p. 353.

50. Pfeiffer, *op. cit.*, chapters 8, 9.

246

51. A.S. Diamond, *The History and Origins of Language* (New York, 1959), p. 267.
52. Willard Van Orman Quine, *Word and Object* (New York, 1960), p. 170.
53. Jacques Derrida, *Writing and Difference* (Chicago, 1978), p. 4.
54. Sigmund Freud, *The Future of an Illusion* (New York, 1955), p. 10.
55. Claude Levi-Strauss, *Tristes Tropiques* (New York, 1961), pp. 292, 293.
56. Jacques Derrida, *Edmund Husserl's Origin of Geometry* (Stony Brook, New York, 1978), pp. 87-88.
57. Eugenio Trias, *Philosophy and its Shadow* (New York, 1983) p. 74.
58. It is noteworthy that this literary revolt against language has coincided with a very significant resistance to time as well. Proust, Joyce, Dos Passos, Faulkner, Gide, Virginia Woolf, Borges, among others, have all tried to challenge the given dimension of time.
59. Elias Canetti, *The Conscience of Words* (New York, 1979), p. 142.
60. Robert Harbison, *Deliberate Regression* (New York, 1980), p. xvi.
61. R.D. Laing, *The Politics of Experience* (New York, 1967), p. 11.
Special thanks to Alice Carnes for assistance throughout.

Number: Its Origin and Evolution

1. ". . .the idea of number implies the simple intuition of a multiplicity of parts or units, which are absolutely alike." Henri Bergson, *Time and Free Will* (London, 1910), p. 76.
2. H. Dingle, "Physics and God," *Hibbert Journal,* Vol. XXVI, No. 1 (1928), p. 44.
3. Max Horkheimer and Theodor W. Adorno, *The Dialectic of Enlightenment* (New York, 1972), p. 21.
4. Robert C. Neville, *Freedom and Cosmology* (New Haven, 1974), p. 83.
5. J.D. Bernal, *The Extension of Man* (London, 1972), p. 27.
6. Hermann Weyl, *The Philosophy of Mathematics and Natural Science* (Princeton, 1949), p. 144.
7. ". . .the number-language of a mathematic and the grammar of a tongue are structurally alike." Oswald Spengler, *The Decline of the West,* Vol. 1 (New York, 1929), p. 56.
8. Max Black, *The Nature of Mathematics* (London, 1933), p. 4.
9. H. Levy, *The Universe of Science* (New York, 1933), p. 82.
10. Charles Parsons, *Mathematics in Philosophy* (Ithaca, 1980), p. 176.
11. Alfred North Whitehead, *Eine Enfürüng in die Mathematik* (Berne, 1928), pp. 41-47. (Generality and the will to generality not discussed in English edition.)
12. "All human knowledge is either experience or mathematics." Friederich Nietzsche, *The Will to Power* (New York, 1967), #530 (p. 288).
13. Arend Heyting, quoted in Claude Levi-Strauss, *The Savage Mind* (Chicago, 1966), p. 248.
14. Karl Vossler, *The Spirit of Language in Civilization* (London, 1932), p. 212.
15. Theodor W. Adorno, *Negative Dialectics* (New York, 1973), p. 148.
16. Ibid., p. 5.
17. Michel Foucault, *The Archaeology of Knowledge* (New York, 1972), pp. 188-189.
18. Quoted in Morris Kline, *Mathematics: The Loss of Certainty* (New York, 1980), p. 99.
19. Franz Boaz, *The Mind of Primitive Man* (New York, 1938), pp. 218-219.
20. Tobias Dantzig, *Number: The Language of Science* (New York, 1959), p. 5.
21. C.R. Hallpike, *The Foundations of Primitive Thought* (Oxford, 1979), p. 267.
22. Raoul Allier, *The Mind of the Savage* (New York, 1929), p. 239.
23. Cited in Jeremy Campbell, *Grammatical Man: Information, Entropy, Language, and Life* (New York, 1982), p. 153.
24. Leslie A. White, "The Agricultural Revolution," from *A Reader in Cultural Change,* Vol. 1, edited by Ivan A. Brady and Barry L. Isaac (Cambridge, MA 1975), pp. 101-102.
25. Dorothy Lee, "Being and Value in a Primitive Culture," *The Journal of Philosphy,* Vo. XLVI. No. 13 (1949), p. 403.

26. Max Wertheimer, "Numbers and Number Concepts in Primitive Peoples," *A Source Book of Gestalt Psychology,* edited by Willis D. Ellis (London, 1938), pp. 265-267.

27. Bryan Morgan, *Men and Discoveries in Mathematics* (London, 1972), p. 12.

28. Alex Comfort, *I and That* (New York, 1979), p. 66.

29. Eric Partridge, *Origins: A Short Etymological Dictionary of Modern English* (New York, 1983), pp. 435-436.

30. Dorothy Lee, "Lineal and Nonlineal Codifications of Reality," *Psychosomatic Medicine,* Vol. 12, No. 2 (1950), p. 96.

31. Marshall Sahlins, from "Discussions, Part II," in *Man the Hunter,* edited by Richard B. Lee and Irven DeVore (Chicago, 1968), p. 89. Sahlins, *Stone Age Economics* (Chicago, 1972), p. 10.

32. Isaac, Glynn L., "Chronology and The Temple of Cultural Change during the Pleistocene," in *The Calibration of Human Evolution,* edited by W.W. Bishop and J.A. Miller (Edinburgh, 1972).

33. Sahlins, *Stone Age Economics,* pp. 278-279.

34. Albert Spaulding Cook, *Myth and Language* (Bloomington, 1980), p. 9.

35. C.S. Belshaw, "Theoretical Problems in Economic Anthropology," in *Social Organization,* edited by Maurice Freedman (Chicago, 1967), p. 35.

36. Pierre Clastres, *Society Against the State* (New York, 1977), p. 7.

37. Sahlins, Ibid., p. 82.

38. John E. Pfeiffer, *The Creative Explosion* (New York, 1982), p. 64.

39. Lewis Mumford, *The Myth of the Machine* (New York, 1967), pp. 139-140.

40. Jacques Derrida, *Edmund Husserl's Origin of Geometry: An Introduction* (Stony Brook, NY, 1978), p. 128.

41. Hannah Arendt, *The Human Condition* (Chicago, 1958), p. 265.

42. Weyl, *Ibid.,* p. 66.

43. A.L. Kroeber, *Anthropology* (New York, 1948), p. 471.

44. Carleton S. Coon, *The Story of Man* (New York, 1954), p. 322.

45. Frederick Turner, *Beyond Geography: The Western Spirit Against the Wilderness* (New York, 1980), p. 66.

46. Lawrence Kubie, *Practical and Theoretical Aspects of Psychoanalysis* (New York, 1950), p. 19.

47. Morris R. Cohen and I. E. Drabkin, *A Sourcebook in Greek Science* (Cambridge MA, 1966), p. 34, n. 13.

48. Joseph Campbell, *Oriental Mythology (The Masks of God,* Vol. 2) (New York, 1962), pp. 41-42.

49. Richard Olson, *Science Deified, Science Defied* (Berkeley, 1982), p. 30.

50. J.D. Bernal, *Science in History,* Vol. 1 (Cambridge MA, 1971), p. 120.

51. Frederick Bodmer, *The Loom of Language* (New York, 1944), p. 44.

52. Charles J. Brainerd, *The Origin of the Number Concept* (New York, 1979), p. 6.

53. *Ibid.,* p. 9.

54. William M. Ivens, Jr., *Art and Geometry* (Cambridge, 1946), p. 30.

55. C.I. Lewis, *Mind and World Order* (New York, 1956), p. vii.

56. Olson, *Op. cit.,* p. 112.

57. Plato predicated the beginning of the state on the "natural" inequality reflected in division of labor. Productive endeavor is from the beginning organized through specialization and division of work, and the state is not only derived from it but acquires stabilility via this fragmentation and coordination. *The Republic,* translated by G.M.A. Grube (London, 1981), sections 369, 370.

58. It can be cogently argued that Plato and Aristotle share essentially the same reductive method. For example, Burt Alpert, *Inversions* (San Francisco, 1973), chapters 5 and 6.

59. David S. Landes, *Revolution in Time* (Cambridge MA, 1983), p. 78.

60. Lewis Mumford, *The Myth of the Machine* (New York, 1967), p. 278.

248

61. A.C. Crombie, *Medieval and Early Modern Science,* Vol. 1 (Cambridge MA, 1967), p. 178.

62. Ibid., pp. 74-75.

63. Lewis Mumford, *The Condition of Men* (New York, 1944), p. 176.

64. Arnold Pacey, *The Maze of Ingenuity* (Cambridge MA, 1976), p. 96.

65. George Sarton, *Sarton on the History of Science* (Cambridge MA, 1976), p. 96.

66. Edwin Arthut Burtt, *The Metaphysical Foundations of Modern Physical Science* (London, 1925), p. 56.

67. Karl Jaspers, *The Origin and Goal of History* (New Haven, 1953), p. 89.

68. Franz Borkenau, *Die Ubergang vom feudalen zum burgerlichen Weltbild* (Paris, 1934). The division of labor thesis is central to Borkenau's attempt to establish the origin of manufacturing period's mentality. Descartes' view of animals as merely cleverly contrived mechanisms - machines - is a product, for example, of the heightened objectification involved in the jump in fragmented work.

69. Carlo M. Cipolla, *Clocks and Culture, 1300-1700* (New York, 1967), p. 57.

70. Edmund Husserl, *The Crisis of European Sciences and Transcendental Phenomenology* (Evanston, 1970), pp. 21-59.

71. Gerald J. Galagan, *The Logic of Modernity* (New York, 1982), p. 31.

72. Weyl, *Op. cit.,* p. 139.

73. R.G. Collingwood, *An Essay on Metaphysics* (London, 1940), p. 256.

74. Charles Coulton Gillispie, *The Edge of Objectivity* (Princeton, 1960), p. 81.

75. In the spatialized age of trade and navigation that was the seventeenth century, it is not accidental that these advances in math provide solutions to problems of motion. Similarly, and more concretely, probability and statistics originate at this time to deal with the complexities of insuring ships.

76. There is much validity to the claim that the main thrust of modern intellectual life is to have "followed Plato and Descartes over the abyss into the insane delusion that the true essence of man lies in disembodied mental activity." Norman O. Brown, *Life Against Death* (New York, 1959), p. 34.

77. Quoted from Alexander Rustow, *Freedom and Domination* (Princeton, 1980), p. 402.

78. Quoted in Pacey, *Op cit.,* p. 134.

79. Carolyn Merchant, *The Death of Nature* (San Francisco, 1980), p. 288.

80. *Ibid.,* p. 205.

81. Ernst Cassirer, *The Philosophy of Symbolic Forms* (New Haven, 1957), p. 341.

82. G.H. Baillie, *Clocks and Watches: An Historical Bibliography* (London, 1951), p. 103.

83. Richard Courrant and Herbert Robbins, *What Is Mathematics?* (London, 1941), p. 9.

84. Ernst Cassirer, *An Essay on Man* (New Haven, 1944), p. 217.

85. Burtt, *Op. cit.,* p. 261.

86. Alfred North Whitehead, *Science and the Modern World* (New York, 1948), p. 37.

87. Christopher Hill, *Intellectual Origins of the English Revolution* (Oxford, 1965), p. 245.

88. Lawrence LeShan and Henry Morgenau, *Einstein's Space and Van Gogh's Sky* (New York, 1982), p. 169.

89. Paul Bekker, *The Story of Music: An Historical Sketch of the Changes in Musical Form* (New York, 1927), pp. 77-114.

90. John Katz, *The Will to Civilization* (New York, 1957), p. 85.

91. J.M. Dubbey, *The Mathematical Work of Charles Babbage* (Cambridge, 1978). Douglas Hofstadter, *Gödel, Escher, Bach: An Eternal Golden Braid* (New York, 1979), p. 25.

92. A.N. Whitehead, *Space and the Modern World* (New York, 1931), p. 49.

93. George Boole, *Studies* (London, 1952), pp. 187-188.

94. Theodor W. Adorno, *Against Epistemology: A Metacritique* (Cambridge MA, 1983), p. 55.

95. Bertrand Russell, *Introduction to Mathematical Philosophy* (London, 1919), p. 194.

96. Paul A. Schilpp, editor, *The Philosophy of Bertrand Russell* (New York, 1951). See

especially Russell's "Reply to Criticisms," p. 694.

97. Cassirer, 1957, *Op. cit.*, p. 387, quoting Hilbert from the German. The principal effort was Russell and Whitehead's *Principia Mathematica* (London, 1910-1913). Another try is found in Brouwer's intuitionist approach, which claims that numerical thinking stands at the beginning of all thought and that it should be thought of as "an essentially languageless activity of the mind having its origin in the perception of a move of time." D. Van Dalen, editor, *Brouwer's Cambridge Lectures on Intuitionism* (Cambridge, 1981), p. 4.

98. Yi-Fu Tuan, *Space and Place* (Minneapolis, 1977), p. 200.

99. Fritjof Capra, *The Turning Point* (New York, 1981), p. 74.

100. Gillispie, *Op cit.*, p. 87.

101. Horkheimer and Adorno, *Op. cit.*, p. 24.

102. Rudy Rucker, *Infinity and the Mind* (Boston, 1982), p. 161.

103. Morris Kline, *Mathematics: The Loss of Certainty* (New York, 1980), p. 3.

104. Ernest Nagel and James R. Newman, *Godel's Proof* (New York, 1958), p. 11.

105. *Ibid.*, p. 101.

106. Jurgen Habermas, *Philosophical-Political Profiles* (Minneapolis, 1983),p. 100.

107. Raymond Firth, *Symbols: Public and Private* (Ithaca, 1973), p. 82.

108. Jagjit Singh, *Great Ideas in Information Theory and Cybernetics* (New York, 1966), p. 7.

109. Concerning the inevitability of the "information environment," we are told, even threatened, on all sides. For example: "The sooner this fact and its consquences become part of our consensual reality, the better for everyone..."

110. Amiel Feinstein, *Foundations of Information Theory* (New York, 1958), p. 1.

111. The sharp rise in the number of single-person households since the 1960s, the fact (early 1984) that American's daily consumption of television is more than seven hours, etc.

112. Alan Turing, "Computing Machinery and Intelligence," *Mind*, Vol. LIX, No. 256. (1950).

113. Bruce Mazlish, "The Fourth Discontinuity," *Technology and Culture*, Voi. 8, No. 8. (January 1967), pp. 14-15.

114. Martin Gardner, *Logic Machines and Diagrams* (Chicago, 1982), p. 148.

115. John Haugeland, "Semantic Engines: An Introduction to Mind Design," *Mind Design: Philosophy, Psychology, Artificial Intelligence,* edited by John Haugeland (Montgom VT, 1981), p. 1.

116. Martin Heidegger, *Introduction to Metaphysics* (New Haven, 1959), p. 49.

117. For example: Hofstadter, *Op. cit.*, pp. 677, 696; Igor Aleksander and Piers Burnett, *Reinventing Man: The Robot Becomes Reality* (New York, 1983); Robert E. Mueller and Erik T. Mueller, "Would An Intelligence Computer Have A 'Right to Life'?," Pamela McCorduck, *Machines Who Think* (New York, 1979) *Creative Computing* (August 1983); Geoff Simons, *Are Computers Alive?: Evolution and New Life Forms* (Boston, 1984)—a very tiny sampling. A more popular example is the "Affectionate Machine," special issue of *Psychology Today,* December 1983.

Axis Point of American Industrialism

1. Samuel Rezneck, *Business Depressions and Financial Panics* (New York, 1968), p. 24.

2. Merle Curti, *Social Ideas of American Educators* (New York, 1935), p. 98.

3. David A. Hounshell, *From the American System to Mass Production, 1800- 1932* (Baltimore, 1984), pp. 25-26.

4. Thomas C. Cochran, *Frontiers of Change: Early Industrialism in America* (New York, 1981), p. 53.

5. Rezneck, *op. cit.*, p. 38.

6. Hounshell, *op. cit.*, p. 43.

7. Cochran, *op. cit.*, p. 74.

8. Norman Ware, *The Industrial Worker, 1840-1860* (New York, 1964), p. x.

9. Victor S. Clark, *History of Manufactures in the United States, 1607- 1860* (Washington, 1916), p. 264.

10. Edward Everett, "Fourth of July at Lowell (1830)," Michael Folsom and Steve D. Lubar, eds., *The Philosophy of Manufactures: Early Debates Over Industrialization in the United States* (Cambridge, 1982), p. 292.

11. Marvin Fisher, *Workshops in the Wilderness: The European Response to American Industrialization, 1830-1860* (New York, 1967), p. 38.

12. Thomas C. Cochran, *Business in American Life: A History* (New York, 1972), p. 38.

13. For example, Brooke Hindle, "The Exhilaration of Early American Technology: An Essay," Brooke Hindle, *Technology in Early America* (Chapel Hill, 1966), p. 3.

14. Merritt Roe Smith, *Harpers Ferry Armory and the New Technology* (Ithaca, 1977).

15. *Ibid.* p. 22.

16. Page Smith, *The Nation Comes of Age* (New York, 1981), p. 795.

17. Philip Taft and Philip Ross, "American Labor Violence: Its Causes, Character, and Outcome," H.D. Graham and T.R. Gurr, eds., *The History of Violence in America* (New York, 1969), p. 281.

18. William Faux, "Memorable Days in America," Reuben Gold Thwaites, ed., *Early Western Travels, 1748-1846*, Vol. XI (Cleveland, 1905), p. 141.

19. *Ibid.*, (Nov. 6 and 3, 1819), pp. 227, 215.

20. Jane Louise Mesick, *The English Traveller in America, 1785-1835* (New York, 1922), p. 306.

21. *Ibid.*, p. 152.

22. Bruce Laurie, *Working People of Philadelphia, 1800-1850* (Philadelphia, 1980), p. 33.

23. Daniel J. Boorstin, *The Americans: The National Experience* (New York, 1965), p. 26.

24. Carl Russell Fish, *The Rise of the Common Man* (New York, 1927), p. 91.

25. Clark, *op. cit.*, p. 401.

26. For example, Robert S. Woodbury, "The 'American System' of Manufacture," Edwin T. Layton, Jr., ed., *Technology and Social Change in America* (New York, 1973), p. 54.

27. Cochran, *Frontiers*, p. 135.

28. H.J. Habakkuk, *American and British Technology in the Nineteenth Century: The Search for Labour-Saving Inventions,* (Cambridge, 1967), p. 128.

29. "The business proprietor's desire to substitute machinery was in large part dictated by the impatience of the knowledgeable artisan with working for somebody else. A lathe or drilling machine stayed put while a fine gunsmith might not." Cochran, *Frontiers*, p. 55.

30. Hugo A. Meier, "The Ideology of Technology," Layton, *op. cit.*, p. 94.

31. Foster Rhea Dulles, *Labor in America* (New York, 1960), p. 32; Philip Foner, *History of the Labor Movement in the United States*, Vol. I (New York, 1947), p. 101.

32. Foner, *Ibid.*, p. 108; Thomas C. Cochran and William Miller, *The Age of Enterprise* (New York, 1961), p. 26.

33. Gary Kulik, "Pawtucket Village and the Strike of 1824: The Origins of Class Conflict in Rhode Island," *Radical History Review*, No. 17 (Spring 1978), p. 24.

34. Jonathon Prude, "The Social System of Early New England Textile Mills: A Case Study, 1812-1840," Michael H. Frisch and Daniel J. Walkowitz, eds., *Working-Class America: Essays on Labor, Community, and American Society* (Urbana, IL, 1983), p. 15.

35. Philip Scranton, *Proprietary Capitalism: The Textile Manufacture in Philadelphia, 1800-1885* (Cambridge, 1983), p. 79.

36. Meier, *op. cit.*, p. 88.

37. Edward Pessen, *Jacksonian America* (Homewood, IL, 1967), p. 119.

38. Dulles, *op. cit.*, p. 29.

39. This primary government armory was authorized by Congress in 1798 and conveniently situated on land belonging to George Washington's Potomac Company. "For more

than a generation it was impossible to impose proper industrial discipline on workers from the surrounding area." Cochran, *Frontiers*, p. 74.

40. Merritt Roe Smith, *op. cit.*, p. 256.

41. Herbert G. Gutman, *Work, Culture, and Society in Industrializing America* (New York, 1976), p. 58.

42. Page Smith, *op. cit.*, p. 273.

43. Michael Feldberg, "The Crowd in Philadelphia," John J. Turner, Jr., ed., *Riot, Rout, and Tumult* (Westwood, CT, 1978), pp. 136-137.

44. Jonathon Prude, *The Coming of Industrial Order: Town and Factory Life in Rural Massachusetts, 1810-1860* (Cambridge, 1983), p. 225.

45. Gary B. Nash, "The Failure of Female Factory Labor in Colonial Boston," *Labor History*, No. 20 (Spring 1979).

46. Alexis de Tocqueville, *Democracy in America*, Vol. 2 (New York, 1966), p. 529.

47. Walton Felch, "The Manufacturer's Pocket Piece," Gary Kulik, Roger Parks, Theodore Z. Penn, eds., *The New England Mill Village, 1790-1860* (Cambridge, 1982), p. 326.

48. Quoted in Introduction, *Ibid.*, pp. xxix-xxx.

49. *Ibid.*, pp. 354-355.

50. Merritt Roe Smith, "Eli Whitney and the American System of Manufacturing," Carroll W. Pursell, Jr., ed., *Technology in America* (Cambridge, 1980), pp. 51-53.

51. Quoted in Karl Marx, *Capital* (New York, 1906), p. 477.

52. *The Complete Works of Ralph Waldo Emerson*, Vol. I (Boston, 1904), p. 455.

53. "Factory Work," *The Simone Weil Reader* (New York, 1977), p. 66.

54. Cochran, *Frontiers*, p. 136.

55. George W. White, *Memoir of Samuel Slater, The Father of American Manufactures* [1836] (New York, 1967), p. 122.

56. White, quoted in Kulik, et al., *op. cit.*, p. 351.

57. Rex Burns, *Success in America: The Yeoman Dream and the Industrial Revolution* (Amherst, 1976), p. 91. Also, William A. Sullivan, *The Industrial Worker in Pennsylvania, 1800-1840* (Harrisburg, 1955), p. 50: "...that overpowering sense of degradation which was beginning to be felt [by the 1830s] by large masses of working people."

58. From *The National Laborer*, April 23, 1836.

59. Arthur H. Calhoun, *A Social History of the Family*, Vol. 11 (Cleveland, 1918), p. 179; Jean V. Matthew, *Rufus Choate* (Philadelphia, 1980), p. 74.

60. Habakkuk, *op. cit.*, pp. 54-55; Carolyn Ware, *The Early New England Cotton Manufacture* (Boston, 1931), p. 8; Barbara M. Tucker, "The Merchant, the Manufacturer, and the Factory Manager: The Case of Samuel Slater," *Business History Review* (Autumn 1981), pp. 310-311; John F. Kasson, *Civilizing the Machine* (New York, 1976), p. 102.

61. Quoted in Peter N. Carroll and David W. Noble, *The Free and the Unfree* (New York, 1977), p. 153.

62. Kulik, et al., "Factory Rules and Regulations (1843)," *op. cit.*, p. 463.

63. Merritt Roe Smith, *op. cit.*, pp. 65, 271.

64. Kulik, et al., "Town Clock (1828)," *op. cit.*, p. 265.

65. Leo Marx, *The Machine in the Garden* (New York, 1964), p. 248.

66. Page Smith, *op. cit.*, p. 821. See Tamara K. Haraven, *Family Time and Industrial Time* (Cambridge, 1982) for a New England case study of the "timing" of all aspects of life in the new framework. Paralleling the heightened time-consciousness was "a pre-occupation with punctuality, measurement, and calculation," according to an early 1830s English traveller, Thomas Hamilton. Patricia Cline Cohen, *A Calculating People: The Spread of Numeracy in Early America* (Chicago, 1982), p. 175.

67. Clark, *op. cit.*, p. 540.

68. Prude, *Coming*, p. 47.

69. Cochran and Miller, *op. cit.*, p. 19.

70. Quoted by Steve Dunwell, *The Run of the Mill* (Boston, 1978), p. 15.

71. Quoted by Roland Berthoff, *An Unsettled People: Social Order and Disorder in Ameri-*

252

can History (New York, 1971), p. 167.

72. James Michael Cudd, *The Chicopee Manufacturing Company, 1823-1915* (Wilmington, 1974), p. 10.

73. Prude, *Coming*, p. 138.

74. Alex Inkeles and David H. Smith, *Becoming Modern* (Cambridge, 1974).

75. Cochran, *Frontiers*, p. 77.

76. Fisher, *op. cit.*, p. 33.

77. Cochran, *Frontiers*, p. 123.

78. Peter Dobkin Hall, *The Organization of American Culture, 1700-1900* (New York, 1982), p. 89.

79. Page Smith, *op. cit.*, p. 114.

80. David Grimsted, "Rioting in Its Jacksonian Setting," *American History Review*, Vol. 77, No. 2 (April 1972), p. 370.

81. *Ibid.*, pp. 371-374.

82. Paula Baker, "The Domestication of Politics: Women and American Political Society, 1780-1820," *American Historical Review*, Vol. 89, No. 3 (June 1984), pp. 625-626; Page Smith, *op. cit.*, p. 13.

83. Gary Lawson Browne, *Baltimore in the Nation, 1789-1861* (Chapel Hill, 1980), p. 97.

84. John Mayfield, *The New Nation, 1800-1845* (New York, 1982), p. 99.

85. Quoted by Pessen, *op. cit.*, p. 50.

86. Curti, *op. cit.*, p. 51.

87. Marvin Meyers, *The Jacksonian Persuasion* (Stanford, 1957), pp. 12- 13.

88. Sydney Nathans, *Daniel Webster and Jacksonian Democracy* (Baltimore, 1973), p. 48.

89. Peter Temin, *The Jacksonian Economy* (New York, 1969), p. 18.

90. Charles D. Lowery, *James Barbour, A Jeffersonian Republican* (University, AL, 1984), pp. 217-218.

91. *The Diary of Philip Hone, 1828-1851* (New York, 1851), p. 142.

92. Fish, *op. cit.*, p. 54.

93. Glyndon Van Deusen, *The Jackson Era, 1828-1848* (New York, 1959), pp. 66-67.

94. Bray Hammond, *Banks and Politics in America from the Revolution to the Civil War* (Princeton, 1957), p. 238.

95. Howard Zinn, *A People's History of the United States* (New York, 1980), p. 59.

96. Paul A. Gilje, "The Baltimore Riots of 1812 and the Breakdown of the Anglo- American Mob Tradition," *Journal of Social History*, Vol. 13, No. 4 (Summer 1980).

97. James B. Agnew, *Egg Nog Riot: The Christmas Mutiny at West Point* (San Rafael, 1979), p. ix.

98. John J. Duffy and H. Nicholas Muller, III, *An Anxious Democracy: Aspects of the 1830s* (Westport, CT, 1982), p. 4.

99. Sean Wilentz, "Artisan Republican Festivals and the Rise of Class Conflict in New York City, 1788-1837," Frisch and Walkowitz, *op. cit.*, p. 54.

100. Theodore M. Hammett, "Two Mobs of Jacksonian Boston: Ideology and Interest," *Journal of American History*, Vol. LXII, No. 4 (March 1976), p. 867.

101. Page Smith, *op. cit.*, p. 746.

102. Gilje, *op. cit.*, p. 564.

103. Paul Owen Weinbaum, *Mobs and Demagogues: The Response to Collective Violence in New York City in the Early Nineteenth Century* (Ann Arbor, 1977), p. iv.

104. Michael Chavalier, *Society, Manners, and Politics in the United States* (Garden City, NY, 1961), p. 371ff.

105. Michael Kammen, *People of Paradox* (New York, 1973), p. 253.

106. Lee Benson, *The Concept of Jacksonian Democracy* (Princeton, 1970), pp. 151-152.

107. Walter Hugins, *Jacksonian Democracy and the Working Class* (Stanford, 1960), pp. 45-46.

108. W.J. Rorabaugh, *The Alcoholic Republic* (New York, 1979), p. 25.

109. Jan R. Tyrell, *Sobering Up: From Temperance to Prohibition in Antebellum America,*

1800-1860 (Westport, CT, 1979), p. 107.

110. Richard D. Brown, *Modernization: The Transformation of American Life, 1600-1865* (New York, 1976), p. 155.

111. Foster Rhea Dulles, *America Learns To Play: A History of Recreation* (New York, 1965), p. 90.

112. Rorabaugh, *op. cit.*, p. 169.

113. Bruce Laurie, "Nothing on Compulsion," Milton Cantor, ed., *American Working Class Culture* (Westport, CT, 1979), p. 106.

114. Tyrell, *op. cit.*, p. 127.

115. Rorabaugh, *op. cit.*, p. 15.

116. Rorabaugh, *op. cit.*, p. 8.

117. Joseph R. Gusfield, "Temperance, Status Control, and Mobility," David Brion Davis, ed., *Ante-Bellum Reform* (New York, 1967), p. 126.

118. Rorabaugh, *op. cit.*, p. 187.

119. This generalization does not mean to imply an easy or complete end of the issue. Concerning the severity and persistence of this phenomenon see Jed Dannenbaum's study of nineteenth century Cincinnati, *Drink and Disorder* (Urbana, 1984).

120. Ronald G. Waters, *American Reformers, 1815-1860* (New York, 1978) p. 209.

121. Michael B. Katz, Michael J. Doucet, and Mark J. Stern, *The Social Organization of Early Industrial Capitalism* (Cambridge, 1982), p. 349.

122. Michael B. Katz, *Irony of Early School Reform* (Cambridge, 1968), p. xvii.

123. Faux, *op. cit.*, (August 5, 1819), pp. 130-131.

124. Frederick Marryat, *A Diary in America* (New York, 1962), p. 352.

125. Curti, *op. cit.*, pp. 80-81.

126. Carl F. Kaestle, *Pillars of the Republic: Common Schools and American Society, 1780-1860* (New York, 1983), pp. 96-97.

127. Katz, et al., *op. cit.*, p. 90.

128. Clifford S. Griffin, "Religious Benevolence as Social Control," Davis, *op. cit.*, p. 90.

129. John F. Kasson, *Civilizing the Machine* (New York, 1976), p. 73. Also David J. Rothman's important *The Discovery of the Asylum* (New York, 1971).

130. Rorabaugh, *op. cit.*, p. 213.

131. Page Smith, *Daughters of the Promised Land: Women in American History* (Boston, 1970), p. 64.

132. Quoted by Cochran, *Business*, p. 91.

133. Stephen Nissenbaum, *Sex, Diet and Debility in Jacksonian America* (Westport, CT, 1980), p. 26.

134. Carl Degler, *At Odds: Women and the Family in America from the Revolution to the Present* (New York, 1980), p. 251.

135. Nissenbaum, *op. cit.*, p. 28.

136. Jayne A. Sokolow, *Eros and Modernization* (Cranbury, NY, 1983), pp. 12-13.

137. Degler, *op. cit.*, p. 250.

138. Page Smith, *The Nation*, p. 714.

139. Gerda Lerner, "The Lady and the Mill Girl: Changes in the Status of Women in the Age of Jackson," *Midcontinental American Studies Journal*, Vol. X, No. 1 (Spring 1969), pp. 11-12.

140. Richard Drinnon, *Facing West: Metaphysics of Indian-Hating and Empire- Building* (Minneapolis, 1980), p. 107.

141. Michael Paul Rogin, *Fathers and Children: Andrew Jackson and the Subjugation of the American Indian* (New York, 1975), p. 165.

142. *Ibid.*, p. 13.

143. Quoted by Major L. Wilson, *Space, Time and Freedom* (Westport, CT, 1974), p. 12.

144. Lee Clark Mitchell, *Witnesses to a Vanishing America* (Princeton, 1980).

Origins and Meaning of WWI

1. Jan Patocka, "Wars of the 20th Century and the 20th Century as War," *Telos* 30, (Winter 1976-77), p. 116

2. Guy Debord, *Society of the Spectacle* (Detroit, 1977), thesis 97.

3. Elie Halèvy, *The World Crisis of 1914-1918*, (Oxford, 1930), p. 17

4. V.R. Berghahn, *Germany and the Approach of War in 1914* (New York, 1974), p. 14.

5. S.D. Sazanov, *Reminiscences: Fateful Years, 1906-1916* (London, 1925), pp. 123, 140.

6. Pierre van Paasen, *Days of our Years* (New York, 1946), p. 46.

7. Z.A.B. Zeman, *The Gentleman Negotiators* (New York, 1971), p. 46.

8. L.T. Hobhouse, *The World in Conflict* (London, 1915), p. 15.

9. Stefan Zweig, *The World of Yesterday* (New York, 1943), p. 197.

10. H.G. Wells, *The Salvaging of Civilization* (New York, 1922), p.1.

11. This general idea is sometimes mentioned in passing, rarely explored or developed. David Thomson saw that "The established authorities were everywhere subject [by 1914] to a recurrent challenge which struck at the roots of their power—the challenge of mass revulsion against the exacting disciplines of industrial urban civilization." Thomson, *Europe since Napoleon* (New York, 1962), p. 505.

12. Laurence Lafore, *The Long Fuse: An Interpretation of the Origins of World War I* (Philadelphia, 1965), p. 15.

13. Leo Valiani, *The End of Austria-Hungary* (New York, 1973).

14. Norman Stone, "Hungary and the Crisis of 1914," in Laqueur and Mosse, eds., *1914: The Coming of the First World War* (New York, 1970), p. 147.

15. Peter F. Sugar, "The Nature of the Non-Germanic Societies under Hapsburg Rule," *Slavic Review* XI:1 (March 1963), p. 29.

16. Edward Crankshaw, *The Fall of the House of Hapsburg* (London, 1963), p. 448.

17. Arthur J. May, *The Hapsburg Monarchy, 1867-1914* (New York, 1968), p. 492.

18. Bottomore and Goode, eds., *Austro-Marxism* (Oxford, 1978), p. 132: Marxist leader Max Adler, in "The Ideology of the War" (1915), warned that "the class standpoint of the proletariat does not in any way diminish its duty and natural inclination to defend the fatherland."

19. Zeman, *op. cit.* p. 146.

20. Hans von Bulow, *Memoirs of Prince von Bulow*, Vol. 3, (London, 1932), p. 148.

21. Edmund Taylor, *The Fall of the Dynasties* (Garden City, N.Y., 1963), p. 243.

22. Edward Crankshaw, *The Shadow of the Winter Palace* (London, 1976), pp. 452-453.

23. Edmund Wilson, *To The Finland Station* (Garden City, N.Y., 1953), p. 453

24. Arno Mayer, "Domestic Causes of the First World War," Brody and Wright, eds., *Elements of Political Change* (New York, 1967), p. 207.

25. Meriel Buchanan, *Diplomacy and Foreign Courts* (London, 1925), p. 169.

26. Leon Trotsky, *The Russian Revolution* (Garden City, N.Y., 1959), p. 17.

27. Paul Avrich, *The Russian Anarchists* (New York, 1978), pp. 118-119.

28. Zeman, *op.cit.*, p. 10.

29. F.L. Carsten, *The Rise of Fascism* (Berkeley, 1971), p. 20

30. *Ibid.*, p. 45.

31. von Bulow, *op.cit.*, p. 254

32. Zeman, *op.cit.*, p. 10.

33. John M. Cammett, *Antonio Gramsci and the Origins of Italian Communism* (Stanford, 1967), p. 36.

34. Gramsci expressed this attitude in his first signed published article, in October 1914. James Joll, *Antonio Gramsci* (London, 1977), p. 42.

35. Giampero Carocci, *Italian Fascism* (London, 1974), p. 10.

36. Paolo Spriano, *The Occupation of the Factories: Italy 1920* (London, 1975), pp. 74-76.

37. Quoted by Spriano, *ibid.*, p. 77.

38. Carsten, *op. cit.*, pp. 53-54.

39. A. James Gregor, *The Young Mussolini and the Intellectual Origins of Fascism* (Berkeley, 1979).

40. Gregor, *Italian Fascism and Developmental Dictatorship* (Princeton, 1979), p. 90.

41. Oron Hale, *The Great Illusion, 1900-1914* (New York, 1971), p. 202

42. *Ibid.*

43. Georges Sorel, *Reflections on Violence* (New York, 1941), p. 78.

44. Alfred Cobban, *A History of Modern France, Vol. 3* (Middlesex, 1963), p. 104.

45. von Bulow, *op. cit.*, p. 173.

46. Prince Lichnowski, *Heading for the Abyss* (New York, 1928), p. 362.

47. Cobban, *op. cit.*, p. 102.

48. David Thomson, *Democracy in France Since 1870* (Oxford, 1969), p. 174.

49. Peter Stearns, *Revolutionary Syndicalism and French Labor* (Rutgers, 1971), p. 69.

50. Halèvy, *op. cit.*, p. 14.

51. *Ibid.*, p. 20.

52. Taylor, *op. cit.*, p. 238.

53. Henry F. May, *The End of American Innocence* (New York, 1959), p. 334.

54. Graham Adams Jr., *The Age of Industrial Violence, 1910-1915* (New York, 1966), p. xii.

55. *Ibid.*, p. 219.

56. Christopher Lasch, *The New Radicalism in America, 1889-1963* (New York, 1965), pp. 202-203.

57. Jacques Ellul, *The Technological Society* (New York, 1967). pp. 365-366.

58. Zeman, *op. cit.*, p. 162.

59. John Higham, *Strangers in the Land* (New York, 1968), p. 195.

60. Hale, *op. cit.*, p. 163.

61. *Ibid.*, p. 153

62. Roger Shattuck, *The Banquet Years* (New York, 1967), p. 283.

63. *Ibid.*, p. 279.

64. Harry Golumbek, *The Game of Chess* (London, 1954), p. 222.

65. Zweig, *op. cit.*, p. 195.

66. R.W. Flint, ed. Marinetti *(New York, 1972), p. 14.*

67. *Shattuck, op. cit.*, p. 353.

68. Discussed by Carolyn E. Playne, *The Neuroses of Nations* (London, 1925), p. 49.

69. Paul Ricoeur, *History and Truth* (Evanston, 1965), p. 213.

70. David Landes, *The Unbound Prometheus* (London, 1969), p. 316.

71. Siegfried Giedion, *Mechanization Takes Command* (New York, 1969), p. 41.

72. Hilton Kramer, "German Expressionism," *San Francisco Examiner-Chronicle*, October 12, 1980.

73. Berghahn, *op. cit.*, p. 78.

74. *Ibid.*, p. 81.

75. von Bulow, *op. cit.*, p. 103.

76. *Ibid.*, p. 102.

77. Playne, *op. cit.*, p. 88.

78. James Gerard, *My Four Years in Germany* (New York, 1917), p. 75. Gerard saw the popular reaction to the Zabern incidents as "perhaps the final factor which decided the advocates of the old military system of Germany in favor of a European war" (p. 91).

79. John T. Flynn, *As We Go Marching* (New York, 1973), p. 81.

80. Arthur Rosenberg, *Imperial Germany* (New York, 1970), p. 58.

81. Gordon Craig, *Germany, 1866-1945* (New York, 1978), p. 337.

82. D.A. Smart, *Pannekoek and Gorter's Marxism* (New York, 1977), p. 20.

83. *Ibid.*, p. 21.

84. Austin Harrison, *The Kaiser's War* (London, 1914), p. 197.

85. James Joll, *The Second International* (New York, 1956), pp. 166-167.
86. Robert Looker, ed., *Rosa Luxemburg: Selected Political Writings* (New York, 1972), p. 40.
87. *Ibid.*, p. 197.
88. *Ibid.*, p. 222.
89. Theo Pinkus, ed., *Conversations with Lukacs* (Cambridge, 1975), p. 148.
90. Hannah Arendt, *Totalitarianism* (New York, 1968), p. 26.
91. Quoted by Arendt, *ibid.*
92. Hannah Hafkesbrink, *Unknown Germany: An Inner Chronicle* (New Haven, 1948), pp. 30-32.
93. Reginald Pound, *The Lost Generation* (New York, 1964), p. 73.
94. Joseph Bibby, *The War, Its Unseen Cause and Some of Its Lessons* (London, 1915), p. 12.
95. George Dangerfield, *The Strange Death of Liberal England* (New York, 1961) p. viii.
96. Emanuel Shinwell, *I've Lived Through It All* (London, 1973), p. 12.
97. R.C.K. Ensor, *England, 1870-1914* (Oxford, 1936), p. 557.
98. R.J. Evans, *The Victorian Age* (London, 1950), p. 46.
99. Colin Cross, *The Liberals in Power, 1905-1914* (London, 1963), p. 171.
100. James Cameron, *1914* (New York, 1959), p. 21.
101. Harold Nicolson, *King George the Fifth* (London, 1952), p. 163.
102. Arthur Marwick, *The Deluge: British Society and the First World War* (Boston, 1966), p. 10.
103. William Archer, *The Great Analysis* (London, 1911), p. 19.
104. Zara S. Steiner, *Britain and the Origins of the First World War*, (New York, 1977), p. 153.
105. Elie Halèvy, *A History of the English People, 1905-1915* (London, 1934), p. 457.
106. *Ibid.*, p. 436.
107. *Ibid.*, pp. 446, 451.
108. Elie Halèvy, *The Era of Tyrannies* (Garden City, N.Y., 1965), p. 106.
109. G.A. Phillips, "The Triple Industrial Alliance in 1914," *Economic History Review*, XXIV:1 (1971), p. 63.
110. Cameron, *op.cit.*, p. 46.
111. Pound, *op.cit.*, p. 28.
112. Quoted in Eric J. Leed's "Class and Disillusionment in World War I," *Journal of Modern History*, 50 (December 1978), p. 691.

Taylorism and Unionism

1. David Jenkins, *Job Power: Blue and White Collar Democracy* (Baltimore, 1974), p. 9.
2. Department of Health, Education and Welfare, *Work in America* (Cambridge, Mass., 1973), p. 19.
3. Frederick W. Taylor, *Principles of Scientific Management* (New York, 1911), p. 32.
4. Siegfried Giedion, *Mechanization Takes Command* (New York, 1948), p. 38. C. Bertrand Thompson made the same point in 1917 when he pointed out the absence of competitive pressure behind firms employing scientific management, "for the reason that most of them now using it stand in a quasi-monopoly position in which there is no necessity to reduce their prices..."] See his *The Theory and Practice of Scientific Management* (Boston, 1917), pp. 88-89.
5. Mary Follett of the Taylor Society, for example, claimed that with scientific management, "authority is derived from function" and thus "has little to do with hierarchy of position as such..." [See Taylor Society, H.S. Person, Editor, *Scientific Manage-*

ment in American Industry (New York, 1929), p. 436.] Typical pronouncements claimed that it embodied "a new kind of authority which stemmed from the unveiling of scientific law,"[See Samuel Haber, *Efficiency and Uplift* (Chicago, 1964), p. 25.] and that it substituted joint obedience of employers and workers "to fact and law for obedience to personal authority." [See Robert Franklin Hoxie, *Scientific Management and Labor* (New York, 1915), p. 9.] The time-study man, measuring and manipulating the worker with his stopwatch, relies on "unimpeachable data." [Horace D. Drury, *Scientific Management* (New York, 1915), p. 59.]

6. Taylor Society, *op. cit*, p. 46.

7. Taylor, *Principles, op. cit.*, p. 59. H.L. Gantt, one of Taylor's leading disciples, spoke of implementing the task system as "the standard method of teaching and training children." [See his *Wages and Profits* (New York, 1919), p. 122.] Since "the worker became an object in Taylor's hands," in Jacques Ellul's phrase, it follows easily that he would be seen as an animal or a child by the Taylorites. Another part of the justification was Taylor's notion of the "economic man," that a worker's real motivation is money and nothing else. [See Sudhir Kakar, *Frederick Taylor: A Study in Personality and Innovation* (Cambridge, Mass., 1970) p. 99.]

8. Hugh G.J. Aitken, *Taylorism at Watertown Arsenal* (Cambridge, Mass., 1960) pp. 112, 137, 140, 158, 161, for example.

9. Taylor Society, op.cit., pp. 447, 450, 453.

10. That the fight to control work was the heart of the contest can be seen in such articles as "Who's Boss in Your Shop?" from the August, 1917 *Bulletin* of the Taylor Society. In fact, the first effort of Taylor to lay out his theory, in "A Piece-Rate System" (1895) underlines that fact that the problem to be solved is the antagonism between workers and employers. [See Frederick W. Taylor "A Piece Rate System," *Transactions of the American Society of Mechanical Engineeers* (New York, A.S.M.E., 1895), pp. 891-898.]

11. See, for example, H. Jack Schapiro and Mahmoud A. Wahba's "Frederick W. Taylor - 62 years later," *Personnel Journal*, August 1974, which argues that the "economic man" model, in which money is the prime motivator, still (sic) obtains.

12. Taylor, "*A Piece-Rate System,*" op. cit. (Discussion: Mr. John A. Penton), pp. 888-9.

13. Drury, *op cit.*, p. 187; Milton Nadworny, *Scientific Management and the Unions* (Cambridge, Mass., 1955), pp. 27-28.

14. John R. Commons, "Restrictions by Trade Unions," *The Outlook*, October, 1906.

15. Surveying the notes and bibliography sections of McKelvey's and Nadworny's books on the subject, we find that McKelvey looked at only two contracts (signed in 1925 and 1930) and that Nadworny examined none.

16. Haber, *op cit.*, p. 67.

17. Thompson, *op. cit.*, p. 96 and p. 155.

18. Henry L. Gantt, a conservative Taylor disciple, admired the Leninist dictatorship, especially, of course, its Taylorist component. And Morris L. Cooke, a liberal Taylorite, of whom it was said in 1915 that "no one has done more to broaden the scope of scientific management." was one of the first spokesmen to publicly urge the Taylor Society to recognize its natural partner in unionism. Cooke, not surprisingly, became in the 1930s a prominent CIO advocate. [See Drury, *op. cit.*, p. 153.]

19. Matthew Josephson, *Sidney Hillman* (Garden City, N.Y., 1952), pp. 111-112.

20. Taylor Papers, "Taylor or Ruggles." February 17, 1908.

21. Hugh G. J. Aitken, *Taylorism at Watertown Arsenal* (Cambridge, Mass., 1960), pp. 67-68.

22. "Hearings Before Social Committee of the House of Representatives to Investigate the Taylor and Other Systems of Shop Management Under the Authority of House Resolution 90." Vol. I, p. 230. Other testimony made it clear, furthermore, that workers' resentment was fueled by the anti-workmanship aspects of Taylorism. Isaac Goostray and Alexander Crawford, for example, spoke of the pressures to slight their work and reduce their !level of craftsmanship.

258

23. Aitken, *op. cit.*, pp. 223-224.

24. For example, Haber, *op. cit.*, declares that organized labor was solidly against scientific management during this period (p. 66), but only cites IAM statements (pp. 67-69) to support this view.

25. Jean Trepp McKelvey, *AFL Attitudes Towards Production* (Ithaca, 1952), p. 16.

26. Aitken, *op. cit.*, pp. 183-184.

27. Richard H. Pells, *Radical Visions and American Dreams* (New York, 1973), p. 200.

28. Whereas Irving Bernstein's *The Lean Years: A History of the American Worker, 1920-1933* (New York, 1960) spoke of the 1920s' "sharp reversal in the AFL's historic opposition to scientific management,' more recent efforts repeat the same error. James R. Green's *The World of the Worker* (New York, 1980) quotes Bernstein to the same general point (p. 127), also citing McKelvey and Nadworny. Daniel Nelson's *Frederick W. Taylor and the Rise of Scientific Management* (Madison, 1980) likewise repeats the myth of a pre-War "confrontation between scientific management and labor" (p. 164) which turned into truce and then collaboration during the 1920s (p. 202). *Management and Ideology: The Legacy of the International Scientific Management,* by Judith A. Merkle (Berkely, 1980), also makes this error (pp. 8, 29) without bothering to mention Nadworny in the text or bibliography. This suggests that the mistaken thesis of union opposition to Taylorism has become an axiom. With Peter F. Meiksin's "Scientific Management and Class Relations", in Vol. 13 No. 2 (March 1984) *Theory and Society,* error on this topic takes a quantum leap. On page 184: "...the A.F. of L. was one of the earliest opponents of scientific management, and, while observers disagree as to the *extent* of worker resistance, it seems clear that Taylorism did provoke at least some strikes." Unionism is thus elevated even a bit higher yet, while rank-and-file antagonism is all but liquidated—an achievement which dispenses with the need for evidence. Sad to say, even Harry Braverman's excellent *Labor and Monopoly Capital: The Degradation of Work in the Twentieth Century* (New York, 1974) falls into this kind of distortion; although the work admittedly does not deal with workers' struggles, his sole reference to anti-Taylorism (p. 136) is his judgement that Scientific Management "raised a storm of opposition among the trade unions during the early part of this century."

Organized Labor vs. "The Revolt Against Work"

1. See Herbert Harris, *American Labor* (New Haven: Yale University Press, 1939), p. 272; Sidney Fine, *Sitdown* (Ann Arbor: University of Michigan Press, 1969), p. 55; Mary Vorse, *Labor's New Millions* (New York: Modern Age Books, 1938), p. 59; Charles Walker, "Work Methods, Working Conditions and Morale," in A. Kornhauser, et al., eds., *Industrial Conflicts* (New York: McGraw-Hill, 1954), p. 345.

2. S.T. Williamson and Herbert Harris, *Trends in Collective Bargaining* (New York,: The Twentieth Century Fund, 1945), p. 210.

3. C. Wright Mills, *The New Men of Power: America's Labor Leaders* (New York: Harcourt, Brace, 1948), p. 242.

4. Daniel Bell, "Work and Its Discontents," *The End of Ideology* (New York: The Free Press, 1960), p. 240.

5. Ibid. p. 238.

6. Stanley Weir, *USA—The Labor Revolt* (Boston: New England Free Press, 1969), p. 3.

7. James Boggs, *The American Revolution: Pages From a Negro Worker's Notebook* (New York: Monthly Review Press, 1963), p. 32.

8. E.K. Faltermayer, "Is Labor's Push More Bark Than Bite?" *Fortune* (June, 1964), p. 102.

9. J.C. Leggett, *Class, Race, and Labor* (New York: Oxford University Press, 1968), p. 144.

10. Staughton Lynd, ed., *Personal Histories of the Early CIO* (Boston: New England

Free Press, 1971), p. 23.

11. Stanley Aronowitz, *False Promises: The Shaping of American Working Class Consciousness* (New York: McGraw-Hill, 1973), pp. 44-46.

12. Bill Watson, "Counter-Planning on the Shop Floor," *Radical America* (May-June, 1971), p. 78.

13. Weir, *op.cit.*, p.2.

14. Thomas R. Brooks, "Labor: The Rank-and-File Revolt," *Contemporary Labor Issues*, Fogel and Kleingartner, eds. (Belmont, Calif.: Wadsworth, 1966), p. 321.

15. William Serrin, "The Assembly Line," *The Atlantic* (October, 1971), p. 73.

16. George Lipsitz, "Beyond the Fringe Benefits," *Liberation* (July-August, 1973), p. 33.

17. Daniel Bell, *The Coming of Post-Industrial Society* (New York: Basic Books, 1973), p. 144.

18. Jeremy Brecher, *Strike!* (San Francisco: Straight Arrow Press, 1972), p. 271.

19. *Washington Post*, March 27, 1970.

20. *Workers World*, July 30, 1971.

21. *Cleveland Plain Dealer*, May 11, 1970.

22. Fred Cook, "Hard-Hats: The Rampaging Patriots," *The Nation* (June 15, 1970), pp. 712-719.

23. William Serrin, *The Company and the Union* (New York: Alfred A. Knopf, 1973), pp. 233-236.

24. Cited by Brecher, *op.cit.*, pp. 279-280.

25. Serrin, *op.cit.*, p. 4.

26. *Ibid.*, pp 263-264.

27. *Ibid.*, p. 202.

28. *Ibid.*, p. 306.

29. Roy B. Helfgott, *Labor Economics* (New York: Random House, 1974), p. 506.

30. Aronowitz, *op.cit.*, p. 43.

31. *Wall Street Journal*, December 9, 1972.

32. Michael Adelman, in *Labor Newsletter* (February, 1974), pp. 7-8.

33. *Los Angeles Times*, October 27, 1973.

34. Sidney Lens, *The Labor Wars* (Garden City, N.Y.: Anchor, 1974), p. 376.

35. Richard Armstrong, "Labor 1970: Angry, Aggressive, Acquisitive," *Fortune* (October, 1969), p. 144. William and Margaret Westley, *The Emerging Worker* (Montreal: McGill-Queen's University Press, 1971), p. 100.

36. Harold W. Davey, *Contemporary Collective Bargaining* (New York: Prentice-Hall, 1972), p. 153.

37. Norman J. Samuels, Assistance Commissioner, Wages and Industrial Relations, letter to author, April 19, 1974.

38. Aronowitz, *op.cit.*, p. 214.

39. Richard Sennett and Jonathon Cobb, *The Hidden Injuries of Class* (New York: Alfred A. Knopf, 1972), p. 4.

40. Remark by CWA president, Joseph Beirne, *New York Times*, July 18, 1971.

41. Aronowitz, *op.cit.*, p. 224.

42. See Jack Anderson's "Merry-Go-Round" column, August 23, 1971, for example.

43. Robert V. Roosa, "A Strategy for Winding Down Inflation," *Fortune* (September, 1971), p. 70.

44. Arthur M. Louis, "Labor Can Make or Break the Stabilization Program," *Fortune* (November, 1971), p. 142.

45. Editorial: "Phasing Out Phase Two," *Fortune* (January, 1972), p. 63.

46. Bureau of Labor Statistics, *Work Stoppages in 1972: Summary Report* (Washington: Department of Labor, 1974), p. 1.

47. David Deitch, "Watershed of the American Economy," *The Nation* (September 13, 1971), p. 201.

260

48. Quoted by Serrin, *op. cit.*, p. 24.

49. Thomas O'Hanlon, "Anarchy Threatens the Kingdom of Coal," *Fortune*, (January, 1971), p. 78.

50. Arthur A. Sloane and Fred Witney, *Labor Relations* (New York: Prentice-Hall, 1972), p. 390.

51. From an anti-union article by John Davenport, "How to Curb Union Power" (labeled *Opinion*), *Fortune* (July 1971), p. 52.

52. *Ibid.*, p. 54.

53. *Los Angeles Times*, November 8, 1972.

54. Armand J. Thieblot and Ronald M. Cowin, *Welfare and Strikes—The Use of Public Funds to Support Strikers* (Philadelphia: University of Pennsylvania Press, 1973), p. 185.

55. *New York Times*, April 13, 1974.

56. *Weekly People*, April 27, 1974.

57. Lucretia M. Dewey, "Union Merger Pace Quickens," *Monthly Labor Review* (June, 1971),pp. 63-70

58. *New York Times*, August 3 and 6, 1972.

59. Confirmed by Harry Bridges, letter to author, April 11, 1974.

60. Dick Meister, "Public Workers Union Win a Rare Agreement," *San Francisco Chronicle* (April 13, 1969).

61. *San Francisco Chronicle*, "Union Fee Ruling on City Workers," October 31, 1973.

62. Joel Seidman, "Political Controls and Member Rights: An Analysis of Union Constitutions," *Essays on Industrial Relations Research Problems and Prospects* (Ann Arbor: University of Michigan Press, 1961).

63. Burton Hall, ed., *Autocracy and Insurgency in Organized Labor* (New Brunswick, N.J.: Transaction Books, 1972).

64. H.W. Benson, "Apathy and Other Axioms: Expelling the Union Dissenter From History," Irving Howe, ed., *The World of the Blue Collar Worker* (New York: Quadrangle Books, 1972), pp. 209-226.

65. *Times-Post Service*, "Administration's Tryst with Labor," *San Francisco Chronicle* (April 14, 1969).

66. *New York Times*, "Key Jobs Offered to Labor by Nixon" (December 31, 1972), p. 1.

67. Phil Stanford, "Convention Time," *Oregon Times* (September, 1971), p. 4.

68. See *California AFL-CIO News*, editorial: "The Convention Caper" (January 14, 1972), for example.

69. Robert J. Marcus, "The Changing Workforce," *Personnel* (January-February, 1971), p. 12.

70. *Ibid.*, p. 10.

71. *Business Week*, "The Unions Begin to Bend on Work Rules," (September 9, 1972), pp. 106, 108.

72. *New York Times*, April 27, 1974.

73. *New York Times*, April 26, 1974.

74. Quoted from Serrin, *op. cit.*, p. 118.

75. David Jenkins, *Job Power* (Garden City, N.Y.: Doubleday, 1973), pp. 319-320.

76. *Ibid.*, p. 312.

77. The San Francisco Social Services Union, a rather anti-union union of about 230 public welfare workers, has emphatically rejected these institutions since 1968. This, plus its vocal militancy and frequency exposure of "Organized labor's" corruption and collusion has earned them the hatred of the established unions in San Francisco.

Anti-work and the Struggle for Control

1. William E. Fulmer, "Decertification: Is the Current Trend a Threat to Collective

Bargaining?" *California Management Review,* Fall 1981, p. 14. Also *Dollars and Sense,* "Union Decertification Elections," February 1980, p. 8.

2. Thornton Bradshaw and David Vogel, eds., *Corporations and Their Critics* (New York, 1981), p. xvi.

3. *Nation's Business,* March 1981, p. 20.

4. Peter L. Berger, "New Attack on the Legitimacy of Big Business," *Harvard Business Review,* September-October, 1981, p. 82.

5. Herbert J. Freudenberger, "How to Survive Burnout," *Nation's Business,* December 1980, p. 53.

6. Merrill Cherlin, "Burnout; Victims and Avoidances," *Datamation,* July 1981, p. 92.

7. Rober L. Veninga and James P. Spradley, *The Work Stress Connection: How to Cope with Job Burnout* (Boston, 1981).

8. Robert L. Kahn, "Work, Stress and Individual Well-Being," *Monthly Labor Review,* May 1981; Ahmed A. Abdel-Halim, "Effects of Role Stress—Job Design—Technology Interaction on Employee Satisfaction," *Academy of Management Journal,* June 1981; Orlando Behling and F. Douglas Holcombe, "Dealing with Employee Stress," *MSU Business Topics,* Spring 1981.

9. Frank Kuzmits, "No Fault: A New Strategy for Absenteeism Control," *Personnel Journal,* May 1981.

10. Clarence A. Deitsch and David A. Dilts, "Getting Absent Workers Back on the Job: The Case of General Motors," *Business Horizons,* September-October 1981, p. 52.

11. Robert Holman's "Beyond Contemporary Employee Assistance Plans," *Personnel Administrator,* September 1981, notes that more than 2,000 such EAP's were established in U.S. firms between 1972 and 1978.

12. Richard J. Tersine and Roberta S. Russell, "Internal Theft: The Multi-Billion Dollar Disappearing Act" *Business Horizons,* November-December 1981, pp. 11-12.

13. Malcolm S. Cohen and Arther R. Schwartz, "U.S. Labor Turnover: Analysis of a New Measure," *Monthly Labor Review,* November 1980.

14. Robert Blake and Jane Moulton, "Increasing Productivity Through Behavioral Science," *Personnel,* May-June 1981, pp. 59-60.

15. R.S. Byrne, "Sources on Productivity," *Harvard Business Review,* September-October 1981, p. 36.

16. *Personnel Administrator,* August 1981, p. 23.

17. George Crosby, "Getting Back to Basics on Productivity," *Administrative Management,* November 1981, p. 31.

18. Stanley B. Henrici, "How Deadly is the Productivity Disease? *Harvard Business Review,* November-December 1981, p. 123.

19. Donald V. Nightingale cites evidence of "growing employee disenchantment," such that "The modern work organization faces mounting pressures from within and without to meet the challenge of employee alienation and dissatisfaction." "Work, Formal Participation, and Employee Outcomes," *Sociology of Work and Occupations,* August 1981, p. 277.

20. *Nation's Business,* "Unlocking the Productivity Door," December 1981, p. 85.

21. James O'Toole, *Making America Work* (New York, 1981). Reviews by Amar Bhide, *Wall Street Journal,* October 20, 1981.

22. *Business Week* "The New Industrial Relations," May 11, 1981, p. 85.

23. *Business Week,* "A Try at Steel-Mill Harmony," June 29, 1981, p. 135.

24. Charles G. Burck, "Working Smarter," *Fortune,* June 15, 1981, p. 70.

25. Burck, "What Happens When Workers Manage Themselves," *Fortune,* July 27, 1981, p. 69.

26. M. Scott Myers, *Every Employee a Manager* (New York, 1981).

27. Burck, "What Happens...," p. 69.

28. Burck, "Working Smarter," p. 70.

29. Burck, "What's in it for the Unions," *Fortune,* August 24, 1981, p. 89.

262

30. Burck, "Working Smarter," p. 70.

31. Burck, "What's in it . . . ," p. 89.

32. *Business Week*, "Quality of Work Life: Catching On," September 21, 1981, p. 72.

34. William G. Ouchi, *Theory Z: How American Business Can Meet the Japanese Challenge* (Reading, Mass., 1981), p. 114.

35. David Lewin, "Collective Bargaining and the Quality of Work Life," *Organizational Dynamics, Autumn 1981,* especially p. 52.

36. *Business Horizons*, "The Eighties," January-February 1981, p. 7.

37. Rep. Stanley Lundine, in "Congress Takes a Look at Human Innovation and Productivity," *Enterprise*, December 1981-January 1982 (pp. 10-11), predicts that government will try to establish a "cooperative relationship among government, labor and management" in the interest of resolving work conflict and raising productivity.

38. George Ross, "What is Progressive about Unions," *Theory and Society,* 10:5 (September 1981), p. 639.

39. *Business Week*, "The Reindustrialization of America," June 30, 1980, p. 55.

40. Charles K. Wilber and Kenneth P. Jameson, "Hedonism and Quietism," *Society,* November-December 1981, p. 28.

41. *U.S. News and World Report*, "Why So Many Jobs for Youths Go Begging," November 23, 1981.

42. Frederick I. Herzberg, "New Perspectives on the Will to Work," *Personnel Administrator,* December 1979, p. 72.

BIBLIOGRAPHY

"Cesar Chavez and the Farm Workers: the New American Revolution — What Went Wrong?" *Politics & Society,* Fall 1972.

"Understanding the Anti-Radicalism of the National Civic Federation," *International Review of Social History,* Vol. XIX (1974), No. 2.

"Organized Labor versus 'The Revolt Against Work': The Critical Contest," *Telos* No. 21 (Fall 1974). Also as *Unions Against Revolution* (with G. Munis), 64 pp. (Black & Red: Detroit, 1975). And in *Reinventing Anarchy* Routledge, Kegan Paul: Boston, 1979).

"The Decline and Fall of Everything," *Fifth Estate,* December 1975. Also published as *Breakdown: Data on the Decomposition of Society,* 8 pp. (Lust for Life!: Milwaukie OR, 1976).

"Who Killed Ned Ludd?: Machine-Breaking at the Dawn of Capitalism," *Fifth Estate,* April 1976.

"Medieval Revolts Against Church and State," *Fifth Estate,* July 1976.

"Unionization in America," *Telos* No. 27 (Spring 1976). Also in *Fifth Estate,* August 1976.

"Taylorism and Unionism," *Fifth Estate,* November 1976.

"Multinational Unions," *Fifth Estate,* April-May 1977.

"New York, New York," *Fifth Estate,* August 1977.

Creation and Its Enemies: *"The Revolt Against Work,"* 64 pp. (Mutualist Books: Rochester, 1977).

"Industrialism & Domestication," *Fifth Estate,* October-November 1977. Also as *Industrialism and Domestication,* 18 pp. (Black Eye Press: Seattle, 1979).

"The Practical Marx," *Fifth Estate,* October 1979.

"The Promise of the '80s," *Fifth Estate* (June 1980). Also in *Open Road* (June 1980).

"The Refusal of Technology," *Fifth Estate* (October 1980).

"Origins and Meaning of World War I," *Telos* No. 49 (Fall 1981).

"Anti-Work and the Struggle for Control," *Telos* No. 50 (Winter 1981-82). Also in *Fifth Estate,* June 1982.

"Beginning of Time, End of Time," *Fifth Estate,* Summer 1983.

"The '80s So Far," *Fifth Estate,* (Fall 1983).

"Language: Origin and Meaning," *Fifth Estate,* Winter 1984.

"Number: Its Origin & Evolution," *Fifth Estate,* Summer 1985.

"Present Day Banalities," *Anti-Authoritarian News Network Bulletin,* Winter 1986. Also in *Fifth Estate,* Winter-Spring 1986 and *Popular Reality,* August-September 1986.

"The Case Against Art," *Fifth Estate,* Fall 1986.

"Media, Irony & 'Bob'," *Popular Reality,* October-November 1986.

"Axis Point of American Industrialism," *International Review of Social History,* Vol. XXXI (1986), No. 3.

"The Case Against Art," *Fifth Estate,* Fall 1986. Also in *Apocalypse Culture* (Amok Press: NY, 1987).

"Vagaries of Negation," *Apocalypse Culture* (Amok Press: NY, 1987). Also in *Anarchy* No. 14 (Summer 1987).

"Agriculture" will appear early 1988 in *Lomakatsi* and *Fifth Estate.*

This is essentially a U.S. listing; much credit regarding several of which articles is due Paula Zerzan and Alice Carnes. Some translations, as pamphlets, broadsides, magazine articles, have appeared in France, England, Scotland, Holland and Spain.